MW00343327

THE PERENNIALS

Also by Mauro F. Guillén

*2030: How Today's Biggest Trends Will Collide
and Reshape the Future of Everything*

THE
PERENNIALS

The Megatrends Creating a
Postgenerational Society

MAURO F. GUILLÉN

ST. MARTIN'S PRESS
NEW YORK

First published in the United States by St. Martin's Press, an imprint of St. Martin's Publishing Group

THE PERENNIALS. Copyright © 2023 by Mauro F. Guillén. All rights reserved. Printed in the United States of America. For information, address St. Martin's Publishing Group, 120 Broadway, New York, NY 10271.

www.stmartins.com

Designed by Jen Edwards

Library of Congress Cataloging-in-Publication Data

Names: Guillén, Mauro F., author.
Title: The perennials : the megatrends creating a postgenerational society / Mauro F. Guillén.
Description: First edition. | New York : St. Martin's Press, [2023] | Includes bibliographical references and index.
Identifiers: LCCN 2023015120 | ISBN 9781250281340 (hardcover) | ISBN 9781250281357 (ebook)
Subjects: LCSH: Generations. | Intergenerational relations. | Aging—Social aspects. | Aging—Economic aspects. | Technological innovations—Social aspects. | Technological innovations—Economic aspects.
Classification: LCC HM721 .G85 2023 | DDC 305.2—dc23/eng/20230413
LC record available at https://lccn.loc.gov/2023015120

ISBN 978-1-250-28134-0 (hardcover)
ISBN 978-1-250-28135-7 (ebook)

Our books may be purchased in bulk for promotional, educational, or business use. Please contact your local bookseller or the Macmillan Corporate and Premium Sales Department at 1-800-221-7945, extension 5442, or by email at MacmillanSpecialMarkets@macmillan.com.

First Edition: 2023

10 9 8 7 6 5 4 3 2 1

For Sandra, Daniela, and Andrea

CONTENTS

PERENNIALS AND THE POSTGENERATIONAL SOCIETY IN FIGURES

With life expectancy growing, more generations are sharing the stage. As the economy shifts and technology disrupts, generations are increasingly learning, working, living, and consuming together. The old model of sequentially living our lives from school to work and retirement that defines us as boomers, millennials, etc.—divisions based on hackneyed assumptions of the way these groups do things—is giving way. A revolution has already begun that is creating a multiplicity of pathways enabling people to flexibly adapt to change and unanticipated events. We're witnessing the coming of a postgenerational society by individuals one can call *perennials*—people who are not characterized by the decade in which they were born but rather by the way they work, learn, and interact with others.

32 years: Growth of the average life expectancy at birth of Americans since 1900, from 46 to 78 years.

19–25 years: The average life left at age 60 for Americans, Europeans, Latin Americans, and Asians.

13–17 years: Years of life left at age 60 that will be in good health.

8: Number of generations sharing the world stage nowadays.

18%: Proportion of American households that constitute a nuclear family with two married parents and at least one child under the age of 18 (2021), down from 40% in 1970.

Also 18%: Proportion of Americans living in multigenerational households, with three or more generations living together (2021), up from 7% in 1971.

10–15%: Highest proportions by country of people age 30 and above enrolled in traditional postsecondary education.

30–35%: Highest proportions by country of people age 30 and above learning on a digital platform.

46%: International executives interested in the potential advantages of a multigenerational workforce.

37–38%: Proportion of Generation Zers and millennials in the United Kingdom who say their brand choice is influenced by parents or guardians—higher than celebrities and social media influencers.

INTRODUCTION

BMW is one of the world's most recognizable brands, the maker of "the ultimate driving machine." While Ford became famous for the moving assembly line and Toyota for its participatory work methods, the German firm usually made the headlines thanks to technical breakthroughs. Over the years, BMW's legendary engineering prowess yielded innovations such as the hydraulic front fork to absorb the shock when riding a motorcycle over a bump, the eight-cylinder alloy engine, the electronically controlled antilock braking system, and the fully fledged thoroughbred electric car. These days, however, BMW is turning heads by pioneering a workplace in which as many as five generations of people collaborate and bring to the table their unique skills and perspectives. They have redesigned factories and the various sections within them so that several generations of workers feel comfortable toiling together, leading to productivity increases and higher job satisfaction.

BMW's parent plant is located north of Munich, the capital of Bavaria. "Approximately 8,000 employees from over 50 countries work at this site, 850 of whom are trainees," reads the company's website. "Every day, around 1,000 automobiles and about 2,000 engines are manufactured here, the plant being closely integrated into the Group's global production network."

The multigenerational workplace seems at first sight to be a recipe for cultural misunderstanding, friction, and conflict. Many people believe that generations are motivated by different aspects of the job like satisfaction, money, or employee benefits. They also differ in terms of their attitudes toward technology. For example, younger generations prefer to communicate via text messages and videos, while others use face-to-face modes more frequently. That's why so many companies, including BMW, were once reluctant to mix different generations on the shop floor or the office. However, there are distinct advantages to having several generations collaborate with one another. BMW noticed that more mature workers may gradually lose mental agility and speed, but use other resources to fix problems, often based on experience.

The relationship between age and workplace performance, however, is not a straight line. Researchers at the Ohio State University were stunned to find that creativity peaks when people are in their twenties and again in their fifties. The reason, they discovered, is that early in working life, people rely on cognitive ability alone, but as their brains slow down, they figure out how to use their experience to compensate for the decline. The different abilities of people at different ages is what persuaded BMW to integrate generations into the same workplace. They found that age-diverse work groups offered both speed and fewer mistakes. "A multigenerational team offers a diversified way of looking at a project or problem," argues Helen Dennis, a specialist on the topic. "The more thoughts you have, the greater the advantage you have to accomplish your objective."

The growing potential of the multigenerational workplace challenges the traditional way in which we think about people of different ages and what we can do and accomplish at various points in life. We frequently hear people say, "I'm too young for that job," or "I'm too old to learn a new gig." When universal schooling and "old-age" pensions were first introduced in the 1880s, life became organized into a simple sequence of stages. Infanthood was all about growing and playing. School, and perhaps college, would follow, and then work. Before we knew it, we would be in retirement, looking back at the linear pattern that a full and orderly life was supposed to be, hoping that our children and grandchildren would successfully replicate the very same trajectory in their own life spans. Our time in this world became compartmentalized into a rigid series of distinct stages ever since.

I call this way of organizing our lives the *sequential model of life.* Over the past 150 years or so, every generation has been told to follow the exact same rules all over the world, from Japan to the United States, and from Scandinavia to the southern tip of Africa. Meanwhile, wars were fought, empires came and went, women gained the right to vote, and we set foot on the moon and dispatched robotic rovers to Mars. But we continued to live our lives in the same old way, one generation after another, in endless reprise.

This state of affairs is becoming obsolete due to long-standing demographic transformations.

It's no secret that we now live much longer lives than ever before. In 1900, average life expectancy at birth in the United States was forty-six years; as of 2022, it's seventy-eight, and it will reach eighty-three within two decades, after accounting for the effect of the coronavirus pandemic. Americans who have made it to age sixty can expect to live an average of another twenty-three years, dramatically up from just ten years in 1900. That's another lifetime within a lifetime. Western Europeans are even better off, with a life expectancy at age sixty of twenty-five years. Asians can enjoy twenty additional years on average, and even in Africa, where much progress can be made, the number is already a stunning sixteen years. In addition to greater longevity, we stay in much better physical and mental shape for much longer—the so-called health span. This simply means that a seventy-year-old nowadays can pursue the active lifestyle of a sixty-year-old from two generations ago.

Definitions of *old* and *young* have shifted over time because of the lengthening of both the life span and the health span. In 1875, the Friendly Societies Act of the United Kingdom defined "old age" as above fifty years. "Forty is the old age of youth. Fifty the youth of old age," said the French writer Victor Hugo, who was an old man for 40 percent of his life, given that he died in 1885 at age eighty-three. Since World War II, age sixty has generally been considered as the borderline between young and old. In its statistical reports, the World Health Organization moves back and forth between sixty and sixty-five, a sign that not even the experts know where to draw the line. For its part, the World Economic Forum defines *old* in a dynamic way as the "prospective age" at which life expectancy is fifteen years—or when the average person has a decade and a half of life left. In the case of the U.S., the boundary would be set at sixty-nine today. That's almost twenty years later than if we followed Hugo's categories.

But not everything in this trend of ever-increasing longevity looks rosy. Frictions are proliferating between younger, taxpaying generations and those in retirement enjoying healthcare and pension benefits. In addition, way too many people struggle with transitioning from one stage to another, such as with adolescence, the midlife crisis, or loneliness during retirement, or they get derailed due to a teenage pregnancy, dropping out of school, a family tragedy, a divorce, or substance abuse. It's no news that many mothers find it difficult to balance family and work, and most are far from being treated equitably in terms of career advancement and pay. And while we live and remain fit longer, we are subject to the corrosive effect of technological change, which renders our education obsolete much faster than in the past. As knowledge becomes antiquated at a dizzying rate, gone is the era in which we could go to school when young and use what we learned over the several decades we spend working.

What if we think about life differently?

There's nothing naturally preordained about what we should do at different ages. In fact, the sequential model of life is a social and political

construction, built on conceptions of patriarchy and bureaucracy that classify people into age groups and roles. The fundamental insight of this book is that the confluence of rising life expectancy, enhanced physical and mental fitness, and technology-driven knowledge obsolescence fundamentally alters the dynamics over the *entire* life course, redefining both what we can do at different ages and how generations live, learn, work, and consume together.

Let me call these massive transformations the *postgenerational revolution,* one that will fundamentally reshape individual lives, companies, economies, and the entire global society. As a result, we will witness the proliferation of perennials, "an ever-blooming group of people of all ages, stripes, and types who transcend stereotypes and make connections with each other and the world around them . . . they are not defined by their generation," in the words of Gina Pell, a serial entrepreneur.

"Revolutions are not made; they come," said the American abolitionist Wendell Phillips. "A revolution is as natural a growth as an oak. It comes out of the past. Its foundations are laid far back," he noted. And indeed, the revolutionary rise of the perennials is the result of long-standing trends. Whereas in the not-too-distant past at most four or five generations of people coexisted at any given moment in time, now we have eight inhabiting the planet simultaneously. In the United States, the eight generations include alpha (born 2013 onward), Z (1995–2012), millennials (1980–1994), xennials (1975–1985), the baby-bust (1965–1979) and baby-boom (1946–1964) generations, the Silent Generation (1925–1945), and the Greatest Generation (1910–1924). In Japan, China, and Europe, where population aging has proceeded faster than in the U.S., as many as nine generations share the stage. As longevity continues to soar, nine or ten generations may end up living together before midcentury. Can different generations get along together? Or are they condemned to enter into politically fraught distributional conflicts over who pays for which services and benefits? How will younger generations feel about paying taxes to fund healthcare and pension systems for their parents, grandparents, and great-grandparents? Can we adopt a perennial mindset to overcome these difficulties? And what exactly should that frame of mind be?

One of the pleasant surprises in this book is that greater longevity has positive implications not just for retirees but for everyone at every stage of life. A longer life span creates more opportunities and wiggle room for their grandchildren to change course, take gap years, and reinvent themselves, no matter their age. But that's only possible if governments, companies, and other organizations move away from the sequential model of life. If people could liberate themselves from the tyranny of "age-appropriate" activities, if they could become perennials, they might be able to pursue not just one career, occupation, or profession but several, finding different kinds of personal fulfillment in each. Most importantly, people in their teens and twenties will be able to plan and make decisions for multiple transitions in life, not just one from study to work and another from work to retirement.

The counterintuitive message of the chapters that follow is that the more decades of life people have ahead of them, the more important it is to keep their options open, and the less useful making "big decisions" becomes. In a truly postgenerational society driven by the perennial mindset, for example, teenagers will no longer have to agonize over the best path for them to pursue in terms of their studies or future jobs, knowing that a longer life span will afford plenty of opportunities for course correcting, for learning new skills, and for switching careers, depending on how the circumstances evolve.

That's potentially the world awaiting us—one in which we don't have to make fateful decisions with irreversible, lifelong consequences but rather one in which we can engage in more multigenerational activities and experience a more diverse array of opportunities over time. For example, we might be able to go back to school without being pigeonholed into reified categories such as young/old, active/inactive, full-/part-time, and so on. Technology may render our knowledge and experience outdated, but it also enables more flexible and iterative modes of learning and working. Our experience of life will no longer follow the beaten path prescribed to us in the late nineteenth century, when large-scale industrialization and mass schooling took hold. In fact, we will live several different lives in one, always in interaction with people of different generations in a society that will no longer be constrained by age or by distance, given the widespread use of digital platforms for remote work and learning. Individuals, companies, and governments that understand this potential will enter a new era of unrestricted living, learning, working, and consuming, thus unleashing a new universe of opportunities for people at all stages of life—a truly postgenerational society.

I decided to write this book during the coronavirus pandemic. Confined to my Philadelphia home, I invested in all the gadgetry necessary to teach and conduct webinars from my basement, drawing on the ideas contained in my most recent book, *2030: How Today's Biggest Trends Will Collide and Reshape the Future of Everything,* which was published in August 2020. Speaking from my virtual pulpit, I shared my evolving thoughts and analysis with business executives, financial analysts, headhunters, government officials, school principals, independent bookstore owners, reading club members, high school students, newspaper founders, retirees, and medical personnel, among many others. I propounded to them the virtues of lateral thinking and connecting the dots. It took me several months to realize I had not fully comprehended in *2030* that demography and technology were joining forces to unravel the sequential model of life we inherited from the late nineteenth century.

It was during one of those webinars that I grasped what eventually became the fundamental insight of this book. The audience was comprised of top management teams from some of the most prominent American zoological gardens and aquariums. As I spoke, it dawned on me that zoos cannot possibly succeed unless multigenerational dynamics are taken into consideration. Grandparents take their grandchildren to the zoo, and parents of small children will indulge their love of this or that animal, but the generations in between have scant interest in this type of outing. How does a zoo attract teenagers, adults without children, and those whose children are no longer small? These organizations have begun to add special events or exhibits incorporating video games, virtual reality, and the metaverse to do just that. In this postgenerational world, not just zoos but all organizations need to use every tool at their disposal to capture the imagination of people at different stages in life—all at once.

Thinking about perennials from any generation makes all the sense in the world as we revisit the way we live, learn, work, and consume. The pandemic has opened our eyes to the immense possibilities—as well as to the hardships and limitations—of remote learning and remote work. It has exposed our vulnerabilities relative to robots and intelligent machines. It has exacerbated inequities by race and gender. And it has powerfully reminded us that nothing lasts forever. I wish to encourage you to see learning, working, and consuming in a different light, one that makes it possible for people and organizations to explore new horizons and to push the limits of what they can do and accomplish throughout their lives. This book is meant for both parents and children, women and men, workers and talent managers, would-be retirees and retirees, families and wealth advisors, and consumers and marketers. All of us will be affected by the shifting dynamics of the postgenerational society.

In the chapters that follow, I'll take you on a journey around the world, calling port throughout East Asia, South Asia, Russia, the Middle East, Africa, Europe, and the Americas. I will refer to many novels, films, TV series, and ordinary people to establish how pervasive the sequential model of life has become in our culture and society. I will identify the main frictions and adversities that this way of organizing our lives has contributed to, and their consequences for various groups in society. I will also tell you about shifting trends in living, learning, working, retiring, inheriting, and consuming driven by the postgenerational revolution and the rise of the perennials.

You'll see that I don't have a magical, ready-made elixir to tackle the problems associated with the sequential model of life. Think about the perennial mindset as a *method* rather than a solution. It's a method to make us aware that viewing life as a linear series of compartmentalized stages defined by age imposes very high costs on individuals and families, leaving many people behind. It's a method to challenge antiquated assumptions that we need to reconsider if we wish to take advantage of the opportunities in this technological age. It's a method to persuade governments, companies, educational institutions, and other organizations to experiment with new models of living, learning, working, and consuming that take advantage of an increasingly postgenerational society. It's a method, I hope, to develop new, imaginative approaches to life in the twenty-first century so that we can unleash the full potential inherent to each of us.

THE PERENNIALS

1

THE FOUR STATIONS IN LIFE

Our lives are like the streams
That flow into the sea
And terminate.
—Jorge Manrique (c. 1440–1479),
Verses on the Death of His Father

The year was 1881. Otto von Bismarck, the "Iron Chancellor," was well on his way to turning a unified Germany into an economic and geopolitical powerhouse. The country had vast deposits of coal and iron ore, a swelling population, financial capital, a vibrant university system, and plenty of inventors and entrepreneurs who would bring to the world the internal combustion engine, chemical dyes, aspirin, and the x-ray machine. But Bismarck was fearful of the growing and militant socialist worker movement energized by the revolutionary ideals of political agitators like Karl Marx and Friedrich Engels, who insisted on bringing to the public's attention the horrid working conditions in the "Satanic Mills" that were the factories of the second Industrial Revolution. In a brilliant preemptive strike, Bismarck devised the initiative of offering a guaranteed retirement income beyond the age of seventy. He was a shrewd politician given that the average life expectancy at the time was no more than fifty. In a letter to the German parliament, Kaiser William I wrote on his chancellor's behalf that "those who are disabled from work by age and invalidity have a well-grounded claim to care from the state." The world's first state pension scheme came into being in 1889. The gambit paid off: revolution was averted.

The idea of a national pension system for all laborers spread around the world rather slowly. In 1908, the United Kingdom adopted such an arrangement for people of "good character" above age seventy. France followed suit in 1910, and South Africa in 1928, covering Blacks since 1944. In 1935, the Social Security Act signed into law by President Roosevelt kicked off the American national pension system as we know it today, covering industrial workers, not just soldiers and mothers, as in the late nineteenth century, but neglecting agricultural and domestic laborers, which at the time represented half of the labor force. Several Latin American countries enacted and expanded state pensions from the 1930s to the '50s, but most schemes remained fragmented until the 1960s. For instance, Brazil unified its system in 1966. Japan's national pension system dates to 1942 and was relaunched in its current structure in 1961. In South Korea, a corporate retirement allowance scheme was established in 1953, but the first national pension scheme wasn't put in place until 1988.

At roughly the same time that "old-age" pensions came into being, governments saw the need to provide the population with basic instruction in reading, writing, history, and arithmetic. This was in part motivated by nationalism, to create what historian Benedict Anderson has called an "imagined community." But it was also driven by the labor requirements of the second Industrial Revolution, which ushered in the science-based industries of chemicals, pharmaceuticals, electrical machinery, and automobiles. Employers realized that an educated workforce could be more productive, especially as industry became more capital intensive. The British historian E. P. Thompson documented that factory discipline, punctuality, and readiness to follow directions required a certain level of education. The Reverend William

Turner of Newcastle, England, quoted in 1786 from a manufacturer of hemp and flax in Gloucester to justify schooling because it made children "become more tractable and obedient, and less quarrelsome and revengeful." Schooling became the method of choice for inculcating a "habit of industry."

Thus, the discipline that schools instill in children became an essential element in the rise of the wage-based employment system. The industrial economy required legions of people willing to work for increasingly large employers in exchange for hourly pay, making themselves available to undertake whatever tasks the employer asked them to do. According to sociologist Charles Perrow, "Wage dependency covered about 20 percent of the [American working] population in 1820, and 80 to 90 percent by 1950." As fewer and fewer people toiled the fields, worked from the home under the putting-out system, or were self-employed, schools became even more important, in a mutually reinforcing pattern. For employers, schools provided a pool of standardized labor needed for "continuous, predictable production" of goods and services on an ever-larger scale. The rise of employment bureaucracies at factories was matched by the development of bureaucratized school systems. The sorting, training, and monitoring of an industrial workforce into specific jobs and tasks could not have been accomplished so quickly without a school system subservient to the requirements of industry. Mass schooling and mass production thus became the two sides of the same coin.

Unlike the schemes of nationalist leaders and captains of industry, social reformers saw in compulsory education a way to protect children from abuse in the farming fields or on the manufacturing shop floor. Schools, however, were far from idyllic places of learning. A teacher from the German southwestern region of Swabia kept partial records of the punishments he inflicted on his pupils over half a century: "911,527 blows with a rod, 124,010 blows with a cane, 20,989 taps with a ruler, 136,715 blows with the hand, 10,235 blows to the mouth, 7,905 boxes on the ear, and 1,118,800 blows on the head." Schooling was indeed as much about inculcating discipline as it was about education.

Schooling became the cornerstone of the sequential model of life because it sorted people into different social roles, careers, and jobs, some of which entailed attending college while others did not. In the 1950s, the functionalist sociologist Talcott Parsons sought to answer the dual questions of "how the school class functions to internalize in its pupils both the commitments and capacities for successful performance of their future adult roles" and "how it functions to allocate these human resources within the role-structure of the adult society." Thus, the elementary school class became "an agency of socialization." In his view, the educational system both reflects the prevailing social structure and creates change and mobility. "To be sure, the high-status, high-ability boy is very likely indeed to go to college, and the low-status, low-ability boy is very unlikely to go. But the 'cross-pressured' group for whom these two factors do not coincide is of considerable importance." Given that schooling is geographically bound, especially at the elementary level, it creates an "initial equalization of the contestants' status by age and by 'family background,' the neighborhood being typically much more homogeneous than is the whole society." In addition, a certain proportion of parents send their kids to private school in every country around the world. In the decades since Parsons wrote his famous essay, we have come to see schooling as both a haven of opportunity and a harbinger of inequality. Thus, the school system, presumably based on meritocratic principles, became a gigantic machine both for sorting children into adult roles and for reproducing the prevailing social hierarchy.

The origins of the idea of compulsory primary education go back to Martin Luther (1483–1546), who proposed that salvation depended on one's own reading of the scriptures and on following a lifestyle congruent with their teachings. Deliverance thus required literacy; promoting education became a Christian duty. The Puritans who sailed across the North Atlantic in search of religious freedom mandated schooling as early as 1690, making the Massachusetts Bay Colony a global pioneer. State-sponsored mass schooling was adopted in Prussia—which was Germany's most politically pugnacious region—as early as 1763, when Frederick the Great made attendance at village schools compulsory for children not belonging to the elites (the latter were already schooled). In 1774, Austrian emperor Joseph II sanctioned a universal compulsory education law. The French Constitution of 1791 promulgated "a system of public instruction, common to all the citizens and gratuitous in respect to those subjects of instruction that are indispensable of all men." Denmark (1814), Ontario, Canada (1841), Sweden (1842), and Norway (1848) were among the first to launch new schooling initiatives.

Mass schooling was not embraced more broadly around the world until the late nineteenth century. In Britain, after decades of limited actions to broaden access to an education at parochial and other private schools, the Forster Elementary Education Act of 1870 created the foundations of a state educational system. In 1876, schooling to the age of ten was made compulsory, and expanded in 1899 to age twelve. In France, primary education was made free in 1881, and compulsory to age thirteen in 1882. In most European countries, girls were initially taught a different curriculum at separate schools, but by World War II, a unified curriculum for boys and girls had become the norm. In the United States, schooling became mandatory in most states outside of the South, and in 1924, all Native Americans became citizens with access to education.

In combination, compulsory schooling, wage-based employment, and pension schemes became the foundation for the sequential model of the "four stations in life," a poetic term resembling the cosmic seasonal calendar. Indeed, by the turn of the twenty-first century, virtually every country in the world had embraced the idea that life proceeds in the four separate and sequential stages of play, study, work, and retirement. It came to be taken for granted as if it were the natural, ideal, and inevitable way of organizing our lives.

THE VIRTUES OF THE SEQUENTIAL MODEL

Perhaps the key advantage of the sequential model of life was its predictability. It enabled a simple and straightforward classification of people into different population groups defined by age. The *passive* population was neither working nor looking for a job. It comprised the individuals at either end of the age distribution: babies and children of "school age," and "old-age" retirees. Women from middle- and upper-class backgrounds also became part of the passive population as they prepared to be married or devoted themselves to their children and ran their households, with the aid of working-class women who had no choice but to be part of the *active* population. Males of "working age" constituted the largest contingent of the active group. Most of the active laborers were employed during what Charles Dickens called the "best of times," while many became unemployed or underemployed during the "worst of times." These categories of people in relation to work continue to hold to this day not just in labor statistics but also in the labor market itself and in our daily lives.

There's no better way of grasping how much our culture is driven by the four stations in life than to spend a bit of time browsing at a local bookstore. Shelf after shelf of how-to and self-help volumes are filled with advice as to how to make it through each of the four stations in life, as if it were (literally) a matter of surviving from one stage to the next. For children, it's all about self-esteem, as in *Helga Makes a Name for Herself, The World Needs Who You Were Made to Be,* or *I Am Confident, Brave & Beautiful* (a coloring book). Teenagers and young adults are the target of so many books that it's actually better not to mention any of them in particular. But never fear: once you've made it to "true adulthood," there's a book on *How to Survive Your Childhood Now That You're an Adult,* which could be more aptly titled, *Freud Unhinged.* Next, there are myriad books on how to put up with those decades we spend working, a genre launched in 1936 with the publication of Dale Carnegie's *How to Win Friends and Influence People.* More recently, this subset of the literature has degenerated into topics such as *Am I the Only Sane One Working Here?: 101 Solutions for Surviving Office Insanity* or *The No Asshole Rule.* And for those in retirement, no shortage of books either: *Not Fade Away: How to Thrive in Retirement; Retirement for Beginners; Retire Young, Retire Rich;* or the inevitable *How to Survive Retirement,* as if this world had something else in stock for us beyond that stage.

The sequential model of life runs deep in the culture and is also encrusted in the law. Most national constitutions enshrine separate rights and obligations for underage children, students, workers, and retirees as distinct from citizens in general. The United Nations has created separate organizations to promote them around the world: UNICEF (for children), UNESCO (for education), and the International Labour Organization (for both workers and retirees). Moreover, it has designated World Children's Day (November 20), International Day of Education (January 24), International Day of Labor (May 1), and International Day of Older Persons (October 1) so as to remind us annually about the different stages of life.

The compartmentalization of life invited experts and scholars to tell us about what each of the stages meant. The popular psychosocial theory of personal development proposed by Erik Erikson (1902–1994) in his book *Childhood and Society* (1950), distinguished among eight stages, each associated with a pair of conflicting tendencies: infancy (zero to two years of age; trust versus mistrust), early childhood (two to three; autonomy versus shame and doubt), preschool (three to five; initiative versus guilt), school age (six to eleven; industry versus inferiority), adolescence (twelve to eighteen; identity versus role confusion), young adulthood (nineteen to forty; intimacy versus isolation), middle adulthood (forty to sixty-five; generativity versus stagnation), and maturity (sixty-five onward; ego integrity versus despair). Each stage is cumulative in the sense that resolving the inherent conflict of a given stage prepares the individual for the next. And each stage entails mastering a key skill: feeding, toilet training, exploration, learning, social relationships, relationships, work and parenthood, and reflection on life, respectively. Failure to effectively master each skill carries dire lifelong implications given that the sequence of stages is predetermined.

The reification of the four stations in life is so deeply ingrained in our minds that we have come not only to take them for granted but also to castigate those who do not make progress from one stage to the next on a timely basis, unless some physical or mental disability interferes with what's supposed to be a universal pattern of progression applicable to everyone. Those who do not shift from infanthood to adolescence as a prelude to adulthood are called Peter Pans. An adolescent who never grows up to become an adult is a rebel. A worker who can't afford to retire is a failure, spendthrift, or irresponsible. An army of psychologists and therapists has come to make a living by offering advice and treatment to those who fall behind in the sequence of stages.

It is no coincidence that Erikson proposed his psychosocial theory when he did. By the end of the 1940s, the majority of people in Europe, the United States, and parts of East Asia and Latin America were subject to the sequential model of life as a result of universal schooling, wage-based employment, and mandatory retirement. The architects of this design—and the state bureaucrats tasked with ensuring that everyone complied—shamelessly argued that the sequence of schooling, employment, and retirement were good for the people. I would certainly like to argue that schooling was and still is largely beneficial, although the homeschooling movement of the 1970s made a good point by challenging the state's monopoly over education on the grounds that the classroom environment had become oppressive and mainly driven by the need to turn children into compliant workers. But I would like to take issue with the universalization of wage employment and retirement, and with the one-way street from education to work, with no possibility of a back-and-forth between the two. The increase in self-employment during the 1980s and the phenomenon of gig work in the twenty-first century have added new urgency to the debate on our prevailing age-based organization of life. The financial crunch afflicting pension systems has given the critics of the sequential model of life more ammunition. Let's examine, stage by stage, the inconsistencies and the ill effects of compartmentalizing life into separate, sequential stages.

PARENTING: FROM CHEAPER BY THE DOZEN TO THE LITTLE EMPEROR

"It takes a lot of money to keep this family going," wrote Frank Gilbreth Jr. and Ernestine Gilbreth Carey in their 1948 bestselling book, *Cheaper by the Dozen,* which inspired four feature films (including two starring Steve Martin and Bonnie Hunt), a stage play, and a musical. They were two of the twelve children raised by industrial efficiency experts Lillian Moller Gilbreth and Frank Bunker Gilbreth, who had joined forces to help companies increase productivity by improving the methodology of time and motion study. Their work inspired not only employers but also modernist architects, Bauhaus founder Walter Gropius among them. They thought it wise to apply the principles of scientific management not just to unwitting workers on the factory shop floor but to their household as well. "To be efficient, in the Gilbreth family, was a virtue on a par with veracity, honesty, generosity, philanthropy, and tooth-brushing." They pioneered the use of cameras to improve the efficiency of manufacturing operations. "Dad took moving pictures of us children washing dishes, so that he could figure out how we could reduce our motions and thus hurry through the task." Frank Sr. would frequently confront the question, "How do you feed all those kids, mister?" His reply would simply be, "Well, they come cheaper by the dozen, you know."

The Gilbreths were outliers not just in fertility but also in social status and education. Lillian was born into a well-to-do California family, attended college at Berkeley, and received a Ph.D. in applied psychology from Brown. It was highly unusual, even at the time, for a woman with her educational credentials to have so many children. For his part, Frank passed on the opportunity to study at MIT to begin a career in industry and consulting that would bring him world fame as one of the key exponents of scientific management. By the time he died in 1924 from heart failure, their oldest child, Anne, was a sophomore at Smith, and their youngest, Jane, just two years old. For four decades, Lillian went on to manage the consulting business while raising her numerous offspring. She found the time to write several landmark books on psychology and efficiency at the factory and in the household, including *Living with Our Children* (1928), in which she rhetorically asked the question, "Why should not a family life have a plan?" She was at the time facing the gargantuan dual tasks of procuring for their children and giving them good opportunities in life. "We shall here consider family life as an educational process for the child, in which we can use all available methods that have proved successful in other fields." For her, "the amount of planning that is done to give him [sic] opportunity for living and richness of experience has an enormous influence on what he will do and be." Unlike many parents nowadays, she argued that "a college diploma and a place in Who's Who mean something, but success as a teacher in a small town or leadership in industry may mean as much." Perhaps it was because of her large family that one of the most celebrated efficiency experts ever did not obsess about any particular way of ensuring that her children would be successful in life. There were many paths to success, and her different children certainly took them.

Fast-forward to the early part of the twenty-first century. Fertility has declined precipitously to the point that throughout East Asia, Europe, and North America, women have far fewer than two children over their lifetime on average, thus falling short of population replacement. According to a report from the National Center for Health Statistics published in 2018, the mean number of children ever born to American college-educated women aged twenty-two to forty-four was *exactly* 1.0, compared to 2.6 for those without a high school diploma. (It was 0.9 for college-educated men). A college education for women thus became America's equivalent to China's one-child policy, if only a lot less intrusive.

With fewer children comes a flight to quality, as the Chicago economist Gary Becker famously proposed. He reasoned that instead of increasing quantity, rising incomes lead people to focus on quality—that is, they replace their clunkers with newer, larger, or more luxurious sedans or SUVs as opposed to adding more subpar cars to their fleet. "The interaction between quantity and quality of children," he wrote, "is the most important reason why the effective price of children rises with income," meaning that as parents see their earnings rise, they prefer to invest more in each child, giving them better opportunities in life. From East Asia and India to Europe and the United States, parents have become obsessed not with raising children successfully but with raising *successful* children—or *a* successful child, in the case of college-educated parents.

Contemporary parenthood has become all about maximizing the chances of sending the offspring to the best possible college. The most watched TED Talk ever, by education professor Ken Robinson, blamed parents for corrupting the goal of education in life. "If you think the whole purpose of education is to get your kid to university, or a particular university; and if you think the reason to do that is because they'll have a degree and their future will be secure and they'll have a nice middle-class job and a long-term income; if that's the mindset, you can see why parents add to the pressure," he noted at a Talent Summit in Dublin in 2018. "The problem with that preoccupation of a certain style of education is that it marginalizes a great many of the other abilities and talents that kids have, and that they'll need now and in the future." The issue has spread to every corner of the world. In India, the combination of high parental expectations and an examination-based curriculum has proved to be detrimental to learning. "Excessive parental aspirations can be detrimental to a child's development, because then the child only looks for ways to swell its grades," argues Avik Mallick. "Neglecting the most important part of education in this process which is to retain the knowledge that has been imparted by the pedagogue, the mental faculty of a child is wasted in trying to make its report card devoid of red ink instead of comprehending the theme of the subject at hand."

Parenting didn't become a widely used gerund and practice until recently, as Alia Wong noted in a 2016 essay in *The Atlantic*. For the longest time, people simply had children and raised them. By the 1990s, she argues, "at least for members of the middle class, being a parent didn't just mean serving as an authority figure and a source of sustenance and support for a child—it meant molding that child's life, flooding her with opportunity so she could have a competitive edge in the long-term, and enriching her with all kinds of constructive experiences." Children of highly educated parents visit museums, attend concerts, and watch stage plays twice or even thrice as frequently as the rest. This trend has exacerbated economic inequality and social reproduction given that, according to sociologist Paul DiMaggio, a family's "cultural capital" is the best predictor of children's grades in primary and secondary school. The staggering American college admissions scandal of 2019—involving scores of admissions staffers, sports coaches, and celebrity, or plainly wealthy, parents criminally charged with bribing testing officials—made it readily apparent that the obsession with preparing children for success in life not only has led to detrimental implications but has acquired comical overtones as well.

Underpinning the urge felt by so many parents to maximize their children's opportunities lies the sequential model of life, whose linear structure simply raises the stakes. If children lag behind, it is commonly assumed, if they fail to keep up with the Joneses' children, they might not be able to make the most out of their lives. Because we move from playing to studying, and then to working, with no chance whatsoever of a feedback loop, we must maximize performance from day one—or inevitably and perhaps irreversibly fall behind. And after we've learned as much as possible by attending the best available educational institutions, we must work like there's no tomorrow in the hope of one day being able to retire.

TEENAGE WOES: BETWEEN *REBEL WITHOUT A CAUSE* AND *MOONLIGHT*

"She'll outgrow it, dear," says Judy's mother (played by Rochelle Hudson) in *Rebel Without a Cause,* the 1955 blockbuster film. "It's just the age . . . It's the age when nothing fits." The social construction of *teenage* and *young adulthood*—two terms that have occupied experts for centuries—involves a series of juxtaposed concepts: dependence and independence, order and rebellion, certainty and risk, stability and adventure, and so on. "I want answers now," protests Jim Stark (James Dean) in response to his father's refusal to even acknowledge the big issues he confronts. "I'm not interested in what I'll understand ten years from now."

The film stands as a monument to the misunderstandings and conflicts between generations in suburban, middle-class households and as an illustration of yet another key shortcoming of the sequential model of life. While the trials and tribulations of the teenage years and early adulthood have occurred ever since the beginning of settled societies some ten thousand years ago, the idea of a natural progression through four concatenated stages that must be experienced in sequence exacerbates the cultural clash between parents and their children as the parents can't see the day their children will become full adults, and the children can't wait to break loose—the perfect recipe for intergenerational conflict.

"At some point, you gotta decide for yourself who you gonna be," Juan (played by Mahershala Ali) tells the protagonist in *Moonlight,* the first LGBTQI+ and all-Black-cast movie to win the Oscar for Best Picture. "Can't let nobody make that decision for you." During the daunting transition from childhood to adulthood, many teenagers struggle with issues of identity, filtered through the prisms of gender, race, and religion. But the sequential model assumes a linear path, a single option, a unique identity at each of the stations in life.

Research has shown that parental pressures for teens to conform with the social expectations of the sequential model can put them at risk of substance use and abuse, among many other ailings. What's more, "pressure on developing minds has the potential to change the circuitry of the brain," says Dr. Joseph Garbely, vice president of medical services and medical director at Caron, a Florida nonprofit dedicated to helping youth suffering from substance addiction. "It's a very serious concern because this biological change can place teens at greater risk for mental health disorders as well as substance use and abuse."

One of the greatest fears parents have under the sequential model of life is for their adolescent children to become a Peter Pan, a socially immature adult, a term popularized by psychologist Dan Kiley in his book *The Peter Pan Syndrome: Men Who Have Never Grown Up* (1983). While the condition is not recognized by the American Psychiatric Association as a mental disorder, it has gained much traction among parents and therapists alike. Signs of this pop syndrome include the unwillingness or inability to take on responsibilities associated with adulthood, lack of self-confidence, and excessive selfishness. In the movies, the classic Peter Pan situation involves a woman stuck with an immature boyfriend—a man-child—who is not willing to "settle down." Perhaps the classic movie of this genre is *High Fidelity* (2000), starring John Cusack. "I can see now I never really committed to Laura," he concedes. "I always had one foot out the door, and that prevented me from doing a lot of things, like thinking about my future and . . . I guess it made more sense to commit to nothing, keep my options open. And that's suicide. By tiny, tiny increments."

The concept of adults behaving like younger folk has been given an ugly term, *transageism*. Its origins can be traced back to the ancient world's mythological *puer aeternus* (or *puella aeterna* in the case of women)—the eternal boy or girl, a child-god who is forever young. Aldous Huxley's 1962 novel, *Island,* referred to Adolf Hitler as a Peter Pan whose immaturity led to the huge "price the world had to pay for little Adolf's retarded matura-tion." Psychologists have recently developed scales to measure the extent to which men (or women) succumb to the syndrome. According to Hum-belina Robles Ortega, a professor at the University of Granada in Spain, pa-rental overprotection is a prime cause. "It usually affects dependent people who have been overprotected by their families and haven't developed the necessary skills to confront life." Peter Pans, she argues, "see the adult world as very problematic and glorify adolescence, which is why they want to stay in that state of privilege." It's certainly ironic that Robles Ortega teaches at the university founded after the Christians took over the last Muslim stronghold in the Iberian Peninsula in 1492. According to the legend, the defending ruler Boabdil's mother scorned his son by saying, "Cry like a woman over what you could not defend as a man." In some sense, he had not become an adult man because he had to give up his domain. Time and again over the centuries, social and parental pressures to make it from one stage to the next seemed to provide the backdrop for interpreting people's behavior.

THE MIDLIFE CRISIS

"Half my life is over and I have nothing to show for it. Nothing," Miles (played by Paul Giamatti) tells Jack (Thomas Haden Church) in *Sideways,* the 2004 hit movie. "I'm a thumbprint on the window of a skyscraper. I'm a smudge of excrement on a tissue surging out to sea with a million tons of raw sewage." A depressed teacher and aspiring novelist, Miles takes a weeklong road trip around California's wine country along with Jack, an actor beyond his prime who is about to get married. The basic story line of the forty-year-old who sees little else but boredom and despair in life is a classic theme in movies, with all sorts of identity variations, including *Lost in Translation, The*

Bridges of Madison County, The Descendants, A Single Man, Wonder Boys, and *Thelma and Louise.*

"Midlife—the years between 30 and 70, with 40 to 60 at its core—is the least charted territory in human development," notes psychologist Orville Gilbert Brim, director of an extensive study funded by the MacArthur Foundation. Most psychological research focuses on childhood, adolescence, or old age. Fights with a partner or spouse, finding oneself in a dead-end job, or watching one's parents decline are among the most prominent stressors. "The reason why midlife people have these stressors is that they actually have more control over their lives than earlier and later in life," observes David Almeida, who was part of the research team. "When people describe these stressors, they often talk in terms of meeting the challenge."

The Canadian industrial psychologist Elliott Jaques coined the term *midlife crisis* in 1965. Among the many symptoms associated with it, discontentment with life, self-questioning, and confusion about where one's life is headed are the ones most directly related to the sequential model of life. Asking questions like, "Is that all there is?" or "Am I a failure?" are among the most telling signs of a midlife crisis, supposedly. Labor economists have also jumped into the fray to examine the relationship between work and happiness. Using international survey data on self-reported satisfaction, they identified a "happiness U-curve," whereby people's feelings about life bottom out during their forties or early fifties. Intriguingly, the effect is greater in wealthier countries with longer life spans. Using data from twenty-seven European countries, David Blanchflower of Dartmouth College and Andrew Oswald of the University of Warwick in the UK found that use of antidepressants nearly doubles during people's late forties when compared to the late twenties or early sixties.

Although a similar age-related dip in well-being has been found in great apes, the sequential model of life simply takes it for granted that we cruise through midlife into retirement because, if we have successfully made it to adulthood, we are in control of our destiny. Susan Krauss Whitbourne, a professor emerita of psychological and brain sciences at the University of Massachusetts Amherst, found that people who switch jobs early in their working life feel more productive and believe they are bequeathing something for future generations. "Job changes in people's 20s and 30s tended to be beneficial in midlife," she notes. "The assumption is these people didn't feel stuck." This and other research powerfully indicates that thinking about the stations in life in a different way might help the quarter of Americans who report experiencing a midlife crisis, according to Cornell University psychologist and sociologist Elaine Wethington.

In China, after four decades of intense economic growth during which as many as nine hundred million people have been lifted out of poverty into the middle class, social media's latest trending topic is the midlife crisis. Both married couples and those who decided to remain single are apparently affected as the cross pressures from parents, work, and social expectations mount. A popular writer of the genre is Chen Danyan, whose novella *Snow White's Résumé* features Li Ping, a lifelong puppeteer who has played the role time and again over several decades. "For women, turning 50 is a milestone," she says. "Society tells you it is a crossroad. Your body underscores the point. Every woman over 50 feels it. The kids are going to college; parents are aging . . . It is never easy to cope with life's changes, and the way to deal with them is to let them be." Fairy tales have, according to her, the power to convey relationships and the role that age plays in them in clear, simple terms. "I think this is the condition of many middle-aged women— when you are no longer young but not old enough," she notes. "They always see things in a negative way, become very suspicious and cynical." For her, "being the Witch not only means a certain freedom that is denied to Snow White, but also means that you've developed your own abilities that Snow White doesn't have."

THE AGE OF LONELINESS

"Well, how does it feel to turn eighty?" Billy (played by Doug McKeon) asks Norman (Henry Fonda), the father of his dad's fiancée, in *On Golden Pond*, the 1981 family drama film. "Twice as bad as it did turning forty," goes the reply. The retired university professor is far from feeling lonely. His wife is by his side; they take care of a young boy during the summer. His wife and daughter sense an improvement in his senility and demeanor thanks to his adventures with the thirteen-year-old. Unfortunately, Norman's experience is hardly the norm. By age sixty, nearly 18 percent of Americans live alone, a percentage that grows to 25 percent by age seventy-five, and 42 percent by age eighty-nine. Most above the age of seventy are retired, which means they have fewer opportunities for daily social interaction, especially if their children live far away. Airbnb, the accommodations digital platform, reports that its fastest-growing age group among hosts offering their space for rent is people above the age of sixty, to a very large extent driven by their desire to avoid feeling lonely.

"The misery and suffering caused by chronic loneliness are very real and warrant attention," says Stephanie Cacioppo of the University of Chicago. "As a social species, we are accountable to help our lonely children, parents, neighbors, and even strangers in the same way we would treat ourselves. Treating loneliness is our collective responsibility." The lack of social connectivity has biological in addition to psychological implications. "Loneliness acts as a fertilizer for other diseases," notes Steve Cole, director of the Social Genomics Core Laboratory at UCLA. "The biology of loneliness can accelerate the buildup of plaque in arteries, help cancer cells grow and spread, and promote inflammation in the brain leading to Alzheimer's disease." Loneliness and its adverse effects are felt more strongly among people living in dangerous neighborhoods. "In my prior investigation of older residents of high-crime neighborhoods, who were mostly African American older adults, a tension emerged between participants' longing to participate in society and obstacles that made this participation difficult to attain," says Elena Portacolone, a sociologist at the University of California San Francisco.

While feelings of loneliness can occur at every age, the sequential model of life exacerbates the effect as people withdraw from social life. In one study, 18 percent of the people surveyed started to feel lonely after they retired. "Retirement comes as a massive shock to the system. Let's just get out there and find out what others are doing," says a participant in the study. "And let's join them if we can. (And thank goodness for the internet.)" According to the National Institutes of Health, "People who find themselves unexpectedly alone due to the death of a spouse or partner, separation from friends or family, retirement, loss of mobility, and lack of transportation are at particular risk" of worsening health. The problem has become so pervasive that the *Journal of Accountancy* felt it necessary to publish a paper on "The Financial and Human Cost of Loneliness in Retirement," directed at certified public accountants (CPAs) who work as financial planners. "Until recently, social isolation and loneliness were considered purely qualitative factors when it came to retirement satisfaction. They were not something that could be measured with dollars and cents." According to an AARP study from 2017, healthcare costs have increased by $6.7 billion annually due to loneliness and social isolation.

One useful way of gauging the impact of retirement on loneliness is to compare voluntary and involuntary retirees. In a paper published in the *Journal of Applied Gerontology,* a team of researchers used data from the 2014 Health and Retirement Study on just over two thousand American retirees. Their key conclusion was that involuntary retirement (nearly a third of the total) was associated with higher loneliness than voluntary retirement. They also found that "social support may alleviate the negative impact of involuntary retirement," which implies that the feeling of loneliness stems from the severing of ties to coworkers. Using the same data source, another team of researchers explored whether the speed of the transition into full retirement had anything to do with loneliness. "The results suggest that what matters is not the type of transition (gradual retirement or cold turkey)," they concluded, "but whether people perceive the transition as chosen or forced." Taken together, these two studies strongly suggest that retirement increases loneliness above and beyond the disbanding of social relationships at work. It makes people very unhappy when they're forced to give up work.

"There's no such thing as old age," the modernist architect Philip Johnson, who lived to age ninety-eight, once asserted. "I'm no different now than I was fifty years ago. I'm just having more fun." Far from being a biological necessity, retirement somehow became a requirement and a life goal in and of itself. Obviously, some occupations lend themselves better to working well beyond what's normally considered to be the "retirement age." But politicians, financial advisors, and real estate developers have persuaded us that this last stage of life is something to aspire to and to long for.

PAVING THE ROAD TO
INTERGENERATIONAL CONFLICT

Besides the multiple psychological stresses that it creates at different junctures in time, the worst consequence of the sequential model of life has been the rise of intergenerational frictions and tensions because of its rigid classification of people into compartmentalized age groups. Adolescents increasingly challenge their parents for their fixed ideas about gender and racial identities and about personal relationships, young adults blame older generations for climate change and a lousy labor market, working adults resent paying for the pensions and healthcare of those in retirement (who now outnumber them at the polls), and retirees rail against the selfishness and immaturity of younger generations. It's only a mild exaggeration to argue that intergenerational conflict could well be to the twenty-first century what the world wars were to the twentieth, mainly as a corollary of the rapid transformation of the population age structure.

A recent research article on "Understanding and Managing Intergenerational Conflict" argues that the classic conflicts between parents and adolescents, and between retirees and workers, are now eclipsed by the interplay among several generations in the workplace. "Senior leadership in many organizations is from a different generation that believes much more in face time and working certain hours, whereas many young professionals have grown up learning how to work smarter, not harder," one study participant mentioned. "I've always been entered into positions where I've had to go head to head in some cases with certain (older) individuals who I would consider complacent in their positions," another noted. Some of the differences are attributable to broader societal trends like secularization: "There is a strong religious value [with older generations], regardless of what religion you were. I mean, how many of the younger generations went to Sunday school?"

In the age of identity politics, intergenerational relations can become tricky.

"Older generations were defined by their work where younger generations are defined by a lot of different things. Like, I'm a certified financial planner, but also a cyclist. I'm also a triathlete. I'm also a coach. I'm also a dad. I coach for my kids. I'm a husband. I'm involved." Technology is also blamed for creating misunderstandings and complicating interaction. "The societal influences that we [older generations] really didn't have much of . . . they [younger generations] are under tremendous pressure. And yeah . . . there are times when they walk away and I think it's because of the societal pressure, again, that the 24/7 mentality has brought us." And also for making communication difficult. "The communication skills of some of the younger people that I meet on a weekly basis are absolutely nil. There are absolutely no communication skills because they learn how to communicate via Twitter and talk in abbreviated words and abbreviated sentences. So if I had to communicate for any length of time with someone in their 20s, I probably couldn't."

But these issues pale by comparison with the potential for intergenerational finger-pointing over existential issues like climate change. "Consumption-crazed baby boomers are leaving millennials with a mountain of debt and a destabilized climate," proclaims the website of ClimateOne.org. After all, it was my parents' generation and my own that became hooked on oil from the 1950s to the '70s as a result of the vast expansion of the economy and the suburbs, and innovations such as the supertanker and the jetliner. One extreme manifestation of this tension is Bruce Gibney's provocative book *A Generation of Sociopaths: How the Baby Boomers Betrayed America* (2017). A Generation Xer and early investor in PayPal, Gibney anticipates that baby boomers are "gonna die before climate probably has a very significant impact on their lives." Therefore, "it's time for them to get out of the way." He sees the issue as in the classic principal-agent dilemma, in which the party that has the lesser stake in the issue is the one making decisions that will mostly affect the other party.

The problem is wider than the controversy created by a book. In 2013, the United Nations called for intergenerational solidarity in the context of its sustainable development goals. "The dedication to future generations is visible worldwide and across cultures," reads the report of the secretary-general on the topic. "It is a universal value shared amongst humanity." It's hard to take issue with that statement, but it clearly reveals a built-in bias that looks at intergenerational solidarity from one perspective alone, that of the younger generations and those to come into being in the future. Meanwhile, the UN continues to ceaselessly promote through its specialized agencies a rigid, age-based system of universal schooling, wage employment, and compulsory retirement that ultimately undermines its own goals of intergenerational justice and equity. National governments and companies are equally wedded to it. As we shall see in the next chapter, the sequential model of life might well survive the current socioeconomic turmoil if it weren't for the seemingly never-ending increase in life expectancy.

2

SOARING LONGEVITY AND HEALTH

I don't work on longevity,
I work on keeping people healthy.
—Aubrey de Grey (1963–)

Joseph Stalin didn't want to die. The ruthless dictator had industrialized the Soviet Union and emerged victorious from World War II—both at a staggering human cost. He was confident he could win the arms and space races. He passed away in 1953 at age seventy-four, just a few years short of the detonation of the first Soviet hydrogen bomb and the launching of Sputnik. It would not have been surprising for him to have lived to age one hundred, if the statistics from his native republic of Georgia were to be believed. In fact, Soviet propaganda touted the entire country as the "State of Longevity." But, as my demography professor Neil Bennett and his colleague Lea Keil Garson have thoroughly documented, bureaucrats and apparatchiks exaggerated the number of centenarians in the Soviet Caucasus region so as to please the

"Father of Nations," as Stalin was called, and make him believe he could live to age one hundred. The Soviet Union was, after all, a gigantic cascade of lies. Not even the Red Tsar was shielded from them.

Longer average life spans, however, aren't fake news. Over the past 250 years, we have witnessed dramatic increases in average life expectancy. It makes a big difference that the average American born in 2022 is expected to live thirty-two years longer than in 1900: seventy-eight compared to forty-six. The global average grew from thirty-one years to seventy-two in 2022, more than doubling. That huge leap forward challenges conventional assumptions about schooling, working, and retirement. "This is the crowning achievement of the modern era," writes historian James Riley, "surpassing wealth, military power, and political stability in import." But it does raise a number of questions. Should we go to school only once? Are we condemned to having only one career, occupation, or profession in such a long life span? Can we afford to retire at age sixty-five if we live another twenty-five years on average? How can our savings last that long? What retirement age makes sense from the point of view of intergenerational fairness?

A BRIEF HISTORY OF THE LIFE SPAN

The fifteen kings of Judah (6000–1000 BC) averaged 52 years of life. Before the Roman sack of Athens, the twenty-nine main classic Greek philosophers, poets, and politicians for whom birth and death dates are known averaged 68 years. The mean was 71.5 years for the thirty who survived that fateful event. By contrast, the thirty-nine Roman philosophers, poets, and politicians from 30 BC to AD 120 averaged only 56.2 years, perhaps because of the widespread impact of poisoning from lead plumbing. The life spans of privileged, presumably well-fed, elite males continued to fluctuate to the present time. The eighteen fathers of the Christian Church (150–400 AD) lived an average of 63.4 years, the twenty-one leading Italian painters of the Renaissance (1300–1570), 62.7 years, and the twenty-seven leading Italian philosophers, 68.9 years. The fellows of the Royal College of Physicians lived an average of 67 years between 1500 and 1640, but only 62.8 years between 1720 and 1800.

Thus, longevity seems to have oscillated throughout the last few millennia around a relatively high level—at least for elite men. Prior to 1800, turning sixty or seventy implied having survived horrific rates of infant and child mortality, famines, plagues, and incurable diseases. Women's life expectancy beyond childhood also went through several ups and downs. For both males and females, life expectancy improved markedly after the Industrial Revolution, except for relatively brief episodes of war or epidemics. In 1785, life expectancy at birth in the United Kingdom was thirty-seven years. By 1900, it had risen to forty-seven years, an increase dwarfed by twentieth-century advances that produced an estimated eighty-two-year average life span in 2022.

Contrary to the conventional wisdom, progress in life expectancy is not primarily due to reductions in infant and child mortality. Mortality rates have declined at every age. In the United States, the average life expectancy for white males at age ten grew from fifty-one years in 1900 to sixty-eight in 2020. At age sixty, it nearly doubled from fourteen to twenty-three years. Similarly, American white women saw their remaining life spans at age ten rise from fifty-two to seventy-three years, and at age sixty from seventeen to twenty-six. Nonwhite males' averages are three to four years lower than for whites, and nonwhite females fall about two years short of their white counterparts. But *every* group has seen life expectancy increase at every age over most of the last 250 years.

Largely because of inequality by race and income level, the U.S. is far from leading the world in life expectancy at birth. In fact, while in 1960, Americans were ranked twenty-second among all countries at the time, by 2022, they were only in forty-eighth place, and the U.S. Bureau of the Census estimates that by 2060, they will fall further to forty-ninth. Leading the pack in 2022 were Monaco, Macao, Japan, Liechtenstein, Hong Kong, Switzerland, Spain, Singapore, and Italy, in that order. Some of these countries are very rich and resourceful. The Mediterranean diet and widely available primary health-care seem to be behind Spain's and Italy's high ranking. Among developed countries, Russia's excessive alcohol consumption and historical disdain for human life—"It loves blood, the Russian soil," goes the saying—has resulted in it being among the mostly poor seventy countries in the world with the lowest average life spans.

"The story of our extra life is a story of progress in its usual form: brilliant ideas and collaborations unfolding far from the spotlight of public attention, setting in motion incremental improvements that take decades to display their true magnitude," writes Steven Johnson, author of *Extra Life,* a major book on life expectancy. Better overall nutrition, improvements in personal hygiene, water chlorination, pasteurized dairy products, antibiotics, mass vaccinations, and advancements in epidemiological analysis are among the plethora of tools that have helped humanity prolong life spans since the Industrial Revolution. As a result of the doubling in life expectancy over the last 250 years, most parents can today live long enough to play with their grandchildren, and at least one in three can have the joy of seeing their great-grandchildren. But not all groups in society have seen their life span increase.

WHAT'S THE MATTER WITH
MIDDLE-AGED WHITE MEN?

"This paper documents a marked increase in the all-cause mortality of middle-aged White non-Hispanic men and women in the United States between 1999 and 2013." Thus reads the first sentence of a thought-provoking paper published in the *Proceedings of the National Academy of Sciences* in 2015 by Princeton economists Anne Case and Angus Deaton (he subsequently won the Nobel Prize). Their careful statistical work triggered a veritable political and intellectual storm in the age of resentment politics. "This change reversed decades of progress in mortality and was unique to the United States; no other rich country saw a similar turnaround." Perhaps the most shocking finding was that "the midlife mortality reversal was confined to White non-Hispanics; black non-Hispanics and Hispanics at midlife; and those aged 65 and above in every racial and ethnic group, continued to see mortality rates fall," albeit, I hasten to add, from higher levels to begin with.

They proceeded to painstakingly document that most of the mortality increase was due to "drug and alcohol poisonings, suicide, and chronic liver diseases and cirrhosis," all of them ominous signs of social dislocation. Even more tellingly, the mortality crisis beset non-Hispanic white males with a high school diploma or less to a much greater extent than the more highly educated. To make matters worse, this demographic suffered from higher rates of mental illness, chronic pain, and inability to work. The emerging overall picture was one of pain, stress, isolation, desperation, illness, and premature death. They called the phenomenon *deaths of despair,* a label that struck a chord with the public's imagination.

The fact that a dry scholarly paper caused a media uproar is news in and of itself. In the run-up to the 2016 presidential election—when candidate Trump made his fateful appeal to the grievances of middle-aged white males in a handful of blue states—it turned into the academic equivalent of a tsunami. The authors followed up in 2017 with an even more provocative analysis in which they proposed a theory of cumulative disadvantage in the labor market among white males with low levels of education when compared not only to other whites but to minority groups as well. According to Case and Deaton, the unraveling of the "blue-collar aristocracy" began with the demise of manufacturing, the reduction in marriage rates in favor of other forms of partnership, and the declining role of traditional religious congregations as sources of social support. In this context, globalization and technological change assessed the decisive blow to the economic opportunities of the lesser educated, who stood to lose from the rising tide of global competition. Lower wages further reinforced the vicious cycle by prompting many non-Hispanic white males to withdraw from the labor market and enter a path of social isolation and financial instability. According to their late Princeton colleague Alan Krueger, about half of men not in the labor force at the time took pain medication, with two-thirds of them taking a prescription painkiller, oftentimes an opioid.

While non-Hispanic white males in their fifties represent less than 5 percent of the American population, their increasingly dire predicament was significant enough to tilt the balance in favor of a candidate who, once in office, revolutionized American and global politics, perhaps for a long time to come. His was a message that resonated with the fallen white labor aristocracy because it victimized specific individuals as opposed to ideas—namely, immigrants, corporate executives, and liberal elites. Trump's unique brand of populism turned American politics on its head by turning the GOP into the party of the frustrated blue collars. Meanwhile, the coronavirus pandemic further complicated matters by increasing mortality among Black men and women to a much greater extent than whites. But even before the pandemic, the plight of non-Hispanic white men in their fifties was not the only surprising upset in the overall trend toward higher life expectancy.

WHAT'S "KILLING" CAREER-ORIENTED WOMEN?

Another peculiarly American tragedy is the narrowing of the life expectancy gap between women and men. Women's projected life span advantage over men at age 60 peaked in 1975 at 4.9 years, a considerable difference in life expectancy. By 2022, it had dropped to 3.3, and the most recent forecast by the United Nations Population Division is that it will continue to slide to under 2 years by 2050. This dramatic decline is much more pronounced in the U.S. than in the UK, Sweden, France, Germany, Spain, Italy, and South Korea. Among large rich countries, Japan is the exception in that women's advantage continues to grow, as is the case in most emerging and developing countries.

Don't get me wrong. American women continue to see their life expectancy increase, but much more slowly than in past decades and at a lower rate than men's. Historically, men have experienced higher mortality rates than women at every age. The reasons for the decline span the whole spectrum, from biology to social behavior. "Female hormones and the role of women in reproduction have been linked to greater longevity," notes *Scientific American*. "Estrogen, for example, facilitates the elimination of bad cholesterol and thus may offer some protection against heart disease." By contrast, hormones seem to be detrimental to men's life span. "Testosterone, on the other hand, has been linked to violence and risk taking." Women's reproductive role also plays to their advantage. "The female body has to make reserves to accommodate the needs of pregnancy and breastfeeding," which may appear to be a disadvantage at first, if it weren't for the fact that "this ability has been associated with a greater ability to cope with overeating and eliminating excess food."

Work outside of the household is a key factor associated with higher mortality. Men have been historically more exposed to the so-called man-made diseases, including "exposure to the hazards of the workplace in an industrial context, alcoholism, smoking and road accidents, which have indeed increased considerably throughout the 20th century." American women today, especially those below the age of forty, have labor force participation rates only a few percentage points smaller than men's, up from very low levels two generations ago.

While women increasingly participate in the labor force, they continue to be responsible for the lion's share of household tasks, including shopping, cooking, and attending to their children. Besides, there are nearly six times as many single mothers as single fathers taking care of their children. As Lisa Berkman, director of the Center for Population and Development Studies at Harvard, notes, women's new role in the U.S. economy has created a perfect storm: they are more exposed to the stress of the workplace, marriage, and, for 11.5 million of them, single motherhood. "Chronic stress may promote earlier onset of chronic diseases," says University of California San Francisco psychiatry professor Elissa Epel. She became somewhat of a celebrity for helping discover that stress tends to wear down the protective tips of chromosomes believed to be associated with longevity, in a finding that comes as close to a smoking gun as there's ever been in the study of women's lost years of life. To make matters worse, women are more likely than men to soothe themselves by eating, and to reduce the time they spend exercising to balance their work and family lives. A perfect storm it is.

DESPAIR IS MORE WIDESPREAD THAN PREVIOUSLY THOUGHT

As if that weren't enough, things are getting even worse for other categories of women. The evolution of female life expectancy displays a continuing bifurcation in the U.S. by education and place of residence, with educated women living in metropolitan areas faring much better than the rest. Between 2009 and 2016, "women experienced life expectancy declines" in eight of the forty American regions analyzed by a team of demographers led by my University of Pennsylvania colleague Irma Elo. It's important to highlight that the data refer to non-Hispanic white women. "In all 40 areas, White men's life expectancy gains outpaced White women's life expectancy gains." Women in nonmetropolitan areas in Alabama, Arkansas, Kentucky, Louisiana, Missouri, Oklahoma, Tennessee, and Texas "lost nearly a year in life expectancy" between 1990 and 2016. Detailed epidemiological studies identify the culprits: smoking, mental and nervous system disorders, and drug overdoses.

Perhaps the most shocking recent research finding in the field of mortality is that even some women who don't work outside of the household are losing out. My coauthor and former student Arun Hendi, now at Princeton University, found that "life expectancy increased or stagnated since 1990 among all education-race-sex groups except for non-Hispanic White women with less than a high school education," for whom there was a sharp *decline* of 2.5 years in life expectancy over two decades. That's a huge change in such a short time. The data and the fancy statistical methods can't even begin to tell the tragic personal stories behind them. Crystal Wilson of Cave City, Arkansas, where most residents are white, passed away at 38. She was a stay-at-home mom suffering from obesity and diabetes. She "dropped out in the tenth grade because she had married," writes Monica Potts in *The American Prospect*. "That was the way things were." Her premature passing is just one example among many in the same community. According to Julie Johnson, the technology coordinator at the local school district, "If you are a woman, and you are a poorly educated woman, opportunities for you are next to nothing. You get married and you have kids . . . You're better off if you're not working . . . It's a horrible cycle." Johnson has a simple answer to what's killing white female high school dropouts, one that parallels the experience of non-Hispanic white men with little education. "The desperation of the times. I don't know anything about anything, but that's what kills them."

The malaise extends well beyond young mothers of low educational achievement. Overall, mortality continues to increase rapidly among all Americans in the twenty-five-to-forty-four age group. "Young adults today have experienced difficulties coming of age during the Great Recession of 2008–2010, that is, delayed transition to adulthood, declines in marriage, and increased rates of co-residence with parents," note Elo and her coauthors. "Adults in this age group have increased rates of drug and alcohol abuse and may experience increased morbidity and mortality related to these behaviors in future decades." That's the future awaiting a sizable number of millennial women and men for whom globalization and technological change represent headwinds. And as if it weren't enough, the coronavirus pandemic increased death rates among the most disadvantaged groups, especially among those fifty years and older.

In stark contrast with the phenomenon of deaths of despair, however, we find a technology-enabled quest for eternal life that aims at challenging inherited assumptions in yet another way.

THE FOUNTAIN OF YOUTH, GOOGLE'S CALICO, AND GOD'S MOLECULE

"When the Ichthyophagi [coast-dwellers] showed wonder at the number of the years, he led them to a fountain, wherein when they had washed, they found their flesh all glossy and sleek, as if they had bathed in oil—and a scent came from the spring like that of violets," wrote Herodotus (ca. 484–ca. 425 BC), the Greek geographer and founder of history as an organized intellectual endeavor. "The water was so weak, they said, that nothing would float in it, neither wood, nor any lighter substance, but all went to the bottom. If the account of this fountain be true, it would be their constant use of the water from it which makes them so long-lived." The mythical fountain of youth had become one of the most mesmerizing concoctions of all time.

I got married at the San José Parish Church in Guaynabo, Puerto Rico, across the road from the ruins of the house of Juan Ponce de León, the conquistador who claimed the island for the Spanish Crown in 1508. He led the first European expedition to Florida in 1513, purportedly to search for the fountain of youth. "At a distance of 325 leagues from La Española [Hispaniola], they say there is an island called Boyuca or Ananeo," wrote Peter Martyr, a contemporaneous Italian scholar in the court of Spain's Ferdinand the Catholic, who referred to the location of the fountain without mentioning Florida or Ponce de León. "And those who have explored the island's interior tell of a remarkable spring that rejuvenates the old through the drinking of its waters. Do not think, Your Holiness," he warned, "that they say this in jest or take it lightly. So formally have they dared to circulate this information throughout the court that the entire town, and more than a few of its most-distinguished members, through virtue and fortune, take it as true."

The first specific reference to Ponce de León's quest for the fountain in Florida dates back to the chronicles of Gonzalo Fernández de Oviedo, printed in 1535, two decades after the conquistador's death. "And then he told that tale about the Fountain that rejuvenates the old or makes them young . . . And this story was so widely-known, its truth so asserted by the Indians from those parts, that Captain Juan Ponce and his people, and lost caravels went . . . to seek this fountain. This was a great joke among the Indian." He was thirty years old at the time of his first voyage to what would later become the Sunshine State, passing away eight years later from wounds sustained during a skirmish with the Calusa people while attempting to establish a permanent settlement in southern Florida. Little did he know that the peninsula would one day become one of the most important retirement destinations in the world.

Fast-forward to the internet age. Google changed the way in which we search for information, find our destinations on a map, and receive messages from advertisers. Flush with cash, they founded the California Life Company (Calico) in 2013, with the express purpose of promoting life expectancy. Two years later, they spun off Verily, formerly Google Life Sciences, a division within the sprawling company. This venture seeks to design intelligent health solutions, including wearable medical devices and monitors, disease management, surgical robotics, bioelectronic medicines, and smart shoes for health tracking and fall prevention. In 2014, reports leaked a baseline study billed as the "most ambitious and difficult science project ever" and "a giant leap into the unknown." Its aim is to "know the structure of thousands of people's bodies—down to the molecules inside their cells" so as to establish biomarkers that can detect diseases.

The quest for a "God molecule" that might retard or even reverse aging has captured the imagination of Hollywood stars and Silicon Valley moguls, both eager to continue enjoying their good fortunes indefinitely. According to Tad Friend's story in *The New Yorker* about their obsession with longevity, the assumption made by actors and "masters of the universe" alike is that some kind of a "cure" for aging is right around the corner. "I have the idea that aging is plastic, that it's encoded," said Joon Yun, a physician and manager of a healthcare hedge fund at a meeting on the subject at the National Academy of Medicine. "If something is encoded, you can crack the code." To growing applause, he went on, "If you can crack the code, you can *hack* the code!" And in keeping with the best sci-fi rhetoric, he added: "We can end aging forever."

Yun's bold assertions are hardly an exaggeration. The truth of the matter is that cells can be genetically manipulated so that they multiply forever, or at least for an extended period, thus arresting aging. The trouble is that humans are a complicated species genetically, behaviorally, and ethically. "In humans, it is not ethical to perform mutations, and there are so many conflicting forces at work that it is difficult to assess the impact of dietary restrictions," notes Janet Thornton, an antiaging expert at the European Bioinformatics Institute. "In the lab, worms' life span can be increased 10-fold; in flies and mice, the max increase is just 1.5 fold, but an equivalent measure is not available for humans. It is likely that the human system is complex with many interconnections and buffering, so such extensions may not be accessible." These efforts notwithstanding, I'd rather be a mortal human than an everlasting worm.

Prolonging life indefinitely may be contrary to religious belief, interfere with the incentives we face at different stages in life, and ultimately make the planet uninhabitable due to overcrowding. But that's not preventing hundreds of millions of dollars from being spent on a panoply of technologies to defeat aging. The idea of immortality is as old as humanity itself. But is it worth the present and future costs, or should we rather focus on living a better, healthier life rather than a merely longer one?

LIFE SPAN VERSUS HEALTH SPAN

"Can We Live Longer but Stay Younger?" That's the question posed by Adam Gopnik in an eye-opening *New Yorker* article. The powerful laws of evolution dictate that human bodies should perform like clockwork and fulfill their mission during the period we pass our genes on to the next generation, but not necessarily later in life. "Once we have passed reproductive age, the genes can get sloppy about copying, allowing mutations to accumulate, because natural selection no longer cares." Thus, the remarkable success in increasing life expectancy has multiplied the rates of all sorts of nasty health problems, including cancer, heart disease, diabetes, arthritis, and dementia. Here's the conundrum. Should scarce research resources be allocated to increasing our life span or ensuring that we remain healthy for most of our lives—our health span? As Tad Friend puts it, this has led to a fierce contest between "healthspanners" and "immortalists." While immortality seems far away, ensuring that we can enjoy life to the fullest for most of our life spans seems entirely within reach. The problem is that health spans have not tended to grow faster than life spans, meaning that the average person still faces a few years—as many as six to eight—of poor health before passing away. Definitely not a good prospect to look forward to.

In 2019, the National Academy of Medicine launched the Healthy Longevity Global Grand Challenge as "a worldwide movement to improve physical, mental, and social well-being for people as they age." The initiative is meant to mitigate the ill effects of population aging, which "is poised to impose a significant strain on economies, health systems, and social structures worldwide. *But it doesn't have to.*" The basic idea involves increasing the health span by spurring "an explosion of potential new medicines, treatments, technologies, and preventive and social strategies that could help transform the way we age and ensure better health, function, and productivity during a period of extended longevity." As is often the case, easier said than done.

While we have excellent measures of life expectancy at various ages based on the timing of mortality, it is much harder—and subject to controversy and debate—to measure people's expected health spans. The World Health Organization has calculated a "healthy life expectancy," defined as "the average life in good health—that is to say without irreversible limitation of activity in daily life or incapacities—of a fictitious generation subject to the conditions of mortality and morbidity prevailing that year." While life expectancy is an on-off switch, the concept of healthy life expectancy suffers from insurmountable methodological ambiguities. Where does one draw the line between healthy and unhealthy? Is there a no-man's-land somewhere in between? Isn't it possible for people to descend into unhealthiness only to bounce back into good health?

Putting such difficulties aside, the evidence points in the direction that better lifestyles, preventative care, early disease detection, and new medical treatments have resulted in a steady increase in health spans beyond age sixty since the indicator was first calculated in 2000. The immortalists might be vindicated by the fact that progress appears to be slow. Average health spans have increased by a mere two or three months per decade—a pace that Google's researchers surely find exasperating and both Hollywood and Silicon Valley dismiss as unacceptable. Still, the good news is that in 2019, the average 60-year-old American male could expect to be healthy for another 15.6 years, and the average woman for 17.1. Given that men's life expectancy was 22.0 at the time and women's 25.0 years, the average American would spend the last 8 years of life with some health condition that implied a limited ability to enjoy it.

Most importantly, since the turn of the twenty-first century, average health spans have increased at roughly the same pace as life spans in most countries in the world, both rich and poor, and especially so in countries as diverse as Angola, Bangladesh, Botswana, China, Denmark, Eritrea, Ethiopia, Finland, India, Ireland, Jordan, Laos, Malawi, Malta, Mongolia, Namibia, Poland, Portugal, Russia, Singapore, South Africa, South Korea,

Thailand, and the UK. As in the case of life spans, when it comes to health spans, the U.S. is an outlier. Health spans have grown only half as fast as life spans, with the ominous implication that the quality of life of gray Americans has deteriorated relative to those in other parts of the world.

What are the intergenerational implications of this state of affairs? Essentially, the average sixty-year-old in most rich countries has another twenty to twenty-five years left of life span, of which ten to fifteen years are expected health span. As a result, does it make sense to retire at sixty-five? Can we afford it as a society? Is it fair to other generations? Those are thorny questions that tend to arouse passions, given what's at stake.

THE IDEA OF (INTERGENERATIONAL) JUSTICE

"When we try to determine how justice can be advanced, there is a basic need for public reasoning, involving arguments coming from different quarters and divergent perspectives," writes Amartya Sen, the Indian Nobel Prize–winning philosopher and economist, in his path-breaking book *The Idea of Justice* (2009). "An engagement with contrary arguments does not, however, imply that we must expect to be able to settle the conflicting reasons in all cases and arrive at agreed position on all issues. Complete resolution is neither a requirement of a person's own rationality, nor is it a condition of reasonable social choice."

Perhaps the best example of the difficulty of arriving at a complete resolution of intergenerational justice is climate change, in which the trade-off between economic well-being today and sustainability into the future is particularly hard to adjudicate. Who pays for pensions and healthcare for those in retirement age is another vexing issue for which it is hard to articulate an argument about fairness. After all, those in retirement gave birth to younger generations, raised them, and provided them with life opportunities. But, as Sen proposes, we can compare and contrast the arguments and perspectives of different generations in the hope of engaging people in a debate that being thorny doesn't make it any less needed.

"The relationship between older and younger generations is still defined by mutual support and affection. However, the action and inaction of successive governments risks undermining the foundation of this relationship," warned a 2019 report by the House of Lords in the UK. "Many in younger generations are struggling to find secure, well-paid jobs and secure, affordable housing, while many in older generations risk not receiving the support they need because government after government has failed to plan for a long-term generational timescale." The committee identified several main areas of friction, including government deficits, access to affordable housing, underfunding of education, and footing the cost of "old age" programs. It bewilders me that they did not include climate change among them.

Society is somehow governed by a social contract providing for some basic rules of engagement. As important as that agreement is, the generational contract is likely to become even more so in the near future. One specific version, the generational welfare contract, stipulates that voters should favor policies that not only favor them but also others at stages of the life course different from their own, for a mix of self-centered and altruistic reasons. Younger generations may want to support pensions and healthcare in anticipation of their needs decades later. Older generations can benefit from childcare services and education if they lead to a bigger and better-prepared workforce willing to pay taxes to fund pensions and healthcare. Still, pensions in particular have become in most rich countries the largest welfare program, upsetting the balance that once existed among various budget categories.

As the cost of pensions and healthcare skyrocketed, "support for pro-old [sic] policies declined in most European countries, although absolute support for government provision of a reasonable standard of living for the old remained high," writes Aart-Jan Riekhoff, a researcher at the Finnish Centre for Pensions. "Decreases in relative preferences for pro-old policies were due not only to decreases in absolute support, but also to increases especially in support for government provision of childcare." In other words, although intergenerational solidarity continues to be strong, the budgetary trade-offs are becoming more salient in the minds of young workers and voters. "This indicates that while the generational welfare contrast may not be under any immediate threat, age-related policy preferences are certainly being re-calibrated in many countries," especially in Europe, the U.S., Canada, and Japan.

A key issue in the recent evolution of intergenerational fairness and solidarity has to do with the extent to which welfare programs are designed for, and delivered to, specific age groups. Public education spending and childcare services benefit the young and their parents, unemployment insurance provides workers with peace of mind should they lose their jobs, healthcare disproportionately benefits those of advanced age, and pension schemes are enjoyed by retirees. In the age of rising debt and budget deficits, intergenerational solidarity gets undermined. This state of affairs is the backdrop for the current showdown over the viability of public pension schemes.

HOUSTON, WE HAVE A PROBLEM

"This is causing me a lot of stress," says Jan-Pieter Jansen, a seventy-seven-year-old Dutchman who retired at age sixty. "The cuts to my pension will mean thousands of euros less that I can spend on the family, and the holidays we like. I'm very angry that this is happening after I saved for so long." After four decades of making contributions to his industry's pension fund, he received a letter informing him of benefit cuts of up to 10 percent.

Longer life spans, combined with falling fertility, represent a formidable double whammy for pension systems, especially those funded through current contributions from employed workers and their employers. Furthermore, many public pension funds have assumed investment returns of 7 percent and above, which are unrealistic at a time when bond yields approach zero. The solutions? Virtually every serious study concludes that some combination of postponing retirement, raising worker and employer contributions and taxes, cutting benefits, or increasing immigration of younger workers is needed. Perhaps all of the above will be needed—which promises to be disruptive and painful. There's a long list of prime ministers and presidents who have seen their popularity eroded over the looming pensions crisis. No politician wants to lose support among contributing workers or pensioners. Meanwhile, the interests are so entrenched that reforms needed to ensure the future viability of pensions seems unlikely.

Fortunately, people seem to be reading the writing on the wall and deciding to retire later. In the early 1970s, men retired at age 69 on average across the developed countries of Europe and North America, and women at age 65. The average age reached a minimum in 2000 at 63 and 61 years, respectively. Over the last two decades, both men and women have postponed retirement by 2.5 years on average.

I find it puzzling that most existing studies of the future viability of pension systems focus on the increase in life expectancy without taking into consideration average health spans. The concepts of both the life span and the health span are central to understanding the future of retirement in a postgenerational society because, when making decisions about retirement, people take into consideration not only how many years they may have left but also how healthy they are or are likely to be.

Let's then crunch the numbers that most experts have surprisingly neglected in the past. The first two columns of table 2.1 show the corresponding figures for major countries, which come from the two authoritative sources discussed earlier, the United Nations and the World Health Organization. The expected health span at age 60 indicates for how much longer we might be able to be fully productive members of society in the sense of being able to work full-time without limitations. The expected life span minus the expected health span shows the *minimum* number of years we might have to be reliant on a pension because we won't be able to work full-time due to poor health. For the average American male, this number is 6.4 years (22.0-15.6), and for the average female, it's 7.9 years (25.0-17.1).

The figures in the table are actually reassuring because Social Security might well survive in its current form *if* we were to work until the end of our health span—that is, until we start to experience serious health issues. This is something that very few people may be willing to do—I certainly wouldn't. That's captured by scenario A, which would lessen the burden on the workers who pay taxes to fund healthcare and pensions. It implies that American men would retire on average at age 75.6 and American women at

TABLE 2.1: LIFE SPAN, HEALTH SPAN, AND RETIREMENT SCENARIOS
FROM THE PERSPECTIVE OF AN AVERAGE 60-YEAR-OLD IN 2019

Country:	Expected Life Span at Age 60 (years)		Expected Health Span at Age 60 (years)		Expected Life Span minus Expected Health Span		Scenario A: Retirement Age if People Stop Working at the End of Their Health Span		Scenario B: Retirement Age if People Stop Working Seven Years before the End of Their Health Span	
	Men	Women	Men	Women	Men	Women	Men	Women	Men	Women
USA	22.0	25.0	15.6	17.1	6.4	7.9	75.6	77.1	68.6	70.1
China	18.6	22.0	15.0	16.9	3.6	5.1	75.0	76.9	68.0	69.9
Japan	24.0	29.2	18.8	21.8	5.2	7.4	78.8	81.8	71.8	74.8
South Korea	22.6	27.3	18.2	21.2	4.4	6.1	78.2	81.2	71.2	74.2
India	17.4	18.6	13.0	13.5	4.4	5.1	73.0	73.5	66.0	66.5
UK	22.7	25.2	17.6	18.9	5.1	6.3	77.6	78.9	70.6	71.9
Germany	22.2	25.6	17.0	19.9	5.2	5.7	77.0	79.9	70.0	72.9
France	23.3	27.6	18.5	20.8	4.8	6.8	78.5	80.8	71.5	73.8
Italy	23.5	27.0	17.9	19.8	5.6	7.2	77.9	79.8	70.9	72.8
Spain	23.4	27.7	18.0	20.3	5.4	7.4	78.0	80.3	71.0	73.3
Mexico	20.0	22.4	15.3	16.8	4.7	5.6	75.3	76.8	68.3	69.8
Brazil	20.1	23.9	15.2	17.4	4.9	6.5	75.2	77.4	68.2	70.4
Turkey	19.2	24	15.8	17.3	3.4	6.7	75.8	77.3	68.8	70.3
Nigeria	13.4	14.3	13.3	13.8	0.1	0.5	73.3	73.8	66.3	66.8
South Africa	14.4	18.3	12.7	14.8	1.7	3.5	72.7	74.8	65.7	67.8

Source: Global Health Observatory of the World Health Organization.

age 77.1, way above today's average retirement ages (the mid-60s). Under that scenario, people wouldn't be able to enjoy a fully active lifestyle during retirement because they would have reached, on average, the end of their health span. It would be especially problematic in Japan, South Korea, France, and Spain, where people would need to retire at or near age 80. Simply put, while very attractive for younger generations, scenario A seems to be socially and politically indefensible. We can't ask people to work until they can no longer do so due to a major health problem. Workers have the right to enjoy at least a few years in retirement while still healthy.

To find some intergenerational balance, one might want to think about intermediate solutions that avoid the extremes of scenario A and of retiring at today's average of sometime in the mid-60s. For instance, we could set things up in such a way that both men and women would spend seven years in retirement before their health span ends, fully enjoying an active lifestyle during that time. I propose seven years mainly because of its biblical connotations. Under this scenario B, American men would retire, on average, at age 68.6 and American women at age 70.1. That sounds more tenable and agreeable than scenario A, but the debate over whether seven years is enough, or intergenerationally fair, would be protracted and fraught politically.

At the root of the problem with every conceivable scenario is the ratio of people of working age to people of retirement age, whose decline poses a

FIGURE 2.1: Number of People Ages 15–59 for Each Person Above Age 60

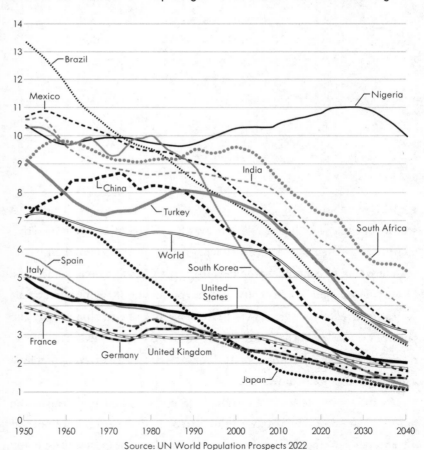

Source: UN World Population Prospects 2022

fundamental challenge to our society. Figure 2.1 shows how bad the situation has become. In 1950, for each person above the age of 60 in the world, we had 7.2 between the ages of 15 and 59. By 2022, that number had fallen to 4.4. In China, it went from 7.1 to 3.5, and in the United States from 5.0 to 2.5. The decline has been even more precipitous in South Korea, from 10.3 to 2.5, and in Japan, from 7.5 to a mere 1.5. These ratios will continue to fall in the next decades given the decline in fertility and the increase in life expectancy, forcing those who work to pay more taxes to pay not just for the pensions but also for the healthcare of those above the age of 60. In Japan and South Korea, by 2040, there will be an average of little more than one person of working age for each person above the age of 60, a ratio so low that seems absolutely unsustainable—unless the robots do all the heavy lifting. In the United States, it will be two. Neither ratio will be enough to deliver on promises made about healthcare and pensions for the simple reason that those commitments were adopted when the ratio was at least three or four people of working age for each person above the age of 60. These figures clearly indicate that the intergenerational trade-offs are complex to navigate, especially when younger workers are supposed to foot the lion's share of the bill.

DISSOLVING VERSUS SOLVING PROBLEMS

I learned many useful things from my late Wharton School colleague Russell Ackoff, the pioneer of systems thinking. The most important lesson came from his eye-opening ninety-minute lecture about the famous London bus strikes of the 1950s. He was brought in by the London transport authorities as a consultant to help address the problem of delays during rush hour, when the number of red double-deckers in circulation exceeded the number of bus stops in the system, a situation that created many delays, as buses could not advance according to schedule. Each bus had a driver at the front and a conductor at the back who collected the fares. The problem was aggravated by the bitter struggles between the bus drivers' and the fare collectors' unions, the former counting many

Pakistanis as members and the latter many Indians. (Mayor Sadiq Khan, first elected in 2016, is himself the son of a Pakistani-born London bus driver.) The drivers and fare collectors blamed each other on a daily basis for the constant delays and bottlenecks—the other side was simply not working fast and hard enough. The drivers would shout back at the collectors that they were slowing things down, and the latter would return the yelling. The verbal abuse made the situation far worse—and made riders very uncomfortable.

There are two ways of addressing any given problem, Russ calmly explained. One is to solve it. That means finding a way to overcome the immediate issue within the existing system design parameters and constraints. In the case of a major city's rush-hour transportation woes, that might involve fine-tuning schedules, adding more bus lanes, anticipating traffic-light changes, directing passengers to less busy routes, or increasing fares during peak hour so as to discourage use. In a way, solving problems is like kicking the can down the road.

The other course of action, Russ would calmly propose, is to dissolve the problem altogether, to eradicate it. This second method consists of redefining the situation in such a way that the problem simply vanishes. In a brilliant stroke, he proposed to the London transit authorities that during rush hour, the fare collectors should not be riding on the back of the bus but standing at each bus stop. If one conductor were not enough for the busiest stops, two should be stationed. Not only would this dissipate the potential for conflict between drivers and fare collectors, but the process of loading passengers at each stop could be accelerated by several orders of magnitude. The problem thus simply went away. I vividly remember the executives attending his lecture at Wharton offering Russ, an octogenarian at the time, a standing ovation. He then proceeded to take questions, delighting the audience with his lucidity.

Solving the looming pensions crisis involves proverbial reforms that lack widespread support: raising the age of retirement, cutting benefits, increasing contributions and taxes, and opening the border to immigration by younger workers. Dissolving the pensions problem requires change at the level of the system—that is, departing from the sequential model of life, plain and simple. Replacing it with a fluid and reversible postgenerational model of life would liberate us from the problem once and for all, a possibility that we will explore later in this book.

3

THE RISE AND FALL OF THE NUCLEAR FAMILY

*Nobody has ever before asked the nuclear family to live
all by itself in a box the way we do. With no relatives,
no support, we've put it in an impossible situation.*
—Margaret Mead (1901–1978)

"As far back as our knowledge takes us, human beings have lived in families. We know of no period where this was not so. We know of no people who have succeeded for long in dissolving the family or displacing it," observed anthropologists Margaret Mead and Ken Heyman in their 1965 book, *Family*. "Again and again, in spite of proposals for change and actual experiments, human societies have reaffirmed their dependence on the family as the basic unit of human living—the family of father, mother and children."

Family is a very important aspect of life. But families come in many shapes, forms, and sizes. We normally think about the nuclear family as including the married parents and their children. But there is also an extended family comprising grandparents, uncles, aunts, cousins, and other relatives.

In addition, single-parent families and families without children have always existed. The frequency of each of these family structures varies across time and space. Contrary to the conventional wisdom, nuclear families with two parents and a certain number of children are no longer the norm throughout most of the developed world. In 1970, 40 percent of all U.S. households were nuclear families with two married parents and at least one child under the age of eighteen, but by 2021, it was just 18 percent, the lowest since 1959. Perhaps that's the reason why the topic has become so political and contentious.

THE NUCLEAR FAMILY AND THE SEQUENTIAL MODEL OF LIFE

"Home is the nicest word there is," declares Laura Ingalls in the opening episode of the megahit TV series *Little House on the Prairie* (1974–1983). *Home* stands here for the "Ingalls family." It epitomizes the ideal of the two-parent-plus-children household, along with the joys, the struggles, and the love that was supposed to permeate life and cure every conceivable setback. Loosely based on the bestselling series of books by Laura Ingalls Wilder and set against the idyllic backdrop of late nineteenth-century rural Minnesota, it struck a chord with audiences worldwide at a time when starting a family and seeing the children form their own was seemingly everyone's dream. As Diana Bruk put it in a *Country Living* article, "It depicted a simpler time when one's life revolved around your church, your school, and your family." The books and TV series didn't shy away from worldly problems and tragedies like a dead baby, blindness, or drug addiction. "Of course they had their hardships, but everyone was always smiling and kind, and there was never a problem that they couldn't all solve together." In post-Vietnam and post-Nixon America, a series that "taught good family values" was perhaps needed. The characters couldn't be more endearing. Charles Ingalls was indeed "the perfect man: reliable, righteous, good-spirited, hard-working." His wife, Caroline, was kind, generous, gentle, and faithful. He hunted, fished, and farmed to procure for the family. She attended to the house. Their children were, well, kids who grew up to become adults.

The 1970s were the heyday of the nuclear family.

In theory, the sequential model of life, with people entering and exiting stages in an orderly and predictable way, became widely adopted around the world at the same time that governments, the media, Hollywood, and the major religions promoted the idea of the nuclear family, consisting of parents raising their children until they finished their education and left the household to start their own families. At the lowest socioeconomic levels, both parents would work, leaving children with neighbors or bringing them with their older siblings. In a development dating back to German unification in the 1870s, women higher up in the social hierarchy were told to stay home and devote themselves to the three k's of *Kinder, Küche, Kirche*—children, kitchen, and church. Companies in most countries, from Japan all the way to the U.S., discouraged or outright prevented married women from working outside the household. By the 1950s, the American nuclear family consisting of two parents, at least two kids, a TV, a washing machine, a car, and a dog had become the standard to emulate around the world, given the growing prosperity of the middle class. Women could work, but only before marriage. Margaret Mead noted that the concept of the nuclear family was detrimental to women's status in society, relegating them to the household, and without the support networks that the extended family offered. Once women started to work in droves outside of the household, many found themselves without family help nearby, and thus decided to have fewer or no children.

There's no consensus, however, around this view. According to historians Peter Laslett and Alan Macfarlane, the nuclear family living in a "simple house" was the norm in England as early as the thirteenth century. In fact, they argue that it was precisely the flexibility and geographical mobility of the nuclear family that made the Industrial Revolution possible, and not the other way around. The logic of the market requires malleable and redeployable individuals detached from the chains of kinship and community. Sociologists like Brigitte Berger and my Penn colleague Annette Lareau further argue that the nuclear family headed by two parents is "child-centered," and thus contributed over the last 250 years to the increasingly important role of education in the modern economy and society. To appreciate the importance of the link between the nuclear family, education, and socioeconomic mobility, suffice it to remind ourselves of the enormous difficulty—and even utter impossibility—for slaves to raise their children as part of a nuclear family, a problem that continues to beset African American communities in the United States to this day, with high unemployment and incarceration rates among Black men. The concept of the nuclear family may have at times subjugated women, but its absence also created problems and social dislocation.

The rise of the nuclear family was underpinned by laws and regulations that encouraged it. Bella DePaulo, a social psychologist, argues that "there are some laws and zoning codes that make it difficult for people to live with the people who matter to them—you know, a Golden Girls–type situation." Essentially, "there are zoning restrictions in some places where only a certain number of unrelated people, often two, can live together." Moreover, in the United States, the Family and Medical Leave Act allows people to take unpaid time off to care for a spouse, but not for an unmarried partner.

The rosy notion of the nuclear family belies a reality of struggle and despair. Its emphasis on "growing up" leads to the enormous pressures placed on children to prepare for achieving as adults everything from a stable romantic relationship to professional success. Moreover, the nuclear family has contributed to social inequality because, predictably, not every group in society is in a position to live up to the ideal prototype. "We've made life freer for individuals and more unstable for families. We've made life better for adults but worse for children," argues *New York Times* columnist David Brooks in a recent *Atlantic* piece. "We've moved from big, interconnected, and extended families, which helped protect the most vulnerable people in society from the shocks of life, to smaller, detached nuclear families (a married couple and their children), which give the most privileged people in society room to maximize their talents and expand their options," and ultimately "liberates the rich and ravages the working-class and the poor." He is referring to the painful fact that the ideal of the nuclear family is far from realized among the poor and underrepresented racial and ethnic minorities.

"UNCONVENTIONAL" HOUSEHOLDS

"I've been chasing this idea about a perfect life, but life is unpredictable and irrational and complicated, and I want a complicated life," decries Judd Altman (played by Jason Bateman) in the star-studded 2014 movie *This Is Where I Leave You*. "Three months ago, I had a great job and a nice apartment and I was in love with my wife." His sister, Wendy Altman (Tina Fey), quickly counters, "No, you weren't." "No?" he replies. "No. She was sleeping with somebody else for a year and you never noticed . . . How in love could you have been?" "Yep . . . That's fair," he concedes. The four Altman siblings are back in their childhood home after the passing of their father, where they spend a week sharing their bruised adult lives with their mother (Jane Fonda) and a whole bunch of spouses (some faithful, others not), exes, and might-have-beens.

Besides cultural shifts in our views about relationships and marriage, the reality is that we no longer live in a society in which life is perfectly sequential and traditional nuclear families are the majority. In both rich and poor countries, households headed by a single parent are on the increase, due to parents separating, divorcing, or never living together. Let's begin the analysis by looking at the proportion of babies born to unmarried women, as reflected in figure 3.1, which is one of the situations that likely, though not always, results in a single-parent household. In the European Union, it was 41.3 percent in 2018, higher than the 39.6 percent of the United States. Even Ireland at 37.9 percent was close to the American average. The proportion was especially high in Spain (47.3), the UK (48.2), Estonia (54.1), Denmark (54.2), Sweden (54.5), Portugal (55.9), Bulgaria (58.5), France (60.4), and Iceland (70.5). Thus, regardless of religious background, latitude, and level of development, babies born to an unmarried woman are now more frequent among the rich countries. Despite its lower level of economic development, in Latin America, the proportions are even higher: 69.3 percent in Mexico, 71.8 percent in Costa Rica, and a whopping 73.7 percent in Chile. It is worth noting that in 1960, only a handful of Western European countries had a proportion greater than 10 percent (Iceland, Austria, and Sweden), and most were below 5 percent. At the time, it was 5.3 percent in the United States, and 4.3 percent in Canada.

The only major exceptions to the overall upward trend are South Korea (only 2.2 percent of babies were born to unmarried women in 2018), Japan (2.3), and Turkey (2.9), where the culture—and government and corporate policies—continue to encourage married women to stop working when they have a baby. There are no official statistics on single motherhood in China, although 5–10 percent of total births is a reasonable guesstimate. The government used to penalize single motherhood within its overall framework for population growth control. But now that the one-child policy is history,

FIGURE 3.1: Proportion of Babies Born to Unmarried Women

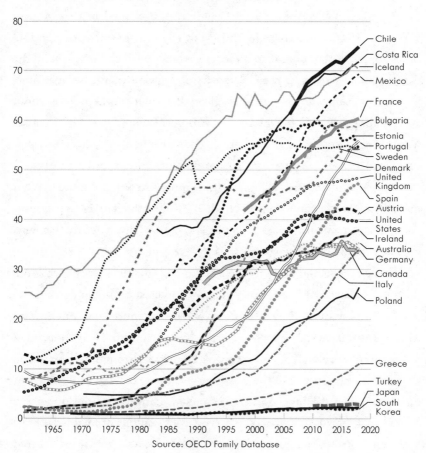

Source: OECD Family Database

it may well be that officials see in this rising global trend a way to reverse the country's demographic decline. In India, a country with a similar proportion to China's (although the statistics do not distinguish between single and widowed mothers), there are probably twice as many single mothers who live with extended family than alone. "From women in my building discreetly moving their husbands away from me in the lift to aunties in the society not allowing their kids to play with my girls cos [*sic*] they come from a 'broken family,' I have seen it all," says Melanie Andrade (not her true name), an Indian mother of two.

However, single-parent households exist for other reasons besides single motherhood, including the death of one of the parents, separation, or divorce. "The U.S. has the world's highest rate of children living in single-parent households," noted a Pew Research Center study published in 2019. "Almost a quarter of U.S. children under the age of 18 live with one parent and no other adults (23%), more than three times the share of children around the world who do so (7%)." The U.S. ranks number one mainly because of its high rates of separation and divorce, given that single motherhood is about average for the world. The lowest proportions of single-parent households were found in countries as different as China (3 percent), Nigeria (4 percent), and India (5 percent). In Canada, it was 15 percent, and the highest in Europe was 17 percent, in Denmark. The report also noted that the U.S. has one of the lowest proportions of children living with relatives (8 percent), compared to a global average of 38 percent, mostly driven by arrangements in emerging and developing countries.

A crucial aspect underlying the nuclear family is the idea that children need to grow up, work, and start their own nuclear family in due course. A 1957 survey quoted by Brooks revealed that more than one in two Americans felt unmarried people were "sick," "immoral," or "neurotic." As we saw in chapter 1, people who do not make it through the prescribed sequential stages of life at the right age risk being labeled as deviants or outcasts. But nowadays, traditional nuclear families are no longer the norm, in at least two respects. First, over 40 percent of married American women already earn more than their husbands, a proportion that may increase to over half by 2030, according to the U.S. Census Bureau. Second, more than half of American households are headed by a single parent, have no kids, or are comprised of single adult individuals. These changes have been driven by globalization, the decline of manufacturing, the feminist movement, secularization, a rising divorce rate, and the rise of the self-expressive culture.

Sociologists Francesca Cancian and Steven Gordon examined the marital advice offered in women's magazines over time. "In place of the old norms of self-sacrifice, avoidance of conflict, and rigid gender roles," they concluded, "there were ideals of self-development, open communication of negative and positive feelings, intimacy, and more flexible roles." Beginning in the 1960s, they identified a "trend toward individualism, emotional expression, and androgyny." For an increasing number of couples, marriage (or cohabitation) is not about children but about fulfillment in life, as my former Penn sociology colleague Kathryn Edin and her coauthor Maria Kefalas have noted. My own take on this remarkable shift is that marriage came to have a very different meaning for educated women who worked outside of the household, with the ultimate evolutionary outcome being fewer kids and more pets. And men had no choice but to adapt to the new situation.

Another aspect of the nuclear family is the impact it's had on social isolation. In the 1985 bestseller *Habits of the Heart,* a team of top American sociologists, led by Robert Bellah, wrote that "American cultural traditions define personality, achievement, and the purpose of human life in ways that leave the individual suspended in glorious, but terrifying, isolation." Making progress in life consists of "finding oneself," "leaving home," "mak[ing] something of yourself" through work, "love and marriage," and "getting involved" in the community and the nation as a neighbor and citizen. But as political scientist Robert Putnam argued in his equally enthralling 2000 hit, *Bowling Alone,* American individualism has triumphed over the traditional sense of community, especially as middle-class families moved into the suburbs and severed traditional ties. "Something important happened to social bonds and civic engagement in America over the last third of the twentieth century," he observed. "We are still more civically engaged than citizens in many other countries, but compared with our own recent past, we are less connected." Among the many culprits (obsession with work, urban sprawl, generational change), he notes that "the downturn in civic engagement coincided with the breakdown of the traditional family unit—mom, dad, and the kids."

Some social scientists feel optimistic about the decline of conventional family arrangements. "To me, the decline of the nuclear family isn't only a story of chaos or trauma," says DePaulo. "For people who never fit comfortably into those nuclear-family structures, it's liberating and opens up a whole panoply of options. The way I think about those options is in terms of the big components of our life—getting married, living together, having sex, having kids." The key point in her reasoning is that "these components all came packaged together, and now they've all come apart. People can pick and choose whatever components they want." For instance, people may live together without getting married or have kids without a romantic partner. The reality, however, is that both nuclear families and hippie communes are on the decline, while other forms of social organization and living are growing rapidly.

FLYING SOLO

"The number of households occupied by just one person is increasing as a trend, and these living a single life have a range of reasons for living alone," announces MBC, the South Korean TV network that airs the world's most famous single-living reality show, *I Live Alone,* featuring the lives of actors, K-pop stars, and leading professional athletes. Known in the nineteenth century as the "Hermit Kingdom" for its attempt to isolate itself from the world, South Korea features the second-lowest fertility rate of any country at a mere 0.87 children per woman (Hong Kong's is 0.76), and has more than six million people living alone out of a population of fifty-two million. Viewers can peek into the lives of assorted celebrities living alone. "This show captures the real image of a single life, the secret and wise tips of household chores, and their philosophy of living alone."

Aggregate statistics show that, indeed, the proportion of households with a single individual is on the increase in many countries, although the data are somewhat patchy, and they include both young people and divorcees or widowers who live alone. In Brazil, it has increased from 5 to 12 percent over the past fifty years, in Mexico from 4 to 10 percent, in Chile from 6 to 9 percent, in Poland from 17 to 24 percent, in Spain from 13 to 23 percent, in Ireland from 14 to 24 percent, in France from 20 to 35 percent, in the U.S. from 13 to 29 percent, and in South Korea from 20 to 27 percent. In most of Europe, a third of households are now comprised of a single individual. Thus, the nuclear family is on the decline because of the increasing proportion of single parents living alone with their children (10 percent in the U.S.), the phenomenon of childless couples living together (a quarter), and the rise in the number of people living by themselves (another quarter). The United Nations estimates that, accordingly, nuclear families with two married parents and at least one child are less than 30 percent of all households in Canada, Japan, South Korea, Russia, and much of Europe. In emerging markets and the developing world, the proportion is even lower, given the historical importance of multigenerational households.

"During the past half-century, our species has embarked on a remarkable social experiment," argues sociologist Eric Klinenberg, author of *Going Solo*. "For the first time in human history, great numbers of people—at all ages, in all places, of every political persuasion—have begun settling down as singletons." The numbers are growing as more people never marry, never have children, and separate or divorce from their partners or spouses.

As DePaulo observes in *Psychology Today*, living alone can be expensive, and thus is more common in richer countries and in those with more affordable housing and better government pension systems. Moreover, "the Internet and other advances in communication technology have made it more possible for people to live alone without feeling isolated." In June of 2021, I completed a five-day quarantine upon arriving in the UK. I never felt more connected in my life, able as I was to video chat with family and friends, to work online, and to access audiovisual entertainment content. But the fact that living alone is possible, and less ostracizing than in the past, doesn't mean that it's desirable. "Living alone may even be stigmatizing," says DePaulo. She attributes the increase in singletons to the rise of individ-ualistic values such as personal independence, self-reliance, self-expression, and personal choice. The breakdown of the sequential model of life and the nuclear family also contribute to this trend.

"The increasing proportion of persons living alone has come to be em-blematic in many ways of modern Western societies because it represents the importance conceded to the individual and to individual goals at the ex-pense, basically, of the family," writes a team of demographers led by Albert Esteve, who works at the Barcelona-based Center for Demographic Studies. Using data on living arrangements in 113 countries representing over 95 percent of the world's population, they found that marital status is the single best predictor of living alone. Thus, the broken sequence from growing up to getting married (or establishing a stable relationship) lies at the heart of this growing trend.

The devil, as usual, is in the details. Among young adults between the ages of twenty-five and twenty-nine, living alone is the exception rather than the rule in most countries outside Europe and North America, where between 15 and 30 percent of women and 20 and 35 percent of men live alone. These pat-terns persist throughout life. In Europe and North America, approximately 8 percent of women and 12 percent of men in their thirties, forties, and fifties—the age groups associated with being a parent in a nuclear family—live alone. While less than 2 percent of African, Asian, and Latin American women live alone at those ages, four times as many African and Latin American men do. Far fewer Asian men live alone given higher marriage rates and cultural stigma. Over time, the number of women who live alone during the first de-cades of adult life is growing only in Europe and North America, while the number of men is rising everywhere except Asia. In sum, living alone is more prevalent among men, in developed countries, and is increasing over time, especially among women and men in their twenties to fifties, especially in developed countries. Behind these patterns is the growing phenomenon of unpartnered individuals. "Men have broken the traditional mold earlier and more decisively than women," conclude Esteve and his colleagues, "though in the most developed world levels of living alone among women are also quite high, an indication that the pace of change may be much more rapid among women than it is among men." Thus, fewer and fewer men and women are making the transition from young adulthood to partnership/marriage and parenthood—as prescribed by the sequential model of life.

EMPTY NESTERS NO MORE

"A Majority of Young Adults in the U.S. Live with Their Parents for the First Time Since the Great Depression," read the headline of a stunning study by the Pew Research Center published in 2020. In 1900, the year President McKinley won reelection, 41 percent of Americans aged eighteen to twenty-nine lived with their parents, a figure that grew to 48 percent during the hardships of the 1930s. The postwar boom and the rise of the nuclear family cut the proportion to just 29 percent by 1960. After two decades of a slow increase, it jumped from 38 percent in 2000 to 52 percent in 2020 (see figure 3.2). This spike started with the 2008 financial crisis, while the coronavirus pandemic of 2019 brought back home millions of college students and young working adults who lost their jobs or had their wages cut, many

FIGURE 3.2: Proportion of Young Adults Living with Parents in the U.S.

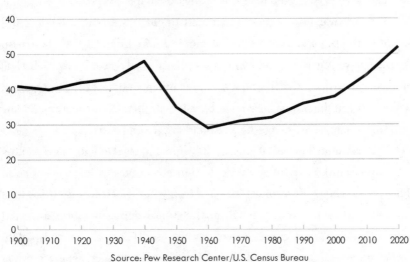

Source: Pew Research Center/U.S. Census Bureau

of them carrying a crushing amount of student debt. But the more years of education, the less likely a young American adult is to live with their parents. "Young adults without a college degree now are more likely to live with parents than to be married or cohabiting in their own homes, but those with a college degree are more likely to be living with a spouse or partner in their own homes." And it's among women, whites, and Asian Americans that the proportion has swollen more rapidly.

The U.S. is not the only rich country where the number of young adults living with their parents is high and growing. As of 2019, the proportion of men and women ages twenty-five to thirty-four in the European Union living with their parents was slightly above 30 percent. In most of Southern and Eastern Europe, it was above 40 percent, while in Germany, France, and the UK, it was under 20 percent, and in Scandinavia below 5 percent, clearly indicating that economic conditions, unemployment, and the affordability of housing play a key role. In March 2021, South Korea's National Statistical Office stunned the world by reporting that 62 percent of unmarried men and women in their thirties, and 44 percent of those in their forties, still lived in the same house with their parents. This means that 26 percent of all South Koreans in their thirties live with their parents (42 percent unmarried multiplied by 62 percent living with their parents), less than the European average. They are referred to as the "Kangaroo Tribe."

The individual stories behind the statistics have been captured time and again in the popular culture. In the movie *Rocky Road* (2014), Harrison Burke (played by Mark Salling) is a successful Wall Street banker who has it all—a sprawling apartment, a spacious office, and an expense account. When his firm goes bust, he moves back in with his parents in a small New England town, where he works on his father's ice cream truck.

"The sizeable number of young adults moving back in with their parents has caused a bit of a kerfuffle among the punditry," notes DePaulo in her book *How We Live Now: Redefining Home and Family in the 21st Century.* "The kids are called the boomerang generation, the go-nowhere generation, and generation stuck." The regression that this represents for parents completely undermines the synchronized sequence of stages that each generation was

supposed to traverse. "The moms and dads who take them in are called heli-
copter parents and worse." At the core of the problem is the mindset we bring
to the different stations in life, as we saw in chapter 1. "The critics, though,
may be appraising this new trend through twentieth-century glasses."

A variation on this theme is the child who never leaves the parental
home. "We are men who still live at home," says Tripp (played by Matthew
McConaughey) in *Failure to Launch* (2006). "We're not here to apologize
about who we are, how we do it, or who we live with." He is thirty-five years
old and still living with his parents in Baltimore. "I'm looking around this
table, hombres, and I see three winners, huh? And to every one of those out
there who sees something different, I say bring it on, 'cause it's gonna take a
stick of dynamite to get me out of my parents' house." His casual girlfriends
invariably dump him when he takes them to "his place." Desperate, the
parents hire Paula (Sarah Jessica Parker), a relationship expert, to persuade
him to move out. After several twists and turns, the two end up in a romantic
relationship.

The sequential model of life assumed that, at some point, parents would
become empty nesters when their adult children established their own residence and started a family. The boomerang and at-home-young-adult phe-
nomena have triggered a wave of articles, books, and self-help guides. Among
the latter, one finds *The Hands-On Guide to Surviving Adult Children Living
at Home* by Christina Newberry. "If you're dealing with adult children at
home—or kids who never left home—you need to know you're not alone,"
she informs us. "Having grown kids living with you can be tough, especially
around the holidays." Being herself a stay-at-home young adult, Newberry
offers not just the 115-page guide but also an 8-page "Adult Children Living at Home Contract," and a "Household Budget Calculator" to help parents through the tricky accounting rules for allocating direct and indirect
expenses, charging their live-in children rent, and helping them "overcome
crippling debt—without taking on the burden yourself."

The growing numbers of young adults who have no choice but to live
with their parents reveals a series of cracks in the intergenerational dynamics
underlying the sequential model of life. First is the assumption that parental

obligations toward children have a date of expiration. The very concept of the empty nest was predicated on that premise. Then there's the issue of who's responsible for the cost of education, given that jobless young adults are in no position to pay down their ever-larger mountains of student debt. And to top it all is the specter raised by Newberry as the "emotional land-mine" of "undermining your adult child's ability to be a good parent" once they have their own children. "When adult children come home with fam-ilies of their own, the ground rules and expectations must be crystal clear," she writes. "And your adult children living at home must understand that no matter what they may be going through in their own lives, it is their respon-sibility to parent their children—not yours." Easier said than done. But—as with all self-help guides—it all boils down to a matter of being willing to take on the challenge.

In some countries, though, the motivations for people in their thirties and forties to live with their parents extend beyond economic necessity. One case in point is South Korea. In 42 percent of the cases, unemployment is the main reason. But that leaves many financially secure young adults who have not moved out. "My parents are afraid, living outside is too dangerous for a single daughter," says thirty-six-year-old Song Jung-hyun, who is unmarried but has a sought-after job as a public high school teacher in Seoul. "Living with parents is happiness." Saving enough money to get married at a later age is also a prime motivation for staying at home. Many point out that it's a two-way street in which the parents give their adult children advice while the children help the parents with their health and certain tasks. If the rea-sons for stay-at-home young adults are so complex, perhaps we should think about the whole business of living arrangements from a better planned, mul-tigenerational perspective.

THE RETURN OF THE
MULTIGENERATIONAL HOUSEHOLD

"My family feels we exemplify . . . multigenerational living," writes architect Robert Habiger in a blog. "We have seven people living on the same property.

This includes my wife's mother, two of our children, one boyfriend, and one grand-daughter. My wife and I act as the de-facto leaders of the household." Robert went to great pains to create the right balance within and across generations when eighty years separate the youngest from the oldest household member in his Albuquerque, New Mexico, home. The Habiger family's experiment is part of a growing trend away from the concept of the nuclear family that emerged a century ago, whereby newlyweds would move out of their respective parents' houses to start a family. "In our multigenerational home we have created four inter-connected living areas. Each living area is independently occupied by one to three family members. This household structure affords each person experiences of solitude/companionship, diversity/unity and independence/support." The benefits of these arrangements can be expansive, according to Habiger. "This pattern of experiential opposites is one of the key aspects of our multi-generation habitation. Attributes such as being close yet apart from each other, having communal activity yet being able to retreat to our own personal sanctuaries are critical lived experiences." It's a compelling narrative.

After centuries, even millennia, of families sharing multigenerational dwellings, the concept of the nuclear family that took root during the twentieth century ushered in a new era in living arrangements that might now be coming to an end, at least partially. The Habigers are no longer a rarity, but rather members of a growing trend, although they are considerably better off economically than most in this growing group. According to data compiled by the Pew Research Center, 59.7 million Americans, about 18 percent of the total, lived in a multigenerational household with three or more generations in 2021, up from 7 percent in 1971. That's exactly the same as the proportion of households that are nuclear families, as we saw earlier. Based on a Harris Poll, Generations United, a nonprofit, estimated that in 2021 about 26 percent of Americans lived in a multigenerational household, up from 7 percent in 2011.

Thus, the estimates are different, but the trend is clear. Before the proliferation of the nuclear family, the percentages were even higher than today (around 30 percent during the Great Depression and 21 percent in 1950), but they dipped until the 1980s and have rebounded since then. Similar increases have occurred recently throughout Europe. Racial minorities are more likely to live in a multigenerational household: about 26 percent of African Americans and Latinx, and 24 percent of Asians, compared to 13 percent of non-Hispanic whites. The foreign-born are also more likely, as are men in general. While economic necessity and cultural norms play a role in the increase, the non-Hispanic white American population in multigenerational households has been growing much faster than the group as a whole.

The motivations for forming a multigenerational household are complex. The Pew survey found that financial issues were the major reason in 40 percent of the cases, followed by those who had always lived that way (28 percent), and taking care of a senior family member (25 percent). In its survey, Generations Together found that there are many reasons to start a multigenerational household: the need for eldercare (34 percent), childcare or child education needs (34 percent), job loss or underemployment (30 percent), high healthcare costs (25 percent), cultural and family expectations (23 percent), high education or retraining expenses (23 percent), divorce or separation (15 percent), and foreclosure or other housing loss (14 percent). Once created, the multigenerational household seems to bring many benefits, recognized by at least 70 percent of those surveyed: it makes it easier to provide for the care of family members, improves finances, improves personal mental and physical health, and makes it possible to continue in school or enroll in job training. It should be underlined that nearly half of them have a total household income above $100,000, indicating that financial considerations are not necessarily the main motivation. Also, 71 percent own the homes where they live. And this arrangement is here to stay. Some 72 percent of those surveyed said they will continue living in a multigenerational household. What's clear is that multigenerational households are less likely to live in poverty, mainly as a result of pooling financial resources, sharing costs, and being in a better position to care for the disabled or seniors. But more than half in the Pew survey said that they found it convenient and rewarding to live in a multigenerational dwelling, and only a quarter to be stressful. We can therefore conclude that perhaps up to a third of all multigenerational households become so by choice rather than strict necessity.

The American Association of Retired People (AARP) has coined the term *grandfamily* to refer to households in which grandparents live with their grandchildren. In 2016, there were 7.2 million such households, more than double the number four years earlier. The opioid addiction crisis is in part responsible for the rapid increase. A survey of more than twenty-three thousand home shoppers conducted in 2016 revealed that 44 percent would like to find a dwelling that could accommodate their parents, and 42 percent anticipate providing shelter to their adult children. Tellingly, 65 percent wished their home had a bedroom with a bath on the ground level, and 24 percent a suite with a kitchenette in addition to living and sleeping areas. Accessory dwelling units, also known as *in-law suites* or *granny flats,* are gaining in popularity. The 2018 AARP Home and Preference Survey showed that one-third of adults would consider building such units on their property if it weren't for zoning restrictions and other rules. Only eight states and the District of Columbia have introduced statewide guidelines. "Removing restrictions and easing the ability to develop housing for multigenerational living provides more options for families to accommodate their changing household dynamics."

One might think that the impetus that multigenerational living has acquired would attract real estate developers. Unfortunately, examples of multigenerational housing projects are few and apart. One example is Grandfamilies Place, a development in Phoenix, Arizona, built in 2012 with fifty-six units specifically designed for grandparents who raise their grandchildren. Funded through private and public sources, it offers affordable rents to residents who earn between 40 and 60 percent of the area's median income. Multigenerational living in homes that weren't designed for such a purpose continues to be the norm, especially because illness, divorce, widowhood, unemployment, poverty, home foreclosure, and recent immigration—not choice—are still the main reasons motivating people to share their living space with several generations, according to Daphne Lofquist, a researcher at the U.S. Census Bureau.

The return of the multigenerational household is thus the direct result of increasing longevity, a declining birth rate, the blurring of generational boundaries, the difficulties faced by young people without strong educational credentials, and a yearning for community. The difficulties young people experience at finding stable employment are also adding to the trend, as are the dire economic straits many families find themselves in. Whether out of necessity or by design, multigenerational living is staging a strong comeback.

What's more, in an article published by the National Institutes of Health, researchers at Columbia University wrote that "multigenerational living arrangements can . . . increase psychological, social, and financial capital—factors associated with improvements in health and longevity." Multigenerational households, by choice or out of necessity, open new horizons for collaboration and mutual understanding which may help overcome the challenges that a rapidly aging population poses. If multigenerational living can increase longevity, can it also help teenagers and people in their twenties better cope with the stress of making life decisions? And can it improve the experience of parenthood?

One doesn't need to embrace the utopias and communes of nineteenth- and twentieth-century America or the kibbutz model—both built on a mix of religious, ethical, and socialist ideas—to obtain the advantages promised by multigenerational households. In some ways, multigenerational living shares with those historical movements a reaction against individualism. Writing about the topic in the late 1960s and early '70s, the sociologist and business consultant Rosabeth Moss Kanter observed that "the commune movement is part of a reawakening of belief in the possibilities for utopia that existed in the nineteenth century and exist again today, a belief that by creating the right social institution, human satisfaction and growth can be achieved." A return to multigenerational living arrangements, if not communal ones, might be a way to cope with the emotional debris created by the pressures of making it from one stage of life to the next without, as the *New York Times*'s Brooks noted, enough of a net of social support.

FROM HE/SHE TO HE/SHE/THEY AND BEYOND

One additional dimension of change engulfing the traditional concept of the nuclear family involves the issue of gendered and ungendered identities. The contemporary debate frequently revolves around the issue of terminology. "Language is a prison we cannot break out of," writes a redditor. "It is a jail to our thoughts. It is a confinement of free thinking." Even worse, language shapes our actions, not just our perceptions. Gendered language has been proven to provide fertile soil for discrimination in the workplace, at school, and in other walks of life. "The world has historically prescribed the male gender as default, a construct that is reinforced through language," argues Nayantara Dutta in a BBC post. "As humans, our collective identity is understood as masculine—we use 'man' to describe our species and 'mankind' as a way to unify us." The most gendered languages among those widely spoken are Spanish, French, German, Arabic, and Hindi. By contrast, Mandarin is a genderless language in that neither nouns nor pronouns have a marked gender. Somewhere in between, we find languages like English with gendered pronouns but mostly genderless nouns. Using a sample of 111 countries, Jennifer Prewitt-Freilino, Andrew Caswell, and Emmi Laakso found that countries "where gendered languages are spoken evidence less gender equality compared to countries with other grammatical gender systems." Furthermore, "countries where natural gender languages are spoken demonstrate greater gender equality, which may be due to the ease of creating gender symmetric revisions to instances of sexist language." In light of this evidence, no wonder that women's advocacy groups and antidiscrimination experts have promoted the more inclusive he/she language for several decades now. In the scholarly world, the word *seminar* is, as it should be, shunned (the female equivalent would be *ovular*), and research insights are no longer *penetrating,* but rather *path-breaking, pioneering,* or *incisive.* In business parlance, *market penetration* is to be avoided, and rightly so as a gendered and plainly ugly term.

But even all those changes are proving to be insufficient to accommodate the diversity of lifestyles people would like to pursue. Since the turn of the twenty-first century, millennials, as well as members of other generations, have challenged the very categories of "male" and "female" in favor of non-binary or nonconforming terminology in order to accommodate a variety of lifestyles. ILGA World, the International Lesbian, Gay, Bisexual, Trans and Intersex Association, America, Australia, and New Zealand, are among the most protective of sexual orientation rights. ILGA publishes a map depicting sexual orientation laws in the world, assigning each country a score on a nine-point scale ranging from "death penalty" (about a dozen countries) to "constitutional protection" (only half a dozen) when it comes to the rights of people with diverse sexual and lifestyle orientations (LGBTQIA+). Not surprisingly, Western Europe, North America, and most Latin American and Caribbean countries are also among the staunchest defenders of sexual orientation rights, as are Angola, Botswana, Mozambique, South Africa, Nepal, Mongolia, South Korea, and Thailand. Many governments, airlines, and universities no longer ask people to self-report their gender, or they offer a nonbinary category.

The LGBTQIA+ revolution has resulted in a wave of moviemaking, yet another sign that it has become part of our collective conscience and culture. "I'm Lisa. I live here," says the new friend of the protagonist of *Tomboy* (2011), the French drama film about the pains of conforming to gender stereotypes while growing up. "You're shy," Lisa says after a pause. "No I'm not," replies Laura, a ten-year-old gender-nonconforming child. "Won't you tell me your name?" After some hesitation, Laura responds, "Mickaël, my name is Mickaël," which she just made up. A similar inner struggle lies at the center of *Carol,* the 2015 romantic drama movie based on Patricia Highsmith's novel *The Price of Salt* (1952), which dwells on the forbidden affair between twenty-year-old Therese (played by Rooney Mara), an aspiring female photographer, and Carol (Cate Blanchett), a glamorous, older woman who is in the process of divorcing. "You're trembling," says Carol while leaning down to kiss Therese. "No, don't. I want to see you." And perhaps the pinnacle of the genre is *Moonlight* (2016), the drama about identity during childhood, adolescence, and early adult life at the intersection of race and sexual orientation. "What's a faggot?" asks Little, the film's protagonist as a child (Alex Hibbert), whose adult name is Chiron. "A faggot is . . . a word used to make gay people feel bad," replies Juan (Mahershala Ali), the drug dealer who becomes a father figure to Chiron. "Am I a faggot?" inquires Little. "No. You're not a faggot. You can be gay, but you don't have to let nobody call you a faggot." The practical implication of *Tomboy, Carol,* and *Moonlight* is that without a mutually exclusive and exhaustive dichotomous classification of people by gender, with all the conventional underlying assumptions about sexual orientation and life roles, the traditional model of the nuclear family gives way to a more inclusive and diverse set of family and living arrangements.

By the turn of the twenty-first century, *The Brady Bunch* felt like a galaxial glow from a distant past, making it readily apparent that the sequential model of life, with its strict ordering and timing, had run its course. Living life one stage at a time and in sequence has become obsolete in the wake of women's new economic and social roles, technological change, cultural globalization, the swelling tide of individualism, rising economic inequality, unconventional living arrangements, and the revolution in non-gendered identities. The nuclear family is no longer the norm in the more developed countries, and it may never become the norm in the emerging and developing world. Do we need to bring some order back into family life? But what definition of *family* should we use? Might tweaking the sequential model of life be enough? Can we dissolve the problem altogether as opposed to implementing patchwork solutions? Or will the cracks in the model make the whole edifice collapse under its own weight? The next chapters explore these possibilities.

4

REBELS WITHOUT A CAUSE?

To be, or not to be, that is the question.
—William Shakespeare (1564–1616), *Hamlet*

"Sixteen-year-old Olivia sat in my therapy office riddled with anxiety because she didn't know what she wanted to do for the rest of her life," writes Janet Sasson Edgette, a psychologist and author. "The urgency, Olivia explained, was that without knowing what she wanted to do, she couldn't pick her college major." Janet reacted in no time by saying, "But you're only a sophomore in high school." Olivia's instinctive response was, according to her therapist, "to roll out a scenario in which equivocating about majors meant you're as good as unemployed, if not homeless." While a third of American college students change their majors before graduating, parents, teachers, and even school counselors insist that they should "hurry up and figure out their future."

Our dominant culture is all about making decisions—the so-called right choices—as early as possible, even while we're still teenagers, while teetering on the verge of one emotional cliff or another. "About three things I was absolutely certain," says Bella Swan (played by Kristen Stewart) in the first *Twilight Saga* film. "First, Edward was a vampire. Second, there was part of him—and I didn't know how potent that part might be—that thirsted for my blood. And third, I was unconditionally and irrevocably in love with him." Bella is the archetype of the indecisive teenager who makes one terrible choice after another. "I'd never given much thought to how I would die. But dying in place of someone I love seems like a good way to go. I can't bring myself to regret the decisions that brought me face-to-face with death. They also brought me to Edward."

The dominant culture gives teenagers a bad reputation when it comes to making decisions. "Cognitive abilities (working memory, digit span, and verbal fluency) seem to be fully developed at age 16 or 17," writes biochemist Elena Blanco-Suarez in *Psychology Today*. "Emotional and social skills need to be developed to reach prosocial adulthood. However, everyone knows that teenagers (being considered between 13 and 17 years of age) are irrational, make poor decisions and take unnecessary risks. But is this true?" Contrary to the stereotype, research indicates that teenagers are as good as adults at making decisions depending on the context. When fast decision-making in real time is needed or when faced by peer pressure, teenagers fare much worse than adults, exercising choice in risky ways.

It seems to me that deploying neuroscience and psychology to understand how teenagers make life-changing decisions such as what education (or even major) to pursue is a solution to the problem, but does not dissolve it, to use the terminology proposed by Russ Ackoff in chapter 2. One great way of eliminating the problem altogether is to challenge the sequential model of life, to enable teenagers and young adults to revisit their choices, to course correct, to adapt in real time through a process of trial and error. Wouldn't that be better than asking them to make momentous decisions that can last a lifetime? The idea that nowadays "kids can't be kids anymore" calls for a reconsideration of how parents—and society—define success, not just academically but also in personal relationships and other walks of life.

Making decisions with lifelong consequences at a young age is always a tall order, and especially so when the economy and the society change so quickly. The decision as to what to dedicate our lives to can no longer be made all at once. To grasp the suboptimal implications of making lifelong decisions only once, and at a very young age, consider the following two possibilities. First, imagine you're throwing a single dart at a target on the wall from sixty feet away. You can win $300 if you hit the center of the target. Now imagine three targets arranged on a straight line, twenty feet apart from one another. In this second situation, you (a) take aim at the first target from twenty feet away for a $100 win, (b) then you walk to the target, pick up the dart, and aim it at the second target situated twenty feet farther away for another $100, and (c) you walk to that second target to aim the dart at the third target twenty feet away for another $100. Which would you rather do, try once from sixty feet or three times from twenty? Hitting the target from sixty feet must be far less likely than hitting the target twenty feet away. If, hypothetically, the probabilities are 1 percent and 5 percent, respectively, the expected gains are five times higher if you take three aims from twenty feet ($100 × 5% + $100 × 5% + $100 × 5% = $15) rather than just one from sixty feet ($300 × 1% = $3).

The point of this example is that it would be much better to go to school every twenty years and decide what type of work to do as opposed to making that decision only once for a period of sixty years, at the risk of seeing your knowledge and skills become obsolete in the meantime. What's more, the odds of hitting the center of the target might improve as you gain experience, an outcome that may also take place when making the decision as to what to study and do for a living every twenty years as opposed to only once for the following sixty years.

Asking young people to "make their minds up" leads to inordinate amounts of stress, missed opportunities, and dissatisfaction with life. Most research on this topic points out that applying so much pressure on teenagers and people in their twenties is usually counterproductive. And it's actually bad for the economy because it makes it harder for the labor market to function properly in its task of allocating talent to jobs. A better alternative is to allow young people to think about their calling in life as a process of experimentation with different jobs and careers, moving back and forth between the classroom and the workplace several times. Moreover, play will not have to be circumscribed to infanthood, evenings, weekends, and vacation time. A less compartmentalized structure of stages throughout life would enable flexible allocations of study, work, and play over one's lifetime, providing people with more freedom to pursue their interests outside of work. Ultimately, these new arrangements might enable an increasing number of people not only to pursue different jobs but also to switch careers.

PARENTAL PRESSURE AND THE PARADOX OF
LIFELONG EARNINGS

"The hardest part of parenting is knowing when to step in and when to step back," wrote Kristin van Ogtrop to her son in a letter of apology published in *Time* magazine. "So I apologize for that, and for all the other times when I took my issues and made them yours," she continued. "One of my greatest mistakes as a mother was to conflate your success with mine. Every accomplishment of yours meant less working-mom guilt for me: if you got an A on a test, I gave myself an A; if you made the varsity team, so did I." And she ended by suggesting that when a child does or accomplishes something, it's better not to say, "I am so proud of you," but to say, "You should feel so proud of yourself." A subtle change of wording that conveys an empowering message.

In 2013, the Pew Research Center published a study suggesting that "Americans say kids need more pressure in school, Chinese say less." In fact, out of twenty-one countries, the U.S. had the highest proportion (64 percent) of people choosing the "not enough pressure" option, compared to China's 11 percent, where 68 percent felt too much pressure was being exerted already. The study noted that average standardized test scores are higher in China than in the U.S., a difference often attributed to stronger parental pressures.

But telling children to achieve more can be counterproductive and often results in higher rates of mental illness, greater risk of injuries, increased likelihood of cheating, self-esteem problems, and sleep deprivation, according to Amy Morin, the editor in chief of Verywell Mind.

The cross-national reality of school performance reveals that the highest average scores are found in countries with high levels of parental pressure as well as in those with lower levels. According to the Organisation for Economic Co-operation and Development (OECD), China, Singapore, Macao, Hong Kong, and South Korea were in 2018 among the countries with the highest average scores for reading, mathematics, and science, and all of them are infamous for the pressure that parents place on their children to achieve. But the top ten also included Estonia, Canada, Finland, Ireland, and Poland, where such pressures are much lower. The U.S. ranked thirteenth, after Sweden and New Zealand. In most countries, including the U.S., boys score higher than girls in mathematics and science, and family socioeconomic status is highly correlated with performance. This study did not ask about race, but the National Center for Education Statistics did. Also in 2018, the status dropout rate, or the proportion of people ages sixteen to twenty-four who are not in school, was depressingly related to race and ethnicity: 1.9 percent for Asian Americans, 4.2 percent for whites, 5.2 percent for people reporting two or more races, 6.4 percent for Blacks, 8.0 percent for Latinx, 8.1 percent for Pacific Islanders, and 9.5 percent for American Indians and Alaska Natives. Men had higher dropout rates than women within each group, and the gender gap was greater for the most disadvantaged groups, except for the last two categories. Intriguingly, children from immigrant families had similar rates to the mainstream.

When examining the impact of parental pressure on these statistics, one must distinguish between the effect of sheer pressure and the influence of role models. Children of better-educated parents are more likely to attend better schools, to graduate from high school and from college, and to get better grades. Moreover, researchers in Sweden found that "gender-atypical" choices—like a woman majoring in mathematics in college—are driven by whether the mother was a science student herself. According to Grace Chen, an education researcher, parental involvement in their kids' education increases academic achievement, classroom behavior, and teacher morale. But parental pressures can be counterproductive.

The negative effect of parental pressure is more widely and deeply felt when it comes to choosing a college to attend, especially in countries like the U.S., where the options are dauntingly complex and difficult to assess. "Families are flunking college selection," argue John Katzman (a cofounder of the Princeton Review, the testing and college admissions firm) and Steve Cohen (an attorney and author). They note that three out of five students transfer to another college because they made the wrong choice. Oftentimes, the issue is money and the stress from having to work while studying to foot the bills.

Parents also tend to exert pressure on what specific career path their children should pursue. In one British study, 69 percent of university students said their parents had tried to influence their choice of university, and 54 percent their specific study and career choices. "Many students from varying backgrounds feel pressure from their parents to pick a certain major or path that will lead to a steady job," wrote Anna Raskind in 2016, at the time a senior at Columbia University, in the *Columbia Daily Spectator,* the student newspaper. At American universities, students from minority backgrounds or who hail from abroad are more likely to experience such pressures, to a large extent because parents are more likely to meddle with their children's choices to begin with. For many parents, majoring in the liberal arts is not as "marketable" as pursuing a degree in business, engineering, or science, or preparing to attend law or medical school. "If parents can give kids the opportunity to be outrageous and work their way backwards, trying to figure it out, and give them some space to figure it out, they will," argues Andrea St. James, a career counselor. "And they'll figure it out in a way in which they will be much more happy in their career versus something they'd get pushed into." In fact, research shows that imposing a career choice can result in lower grades, earnings, and self-esteem, and higher rates of stress, frustration, and even depression.

"What do you want to do with the rest of your life? Is this something you actually want to pursue? There's over a million people going after the same career and there's only a 1% chance that anyone makes it." Those are, according to the *Ledger* editorial board, questions that many parents ask of their children when it comes to picking a course of study and a career. And yet, few parents realize that the top 25 percent of American earners among majors in education, social work, the humanities, or the liberal arts make as much over their professional careers as the bottom 50 percent of those who major in engineering, economics, computer science, business, or accounting. "Students and parents have a pretty good idea of what majors pay the most, but they have a poor sense of the magnitude of the differences within the major," writes Douglas A. Webber, an economist at the Federal Reserve Board, who made the calculations. While it's true that the 25 percent highest-earning engineers or computer scientists will make twice as much as the median humanities or liberal arts major, the bottom 25 percent "quant" will make less or about the same as the median "poet." Thus, picking a major—under pressure or not—simply because it offers a better prospect for lifelong earnings can prove to be based on not only a counterproductive logic but also a feeble one.

In addition to the enormous dispersion in lifelong earnings—not all quants are well paid, after all—there's another reason for not making early career choices in terms of marketability. Let's return to Olivia and Janet, the high school student and her therapist, to illustrate where the biggest problem lies. Janet is rightly concerned with teenagers pursuing a "practical" course of study and not their true passion. She fully grasps the implications of the unraveling of the sequential model of life. "Besides, the idea of one major and one career is becoming outdated; job descriptions now are more fluid, demanding skills of adaptation at least as much as content-based expertise."

THE MYTHS OF YOUTHFUL PERFECTIONISM
AND ADVENTURISM

Another variation on parental pressure is the frequent inversion of the reality of who's pressuring whom. "I just want her to be happy," parents routinely tell Rachel Simmons, an author and cofounder of Girls Leadership. "But she puts *so much pressure on herself.*" The problem with this statement is that it blames the teenager as opposed to the prevailing culture of perfectionism and achievement. In a recent study based on some forty-two thousand American, British, and Canadian college students over the past three decades, psychologists Thomas Curran and Andrew Hill report a growing trend of teens feeling that "I have to excel at everything I do" and "I'm a complete failure if I fall short." The researchers observe that "American, Canadian, and British cultures have become more individualistic, materialistic, and socially antagonistic over this period, with young people now facing more competitive environments, more unrealistic expectations, and more anxious and controlling parents than generations before." The culture of perfectionism stems from the pressure that teens feel from parents and peers alike amid rising individualism and materialism, and is resulting in higher rates of depression, anxiety, and suicidal ideation. The rise of digital social media has exacerbated the trend.

The extreme of perfectionism is matched in the popular culture by its polar opposite of freewheeling adventurism. As far back as 1890, the Irish writer and wit Oscar Wilde was advocating a freer world for his young hero in *The Picture of Dorian Gray.* "Ah! realize your youth while you have it. Don't squander the gold of your days, listening to the tedious, trying to improve the hopeless failure, or giving away your life to the ignorant, the common, and the vulgar," wrote Wilde, his diatribe bordering on hedonism. "These are the sickly aims, the false ideals, of our age. Live! Live the wonderful life that is in you! Let nothing be lost upon you. Be always searching for new sensations. Be afraid of nothing."

Oscar Wilde wrote his only novel just nine years after Bismarck's momentous pension proposal, mounting a frontal attack on the idea that teenagers must make the transition to adulthood at age twenty, give or take a couple of years. *Dorian Gray* was considered scandalous when it was first published. Today, we know that "young adults" being rebellious, adventurous, and enjoying themselves, always looking for the next new experience, is in part the result of biology—teenagers' brains are still developing, which results in an imperfect ability to judge danger and an attraction to the high that comes from risky behaviors. And yet, to this day, parents continue to place enormous pressure on their teenage children to make up their minds, to make big choices that will define their entire lives, to become "grown-ups."

The theme of the rebellious youth has since reverberated throughout our culture, from *Rebel Without a Cause* (1955) to *Bohemian Rhapsody* (2018). In one of the opening sequences of the film about the rock band Queen, Freddie Mercury's strict father decries his scattered lifestyle. "No thought of the future in your head," he lashes out at him. "Thoughts, good works, good deeds. That's what you should aspire to." The twenty-three-year-old airport baggage handler and aspiring rock star simply replies in his signature four-octave range voice, "And how has that worked for you?" In the world Mercury was born into, young adults had to draw plans as to what came next: a vocational training program, a major in college, an occupation, a profession, a career, starting a family. Those decisions made sense during most of the previous century when the average person aged twenty would have already consumed a third of his or her expected life span. But today, how can we even pretend to make decisions for the remainder of our lives when we have six or seven decades ahead of us? Is it good for young people? And how about for the economy? Why do parents continue to insist on making fateful choices so early in life when the employment landscape is changing so fast?

COLLATERAL DAMAGE AND INEQUALITY
OF OPPORTUNITY

Rebellious or not, the fallout from the strict adherence to the sequential model of life extends well beyond disgruntled teenagers and their disappointed parents. At the present time, a substantial proportion of the population in developed countries—ranging from 15 to 30 percent—does not fully benefit from the great things that the model has to offer mainly because they somehow deviated from its prescribed linear path. This sizable proportion includes high school dropouts, teen mothers, foster children and teenagers, substance abusers, and others who went through an abrupt detour in life.

"My childhood was often distressing and chaotic," declared Alexandra

(Lexie) Morgan Gruber at a U.S. Senate Finance Committee hearing in 2015. "As a result, I suffered from severe anxiety and depression. When I entered foster care, I was traumatized from losing the only family and home I had ever known." Lexie prefers not to explain exactly why she became parentless. What followed was a series of failed placements with different foster families and shelters until she landed at a therapeutic group home in her native state of Connecticut. She persevered against the odds, finished high school, and then went on to graduate with honors from Quinnipiac University, right on time, at age twenty-two. She subsequently took a job at a Washington, DC, nonprofit.

Lexie's pedigree, unfortunately, is the exception rather than the rule among foster children. According to the Annie E. Casey Foundation, foster care teenagers attend college at a rate half the average for young Americans, and just 18 percent of those who matriculate in a college earn a degree, on average in over six years. As of 2021, only thirty-five states offered them some kind of tuition assistance for postsecondary education, with twenty-four of them offering statewide tuition waivers, seven offering scholarships, and four offering funded grant programs. In a truly postgenerational society, more resources should be available to level the playing field for children who could not enjoy the emotional and economic support that belonging to a nuclear family can provide. But most importantly, those benefits should be made available at any age, not just upon graduating from high school, if we want to achieve equality of opportunity.

Recovering drug and alcohol addicts are another instance of "collateral" damage. Given that three in four of them eventually recover, it's essential to offer them multiple pathways at different points in time to reenter society and the economy as productive citizens. In 2021, there were 22.3 million Americans successfully recovering from substance abuse—a staggering one in ten adults. Clearly, the dense network of treatment programs, support groups, and even insurance schemes makes it possible to achieve a 75 percent success rate. But putting the addiction behind does not guarantee ideal outcomes in terms of health or employment. They're more likely than the average American to be unemployed and to suffer from a disability.

Unsurprisingly, Latinx and African American addicts are much more disadvantaged than their white counterparts when it comes to quality of life after recovery. Many cannot overcome the stigma and the barriers that companies and society as a whole impose on them.

Taken together, foster care children, teenage mothers, and recovering addicts are not a minuscule fraction of the American population. By my own back-of-the-envelope calculation, there are nearly 50 million living Americans who have been in one or more of those three categories at some point in their lives: 15 million people who went through the foster care system (some 200,000 enter it annually, multiplied by the average life expectancy beyond age eighteen), 15 million women who gave birth as teenagers (calculated following a similar logic), and 30 million who fell to substance abuse (of which 22.3 million have recovered). That adds up to about 15 percent of the American population afflicted by those three problems alone. For them, the sequential model has made it exceedingly difficult to catch up after a major setback. That's how cruelly simple it is: if you fall behind, if you take the wrong turn at one of life's crossroads, if something stands in the way of making steady progress through the various stages of life on a timely basis, chances are you're doomed or you won't fully enjoy everything that one of the world's richest and most advanced societies and economies has to offer, including a job and a certain degree of financial security. COVID-19 represents a stark reminder that global and local crises can make it very hard for young people, especially those with disadvantaged family backgrounds, to keep up with the various milestones in the sequential model of life.

THE JOBS OF THE FUTURE

"Seriously? You're asking about the workforce of the future? As if there's going to be one?" That was the blunt statement from a scientific editor, who preferred to remain anonymous, to the Pew Research Center's canvass of experts. "'Employers' either run sweatshops abroad or hire people in the 'first world' to do jobs that they hate, while more and more unskilled and skilled people end up permanently on welfare or zero-hour contracts. And the relatively 'job-secure' qualified people who work in the 'professions' are probably a lot closer than they think they are to going over that same cliff." The argument is surely an exaggeration, but it serves as a stark reminder that we're not thinking hard enough about what the future of jobs and skills will look like.

People of all ages will need more flexibility when it comes to education and lifelong learning to cope with the enormous changes in the labor market. According to the Federal Reserve Bank of St. Louis, there were 26 percent fewer workers employed in U.S. manufacturing in 2020 when compared to 1987, but they produced a whopping 63 percent more. The economy has been changing for decades due to several overlapping waves of technological transformation. The service sector has expanded dramatically. A majority of Americans are now employed in white-collar occupations, even among those nominally employed in manufacturing. Most white-collars belong to the "professional and technical workforce," which represents 41 percent of all American workers, according to the Bureau of Labor Statistics, a proportion that is similar in Europe, Canada, Australia, Japan, South Korea, Singapore, and other advanced economies. This is a heterogeneous group of people with strong educational credentials and relatively high salaries, including managers, computer programmers, engineers, architects, physicians, lab technicians, lawyers, professors and teachers, designers, artists, and so on. Interestingly, slightly more than half of them are women. Their professional success hinges on being completely up-to-date as to the knowledge underpinning their jobs. They perform mostly nonroutine cognitive tasks, which so far have proved difficult to automate, although artificial intelligence might pose a threat in the future.

The growth of the professional and technical workforce was triggered by increasing demand for analytical skills. But, as labor economists have thoroughly documented, the demand for social skills has grown even faster. These include the ability to communicate, work in teams, make decisions under conditions of uncertainty, and negotiate effectively. In addition, the demand for emotional intelligence has soared—that is, "the ability to carry out accurate reasoning about emotions and the ability to use emotions and emotional knowledge to enhance thought." As Marshall Kirkpatrick, cofounder of Little Bird, previously with ReadWriteWeb and TechCrunch, puts it, "the future will require more soft skills, self-awareness, empathy, networked thinking and lifelong learning."

Tiffany Shlain, a filmmaker and founder of the Webby Awards, cogently notes that "the skills needed to succeed in today's world and the future are curiosity, creativity, taking initiative, multi-disciplinary thinking and empathy. These skills, interestingly, are the skills specific to human beings that machines and robots cannot do." It's perhaps unsurprising that an artist would think that way. But listen to Ben Shneiderman, a computer scientist at the University of Maryland, who takes the argument one step further by arguing that "students can be trained to be more innovative, creative and active initiators of novel ideas. Skills of writing, speaking and making videos are important, but fundamental skills of critical thinking, community building, teamwork, deliberation/dialogue and conflict resolution will be powerful." Needless to say, such social skills are not a central part of the curriculum in either primary, secondary, or tertiary education.

One can also define the skills of the future by describing what they won't be. Justin Reich, executive director at the MIT Teaching Systems Lab, has argued that "the most important skills for the future will be the kinds of things that computers cannot readily do, places where human workers have a comparative advantage over computers." He proposes "ill-structured problem solving and complex, persuasive communication" as examples. As Pablo Picasso once put it, "Computers are useless—they can only give you answers." Asking the right question is always the prerequisite to providing a correct answer. If the issue or challenge at hand is not posed in the right way, the right answer can't be forthcoming.

The emerging consensus among experts is that the jobs of the future will require interdisciplinary training rather than specialization. Meryl Krieger, career specialist at Indiana University Bloomington's Jacobs School, believes that "the most important skills in the workforce of the future are (1) transferrable skills and (2) training in how to contextualize and actually transfer them." J. Trevor Hughes, CEO at the International Association of Privacy

Professionals, agrees in that "many of the skills of the future are hybrid skills—requiring expertise or fluency across some of our traditional domains." He proposes his own field of privacy protection as an example. "Any digital economy professional needs to understand privacy and how it creates risk for organizations. But that means grasping law and policy, business management, and technology. Modern professionals will need to bridge all of these fields." Luis Miron, a distinguished university professor and director of the Institute for Quality and Equity in Education at Loyola University in New Orleans, proposes that "the most important skills are advanced critical thinking and knowledge of globalization affecting diverse societies—culturally, religiously and politically." That was exactly what I taught, in collaboration with anthropologist Brian Spooner, at my popular University of Pennsylvania undergraduate class on globalization for over two decades.

Polina Kolozaridi, a researcher at the Higher School of Economics in Moscow, offers the best possible articulation of the power of an interdisciplinary education. "The most important skills needed to succeed in the workforce of the future are process-oriented and system-oriented thinking, coding, etc." She highlights the importance of technical skills such as AI communication, 3D modeling, and physics. But she also believes that critical thinking, information management, and documentary and evidence skills, especially those developed through the study of history and journalism, will prove essential.

Other experts emphasize learning, unlearning, and relearning. "The key thing to realize about skills and the future is that there is no one set of skills that we can identify as core or important," argues Alf Rehn, a professor and chair of management and organization at Åbo Akademi University in Turku, Finland. "The future of skills is going to be one of continuous change and renewal, and any one special skill we can identify now will almost certainly be outdated in not too long. Creativity and critical thinking will be as important in the future as it is today, but beyond this we should be very careful not to arrogantly assume too much." As Mark Twain shrewdly put it some time ago, "It ain't what you don't know that gets you into trouble. It's what you know for sure that just ain't so."

Analytical and social skills are both critical to success in today's labor market for most people. But are we preparing them in the best possible way? What educational programs are best? And what role should lifelong learning play?

REIMAGINING ELEMENTARY AND SECONDARY EDUCATION—FOR EVERYONE

The fundamental problem besetting the education sector is that it needs to prepare students for jobs that don't yet exist. According to the World Economic Forum, two-thirds of children entering grade school will work in jobs that only the future will tell what they are. "New categories of jobs will emerge, partly or wholly displacing others. The skill sets required in both old and new occupations will change in most industries and transform how and where people work." The National Academies of Sciences, Engineering, and Medicine concluded in a 184-page report that education will need to go through a major transformation given the trends in the labor market, and that "recent IT advances offer new and potentially more widely accessible ways to access education."

The growing consensus among experts is that "the most important skill is a meta-skill: the ability to adapt to changes," argues Calton Pu, a professor at the Georgia Institute of Technology. But it seems at odds with the way in which the school curriculum is organized. "As the rate of technological innovation intensifies, the workforce of the future will need to adapt to new technology and new markets." Technological transformations—as well as population and economic changes—call for flexibility and for an education that is not siloed into different disciplines. "The people who can adapt the best (and fastest) will win." The trouble is that leaders in technology, education, and business do not believe the educational system is ready to meet the challenge, as reported in a Pew Research Center survey among 1,408 experts. What type of schooling will prepare children for the changes ahead?

Barry Chudakov, founder and principal at Sertain Research and Stream-Fuzion, strongly believes that "the first skill needed to succeed in the workforce of the future will be the ability to understand, manage and manipulate data." In his view, in the future, everyone working in technology "will need to be a quant [quantitative analyst] or keep up with the quants." I would argue that *everyone* will need to understand, manage, and manipulate data, in every job and in every part of the economy. Schools have certainly made an effort to incorporate this insight into their curricula.

A second, more important skill to be successful in the future, according to Chudakov, "will be the ability to find meaning and value in data combined with the problem, condition, or opportunity the data is outlining." Now we are moving more in the direction of social and contextual skills rather than technical skills per se. "Said simply, the greatest skill will be the ability to think through the cloud of facts, data, experience and strategic direction that products and services require. Design thinking or visual thinking will be a critical part of managing a data-driven world." In this context, design means framing the problem, issue, or challenge in a way that makes sense. This involves telling the forest from the trees; not just recognizing patterns—which artificial intelligence can do—but finding the meaning of the pattern.

One of the main difficulties involved in reforming elementary education is that modern schooling emerged in the nineteenth century as an institution to create an army of docile industrial workers, as we discussed in chapter 1, and not a legion of critical thinkers. Jeff Jarvis, a professor at the Craig Newmark Graduate School of Journalism at the City University of New York, argues that schools "are built on producing single right answers rather than creative solutions." Echoing the historian E. P. Thompson's analysis of "Time, Discipline, and Industrial Capitalism," he writes that "they are built on an outmoded attention economy: Pay us for 45 hours of your attention and we will certify your knowledge." For him, the solution lies in shifting "to competency-based education in which the outcomes needed are made clear and students are given multiple paths to achieve those outcomes." Accordingly, he prefers students to demonstrate their progress through a portfolio rather than exams or tests.

At the highest level of abstraction, the core problem with modern schooling is that it seeks to turn children into something not aligned with the new economic and technological realities. As Pamela Rutledge, director of the Media Psychology Research Center, puts it, "Traditional models train people to equate what they do with who they are (i.e., what do you want to be when you grow up) rather than to acquire critical thinking and flexible skills and attitudes that fit a rapidly changing world." Compulsory education is, in her view, "invested in learning as a supply-side model rather [than] demand-side that would create proactive, self-directed learners." Given the inertia, bureaucracy, and entrenched interests in elementary education, which has been compulsory in most countries around the world for the last decades, it's hard to envision how this late-nineteenth-century invention we call schools can be reinvented to serve a useful purpose in the twenty-first century. Elisabeth Gee, professor at Arizona State University, argues that "we don't need large-scale training of workers," as during the Second Industrial Revolution. "We need real education (not job-focused) and opportunities for people to pursue diverse pathways for career development and lifelong learning." That's exactly what departing from the sequential model of life entails.

FUNCTIONAL ILLITERACY

My modest proposal for elementary schools is to focus on people's capacity to adapt, learn, unlearn, and relearn. Let's make sure that by the time students start high school or drop out, they can write creatively, read efficiently and make sense out of complex texts, and handle numbers and abstract reasoning with ease. The future belongs to critical thinkers, to people who can process new information and incorporate it into their own model of reality. Unfortunately, we're far from these goals. In the U.S. and the UK, one in seven adults lack basic literacy skills in language and math. It's called *functional illiteracy*. Some of it is due to learning disabilities, but defective schooling is also responsible.

"Walter Long is 59 years old and lives in the town outside of Pittsburgh where he grew up," read the beginning of a CBS News story on functional illiteracy. "He's got a good job with the county water board, a nice house where he has raised four kids, and a wife who loves him." His big secret was that he could not read. "He faked it well, until one night when he was pretending to read a story to his four-year-old daughter, Joanna." The innocence of children that age conceals an uncanny instinct for sensing things that don't fit. "My daughter looked up at me and said, 'That's not the way Mom read it to me.'" Walter remembers thinking, "It's still hard to say to a four-year-old that you can't read."

Walter was one of thirty-two million American adults found not able to read in a study conducted by the National Center for Education Statistics in 2003. The most recent surveys, for 2012–2014 and 2017, revealed that literacy and numeracy average scores have declined. Women trail men in numeracy, but are slightly ahead in literacy. African Americans trail both whites and Hispanics. Hispanics have shown remarkable increases in literacy and numeracy even as the other groups saw a decline. Having said that, the problem is so pervasive that it afflicts not just marginal members of society by people with good jobs. Ford and Motorola have created remedial programs for employees who need to beef up their reading skills.

The OECD compiles comparable data for other countries as part of the Program for the International Assessment of Adult Competencies. Not surprisingly, richer countries have fewer illiterate people than poorer countries. Most European countries, Japan, and South Korea have higher literacy levels than the U.S., and the situation is worse when it comes to numeracy—the U.S. is below the OECD average. Inequality of access to quality schooling is mainly responsible for this situation in which the most technologically advanced country scores so low in international comparisons.

THE ROLE OF LANGUAGES IN EDUCATION

For students whose native tongue is not English, elementary education should make them fluent in what has become the global language of business, science, and technology. Only one in seven people in the world are fluent in English as a second language. The proportion is as high as 70 percent in Northern Europe, but as low as 5 or 10 percent in Southern Europe, Latin

America, the Middle East, Asia, and Africa. Some people surely can read English but not speak it fluently. Still, the numbers mean that more than half of humanity is not in a position to read the contents of websites in English, which still account for more than half of the total.

Learning a second language does not only give people access to information and enable them to interact. It also enriches the mind. The late political scientist and sociologist Seymour Martin Lipset, a Canadian, once said, "Those who know one country know no country." Without knowing another culture, how can anyone be certain of understanding their own? Many years ago, I wrote an opinion piece for *The Chronicle of Higher Education* on the real reasons why people—even if English is their native tongue—should learn other languages. I argued that there is a fundamental misunderstanding of the role that language learning should play in people's education. Languages are far more than useful tools to achieve an end, such as being able to live, work, or learn in a given country. They are a window into another culture, another way of seeing the world. Acquiring another language makes students better problem solvers, unleashing their ability to identify problems, enriching the ways in which they search and process information, and making them aware of issues and perspectives that they would otherwise ignore. I have often observed that students with exposure to two or more languages and cultures are more creative in their thinking, especially when it comes to tackling complex problems that do not have clear solutions.

Learners of languages, by exposing themselves to other cultures and institutional arrangements, are more likely to see differences of opinion and conflicts by approaching a problem from perspectives that incorporate the values and norms of others as well as their own. Knowledge of other languages also fosters tolerance and mutual understanding. Language learning is thus much more than becoming operational in an environment different from one's own. It is a powerful way of appreciating and respecting the diversity of the world.

Another common misconception about the study of languages is that globalization has reduced the market value of most of them while increasing that of English, the lingua franca of business, science, and technology.

According to that logic, students would be wise to invest their time and energy in other subjects once they have mastered spoken and written English. While it is true that major multinational companies use English at their most important meetings, I continue to come across case-based evidence indicating that if you work for a German, Japanese, Chinese, Swedish, or Brazilian company, you'd better speak the language of the home country, or you will be at a disadvantage when it comes to understanding the subtleties of decision-making and advancing your career. English proficiency may have become a necessary qualification for employment at most multinational organizations, but it is certainly not sufficient to pursue a successful professional career in an international context. The argument that the market value of the English language is increasing relative to the value of other languages, if pushed to its logical extreme, would present native English speakers with a false choice between allocating their energies to learning another language and focusing on other academic subjects.

Many universities have lost touch with an evolving reality in the international business world. Some undergraduate and graduate business programs claim to offer an international education, in some cases involving short study trips. But few integrate a rigorous course of study in languages with standard business subjects. At the graduate level, we have convinced ourselves that a one-or two-week trip to meet business leaders in some country can be a substitute for the deep study of at least one foreign language and culture. We are fooling ourselves if we believe that a global management education consists of short study trips instead of serious language instruction.

Students who are serious about engaging in a demanding activity, whether learning to speak a language or play a musical instrument, are more motivated to learn other subjects. The language learner is undaunted by the difficulty of the task and eager to benefit from the discipline that language instruction offers. Before becoming the dean of Judge Business School at the University of Cambridge, I taught sociology and management courses to undergraduate and graduate students for nearly thirty years. Those who have knowledge of languages other than English tended to perform better.

By undermining the importance of learning other languages, we are losing an opportunity to educate our students to be better citizens of the world and failing to provide them with the mindset and the tools they need to understand and solve complex problems. Learning a language exercises the mind and enriches the spirit. It is a fundamentally humbling process by which students learn that their culture and way of expressing it are relative, not absolute. That perspective makes them more open to other points of view and more likely to avoid one-size-fits-all solutions to the problems of the world.

WHAT'S WRONG WITH HIGH SCHOOL AND COLLEGE?

"Suppose you had $100 in a savings account and the interest rate was 2% per year. After five years, how much do you think you would have in the account if you left the money to grow?" This is a standard question about compound interest often used to assess people's level of financial literacy. The options given as potential answers include: (A) more than $102; (B) exactly $102; and (C) less than $102. The correct answer is (A), given that the money is being left in the account for five years.

Now consider another question. "Imagine that the interest rate on your savings account was 1% per year and inflation was 2% per year. After one year, how much would you be able to buy with the money in this account?" The options here are more, exactly the same, or less than today, with the latter being the correct answer. Lastly, let's examine the true/false question, "Buying a single company's stock usually provides a safer return than a stock mutual fund," with false being the correct answer.

It turns out that only 43 percent of American college graduates and 64 percent of people with a master's or doctorate get the answer right to all three questions. That's much higher than the 13 percent of people with less than a high school education, and 19 percent of those with a high school diploma, but not nearly good enough. If after seventeen years of schooling, most American college graduates don't understand the concepts of compound interest, real interest rates, and portfolio diversification, then there's something fundamentally wrong with the educational system. And if only one in five high school graduates know the right answers, that's a national tragedy. How can we expect people to make sound financial decisions, to save for retirement, or to avoid excessive levels of personal debt? The proportions of people who know the answers are nearly twice as large in Germany, the Netherlands, and Switzerland, but still a third of college degree holders and nearly half of high school grads could not get all answers right. And the gender gap is yawning; women trail men by anywhere between 8 and 23 percentage points in those four countries. My Wharton colleague Olivia Mitchell has found that people who lack basic financial literacy skills, as measured by the tests above, are much better at managing their personal finances, including saving enough for retirement.

Much of this appalling situation has to do with underlying patterns of economic inequality. The proportions of financially literate people are lower in the U.S. than in Europe due to inequalities in access to education. European countries tend to have national—in some cases regional—primary and secondary education systems with national standards and centralized funding. In the U.S., by contrast, schools are run at the local level and funded mainly through real estate taxes. Poorer municipalities cannot offer the same quality of education as richer ones. Private schools further magnify preexisting inequalities. At the college level, European universities are on average much better than American universities, although they don't have anything approaching Harvard or Yale.

For Jim Hendler, a professor of computer science at Rensselaer Polytechnic Institute, universities need to double down on what elementary and high school education is supposed to provide. Colleges "will need to be more focused on teaching students to be lifelong learners, followed by more online content, in situ training, and other such [elements] to increase skills in a rapidly changing information world." In spite of the rise of online learning, the "college experience" is still seen by most experts as beneficial and necessary. Frank Elavsky, a data analyst at Acumen, argues that "interpersonal experiences and the liberal arts" are actually the more important skills. "Human bodies in close proximity to other human bodies stimulate real compassion, empathy, vulnerability and social-emotional intelligence." Uta Russmann, a marketing professor at the University of Applied Sciences in Vienna, Austria, argues that mass online programs can't be the solution to developing sophisticated social skills and that colleges are ill-equipped at the present time to do so. She also believes that, increasingly, skills will be learned on the job.

The digital revolution will bring about a shakeout in the world of colleges and universities. "No matter how good our online teaching systems become, the current four-year college model will remain dominant for quite some time," argues David Karger, a professor of computer science at MIT. He believes that online education will benefit the most famous universities because they are a major source of new knowledge. By contrast, less well-known universities will need to change their value proposition. He envisions universities with fewer teaching faculty and more teaching assistants or tutors who help students learn online.

Making the sequential model of life more malleable may help improve the quality and impact of elementary, high school, and college education. If both students and schools had a second or a third chance to adjust and to get it right, then perhaps the outcomes would improve. That's the subject of the next chapter.

5

THREE CAREERS IN A LIFETIME

Life isn't about finding yourself.
Life is about creating yourself.
—George Bernard Shaw (1856–1950)

Anita Williams had been working as a software developer for fifteen years after college. Her company promoted her to team leader, but she was keenly aware that many former clients were now using their own artificial intelligence tools to do the work she once did for them. In a moment of self-reflection, she realized that perhaps the writing was on the wall. Educational institutions around the world had churned out millions of software engineers over the previous two decades. India alone has nearly ten million and produces three hundred thousand new graduates every year. She decided to take several online classes in interior design as part of a nondegree program that enabled her to register with her municipality as a certified designer. Her thinking was that AI could not yet mimic the creativity and sense of beauty of a human being. Some twenty years later, however, machine learning, pattern recognition, and virtual reality had made such inroads that many people found it easy to design their own kitchens online. Some tools even offered automatic filing of all the necessary construction permits and the placement of the orders for all the required materials and specialized labor. Already in her late fifties, Anita decided to double down on her creative bent and become an artist. A degree in fine arts was a longtime aspiration of hers. With her children now in college and a hefty amount of savings in the bank, she had more freedom to pursue her interests. She set up a workshop at home and sold her art online.

The fictional story of Anita is not far-fetched. Real-life people are making such career changes. Alisa M. became a computer programmer after years of helping her ex-husband run a restaurant. "A friend told me to look into SAP [the German IT giant] . . . This was in 2003, and I was 45 years old." She had studied to be a programmer, but in such a rapidly evolving field, her training became so obsolete that she had to go back to taking classes. "So yes, it is possible. . . . I am even looking to change careers in a couple of years when I retire: looking for ideas and maybe it is an idea for you to ask your readers: what to do after you retire from your actual job?!" For his part, Dr. Bernard Remakus had spent decades as a teacher and high school sports coach before becoming an internist. "Because I was older, my motivation was obvious . . . I feel I had many advantages attending medical school as an older student."

Each of those transitions took place at a time when career switching was relatively rare, except for a brief period when finance jobs were scarce after the 2008 financial crisis. "The single career path or job-for-life certainly isn't dead," says Natasha Stanley, a career change coach at UK-based Careershifters, "but it's becoming more and more likely that people will go through at least one career change in their lifetime." At the pace technology disrupts entire occupations and industries, we may have to start afresh in a new line of work or profession every two decades or so. As these changes set in, the possibilities for intergenerational learning will multiply, as will the need to think about how to manage a multigenerational workforce with not only different skills and strengths but also values and attitudes. How will a twentysomething team leader direct a baby boomer? Will n alpha feel comfortable having only xennial and baby-bust colleagues?

LIFE SPAN × HEALTH SPAN × TECHNOLOGY = MULTIPLE CAREERS

We need to connect the dots to see the future. At the root of the new trend toward multiple careers in a lifetime lies the convergence of three unique trends. First, we're living longer. The twelve thousand Americans who on any given day celebrate their sixtieth birthday can expect on average to live another twenty-three years. The number is even higher in some European and Asian countries: twenty-seven years in Japan and Hong Kong, twenty-six years in Australia, France, Spain, and Switzerland, and twenty-five years in Singapore, South Korea, Canada, Israel, Greece, Iceland, Sweden, Ireland, Portugal, Malta, Norway, Finland, and Panama. The immediate consequence of this increasing trend is that few people have set aside enough money for retirement. Second, we're staying healthier than ever for longer, as we saw in chapter 2. This means we can work and have an active lifestyle for many years to come beyond age sixty, what's known as the "health span." And third, technological change, as we saw in chapter 4, is making whatever we learned at school obsolete or antiquated much faster than in the past.

As a result of this coincidence of trends, an increasing number of people in their early forties will soon feel that their knowledge base no longer makes them competitive in the labor market and decide to go back to school. But don't get me wrong. I'm not expecting them to check into a dorm, fraternity, or sorority on campus. Most likely, they will use some kind of digital platform to learn new things. Then they'll go back to work. But by age sixty, realizing that they still have some twenty-five years to live (on average) and not enough savings for such a long retirement, they will go back into learning mode followed by some full-time or part-time occupation.

Many people will not only switch jobs; they will switch careers, professions, or occupations, reinventing themselves each time they go back to school. "It is projected that those entering the workforce today will pursue four or five different careers (not just jobs) over their lifetime. These career changes will require retooling, training, and education," says Ray Schroeder, associate vice chancellor for online learning at the University of Illinois Springfield.

Nowadays, it has become readily apparent that technological change makes it harder for many workers to keep up. Most of us struggle to maintain pace with new developments in our profession or occupation. Entire job classes are shrinking due to such disruptive technologies as robotics, artificial intelligence, and the blockchain. We're used to hearing about how automation has led to job losses for low-skill, routine occupations. In the future, scores of white-collar office workers and managers may be getting pink slips due to how the blockchain can make contracts go digital. Middle management's responsibilities include monitoring performance by suppliers and employees, ensuring that contractual clauses are met, and certifying the completion of tasks. "The smart contract offers an efficiency nearly impossible to match with human effort, especially when verifying for quality," notes Andrew J. Chapin, a technology entrepreneur.

My Wharton colleague Lynn Wu argues that "contrary to the popular notion that robots will replace human labor, we find robot-adopting firms employed more people over time." By contrast, she found in a twenty-year study that most job losses due to automation took place among managers and supervisors. "There is less need for managers to supervise, ensuring that workers show up on time, inspect their work, etc.," she notes. "Robots can record precisely the work they have done, so there's no agency costs, no fudging of the numbers."

And while today, only a few people are going back to school to pursue a different career, the trend is gathering speed. In 2018, *Forbes* published a story with the headline "Going Back to College After 50: The New Normal?" According to survey data, 60 percent of American adults between twenty-three and fifty-five years of age without a college education have considered it. It's shocking to realize that, according to the U.S. Department of Education, more than half of college-degree seekers are adults who could not pursue a postsecondary education earlier in life. The top considerations for attending college later in life, or returning to it, are the fear of being "outsourced or rendered obsolete by new technologies," keeping up with younger workers, and pursuing a new challenge. In China, one in four of the 230 million people above the age of sixty are attending college under a government-sponsored program. According to Xinhua, the official Chinese news agency, "Liu Wen-zhi gets up early, makes breakfast and sends her grandchildren to school." Then she goes to Dezhou College for the Aged, in Shandong Province, one of sixty thousand similar institutions in China. She is taking classes in "stringed instruments, the electronic piano, Peking Opera and paper-cutting." Yang Ruijun, a sixty-three-year-old former farmer, is the first in her village to attend the same college as Wenzhi. She has become a singing teacher.

In 2017, the *Financial Times* published a piece with the eye-catching title "Plan for Five Careers in a Lifetime: Work Is Impermanent—Reinvention Is Rational." Helen Barrett, the author, at the time the newspaper's Work & Careers editor, reflected on her own experience. "Changing careers is difficult, lonely, daunting and expensive," she asserts. "I should know: after a decade in advertising, I switched to journalism in my mid thirties, which not only meant starting at the bottom (one editor helpfully pointed out that I was 'the oldest intern ever') but also halved my pay. It took me four years to catch up." She then recounted the story of a woman in her fifties who was about to qualify as a lawyer, her fourth career after being a professor, a museum curator, and a teacher of would-be entrepreneurs. Her motivation? "She was thinking about her next challenge. She was a perpetual self-improver."

In the era of successful entrepreneurs in their twenties who create unicorns—companies valued at a billion dollars or more—it is also refreshing to reflect on what human ingenuity and creativity can accomplish at age forty. Vera Wang, the famous fashion designer, tried her luck first at figure skating, competing in the U.S. championship at age nineteen, which landed her a feature in *Sports Illustrated*. But she did not make it to the very top in such a competitive field, deciding instead to focus on her studies. After graduating from college, she became the youngest editor at *Vogue* magazine, followed by a short stint at Ralph Lauren. At age forty, she decided to become an independent bridal wear designer. The rest is history.

ONLINE EDUCATION COMES TO THE RESCUE

Lifelong learning and career switching, however, are easier said than done. Both involve a crucial generational aspect. For them to become a reality, massive change must occur at educational institutions—from primary schools to universities—and at companies, as well as the government. The education sector is rigidly stratified by age. My own experience teaching in executive education at Wharton and in the University of Pennsylvania bachelor's degree program for "unconventional students"—a euphemism to refer to those who could not attend college right after high school—showed me that it makes all the sense in the world to invite people to go, or return, to school at any moment in life. In that same vein, dozens of high schools across the United States are engaged in adult and continuing education. And herein lies the big opportunity: intergenerational learning in a multigenerational educational system. The program at Penn separates lifelong learners from young college students, missing out on enormous opportunities for intergenerational learning, something that Columbia University has understood for years, as it allows students in their thirties and forties matriculated in the School of Professional Studies to mingle with Columbia's college-age undergraduate students while taking classes together. The benefits of diversity in schools or universities are frequently touted to illustrate how enriching it is to learn from others. It is time for educators to include generational diversity as they compose their classrooms and educational programs so that learning can also take place across generations, leveraging unique experiences and skills to the benefit of others who lack them.

Digital learning is increasingly enabling career switchers. Hannah Cross, for instance, studied art history as an undergraduate at University College London, working for major institutions such as the Tate Gallery and the Institute of Contemporary Arts in the British capital after graduation. She decided to change tracks and become a programmer. A three-month immersive course helped her get a job at a start-up. It was not easy at first. She would see her colleagues fix coding problems very quickly while she struggled with hers. But she persevered and succeeded at her new job. Martha

Chambers, a former humanities teacher, became a junior JavaScript software engineer at ITV, the British TV station, after completing a similar course. "The great thing about the course is it's a way of getting into it even if you're not one of those types that has spent hours in their bedroom" playing with digital devices. Her current boss is also a career switcher, someone who was previously employed in social work.

Technology both creates a problem by making knowledge obsolete and provides a solution by enabling lifelong learning and career switching. Innovative online programs make it easier for worker-learners to refresh their knowledge while also attending to their families. Low-residency degree programs, for example, could enable people of all ages to continually adapt to a shifting job market. "We will definitely see a vast increase in educational and training programs," says Michael Wollowski, an associate professor of computer science at the Rose-Hulman Institute of Technology. "We will also see what might be called on-demand or on-the-job kind of training programs." David Karger, a professor of computer science at MIT, notes that many online offerings are "little more than glorified textbooks," but he believes in the promise of online education. For his part, Barry Chudakov, founder and principal at Sertain Research and StreamFuzion, believes that we will stop separating schooling and work. "They will seamlessly weave into a braid of learning, realization, exposure, hands-on experience and integration into students' own lives." He firmly believes, as I do, that "one way we will break down these walls . . . will be to create digital learning spaces to rival classrooms as 'places' where learning happen[s]. Via simulation, gaming, digital presentations—combined with hands-on, real-world experience—learning and re-education will move out of books and into the world." Institute for the Future fellow Richard Adler envisions that those technologies will create a unique learning experience "across a broad range of fields." Ray Schroeder goes one step further, saying that "I anticipate the further development and distribution of holoportation technologies such as those developed by Microsoft using HoloLens for real-time, three-dimensional augmented reality." The hope is that these tools will enable very realistic interactions and engagement. For Tawny Schlieski, research director at Intel and president of the nonprofit Oregon Story Board, new technologies like augmented and virtual reality have the potential of truly immersing learners in the context of what they are learning, making the process more experiential and interactive.

The technological revolution in education is not just about the mode of delivery. It's also about the possibility that people may become self-directed learners. "There is no field of work that cannot be learned, totally or in great part, in well-organized and administered online programs, either in traditional 'course' formats, or in self-directed, independent learning opportunities, supplemented, when appropriate, by face-to-face, hands-on, practice situations," says Fredric Litto, a professor emeritus of communications at the University of São Paulo, Brazil. Ian O'Byrne, an assistant professor of literacy education at the College of Charleston, thinks that technology will enable personalized digital learning. "We'll see a rise in the offering of premium or pay content that creates a space where one-to-one learning and interaction will allow mentors to guide learners while providing critical feedback. We will identify opportunities to build a digital version of the apprenticeship learning models that have existed in the past." He finds the possibility of merging online teaching with the blockchain as perhaps the most tantalizing of all given that it promises to create a decentralized digital registry where, on the one hand, workers can post their skills, diplomas, and experience, and, on the other, companies and other organizations can look for the talent they need. "Alternative credentials and digital badges will provide more granular opportunities to document and archive learning over time from traditional and nontraditional learning sources." He anticipates that blockchain technology will enable learners to choose exactly what pieces or modules of a lesson they want to access, and thus create their own, individualized learning journey.

The limits to self-directed study are obvious, and it remains to be seen to what extent technology can help people overcome them. "Self-directed study is [a] variable that changes the alchemy of teaching and learning," says Beth Corzo-Duchardt, a professor at Muhlenberg College. Research shows that self-directed students have a good learning experience to the extent that they have a good educational foundation and a supportive family environment. They tend to be privileged students who have developed the necessary skills to learn on their own and to think critically.

One of the ways in which online education may reduce, not increase, inequality is by delivering high-quality value at a low cost. Baratunde Thurston, a director's fellow at the MIT Media Lab, maintains, "Why go $100,000 in debt for a four-year university, when you can take a more targeted course with more guaranteed income generation potential at the end?" Jeff Jarvis, a professor at the Craig Newmark Graduate School of Journalism at the City University of New York, notes that "we need to see the marginal cost of teaching another student fall to zero to see true innovation come to education . . . I don't think we'll ever reach zero; MOOCs are not the solution!" He predicts a "radical economic disruption" using technology in terms of both delivering a learning experience and certifying it. Marcel Bullinga, a keynote speaker, thinks that "the future is cheap, and so is the future of education." He believes that education will become widely accessible at low cost, thanks to technology. "I saw an ad already for $1,000 bachelor's-level training—with an app, of course. Schools and universities will transform in the same way as shops have done in the past ten years from analog/human-first to digital/mobile/AI-first." He predicts that online educational credentials will become more popular than the traditional system.

There are limitations, however, to what can be achieved online. "Coding, big-data analysis capacities, efficient management of resources, abstract and logical thinking, rapid response, the ability to think across information systems, etc. will be necessary skills in one of the sectors of this new workplace. In another [area], the necessary skills will include obedience, rapid response, efficient management of customers/simple services/machines, ability to maintain order, security, to confront emergencies, etc.," says Simon Gottschalk, a sociologist at the University of Nevada, Las Vegas. He thinks the social skills are more easily acquired through face-to-face learning. Peer-to-peer learning online may help overcome some of the constraints, but perhaps not all. "I suspect that the mass educational approach of MOOCs will be tempered with more sophisticated peer-to-peer connected learning that traverses online and physical realms," notes Marcus Foth, professor of interactive and visual design at Queensland University of Technology. "Most difficult to scale are those skills that require human interaction (e.g., medical skills involving patients)," observes Michael Dyer, a computer scientist at UCLA. He believes that new technologies like virtual reality and AI will make online learning so much more effective, scalable, and enjoyable.

Even faculty in the humanities are starting to recognize the potential of online education, although with some caveats. "The high cost of higher education, desire to make education available to a broader number of people, development of increasingly sophisticated online courses" are all factors that make online options more attractive, says Naomi Baron, a professor of linguistics at American University. For her, the main challenge has to do with deciding which parts of the learning experience can happen online and which need to be face-to-face.

On balance, online learning will play a crucial role in job and career transitions because of its availability, freshness, immediacy, and affordability. Janice R. Lachance, interim president and CEO of the Better Business Bureau Institute for Marketplace Trust, argues that online education is a great option for many learning needs. It "is critical for just-in-time skills or continuing professional development." She thinks that not learning is not an option anymore, regardless of age. The online option will, in her view, offer people unlimited opportunities for career progression or "simply keeping up."

Online learning will evolve quickly as demand grows, offerings differentiate, and new technology becomes available. I taught an online class over the metaverse for the first time in May 2022. I initially thought it was just another fancy approach to digital interaction, another fad, but nothing that could add real value beyond what we can already achieve through existing platforms. I thought the metaverse would revolutionize gaming, shopping, and healthcare, but not education. I was wrong. Once we learn how to use it effectively, the metaverse will open an entire array of new possibilities to immerse students in a learning experience hitherto impossible. I've become a big fan of the metaverse.

Rather than listening to one expert or entrepreneur after another, let's pay attention to what James Hinton, a truck driver and writer, has to say. "A pharmacist in a remote location such as Salmon, Idaho, could achieve a doctor of pharmacy (Pharm.D.) without having to quit her job and move away." Online education promises to open new horizons to people in far-out locations. He believes that rural residents will benefit the most from online education options and may persuade young people not to migrate to a major urban area. "It's quite the exciting development."

It certainly is.

COMPANIES AND GOVERNMENTS
NEED TO CHANGE

According to the Bureau of Labor Statistics, the average American holds twelve jobs between the ages of eighteen and fifty—or a new job every 2.7 years, while in Europe and Japan, it's every 10 years. In the future, it could well be that the metric shifts from jobs to careers as we pursue two or even three different occupations or professions. And that will change not only how we look at our careers but how companies hire. People in their twenties will plan to go through several career transitions as opposed to spending their entire lives in one line of work. Companies will need to adapt to this new situation. From a hiring standpoint, managers and HR can no longer assume that an entry-level employee will be in their twenties since someone in their forties, fifties, or sixties may have decided to enter a new occupation and, if they have attained the necessary skills, will be as qualified as a recent high school or college graduate might be.

Companies, governments, and educational institutions have to change if lifelong learning in a multigenerational context is to realize its full potential. As employers, they will need to see the benefits of sending people back to full-time learning at several points during their careers, potentially learning from the perspectives and capabilities of younger generations. Financing would need to be made available, especially for workers who would lose their earnings while going back to school. Consider the case of Mike, who graduated with a bachelor's in his early sixties after a thirty-year career at a telecommunications company. His employer had established a partnership for online education with Champlain College in Burlington, Vermont, encouraging employees to acquire new skills in areas like cybersecurity.

"We are now in the transitional stage of employers gradually reducing their prejudice in the hiring of those who studied at a distance," notes University of São Paulo's Litto, "and moving in favor of such 'graduates' who, in the workplace, demonstrate greater proactiveness, initiative, discipline, collaborativeness—because they studied online." Charlie Firestone, communications and society program executive director and vice president at the Aspen Institute, is very optimistic. "There will be a move toward more precise and better credentialing for skills and competencies, e.g., badging and similar techniques." Sam Punnett, research officer at TableRock Media, concurs: "I suspect employers will recognize the new credentialing systems . . . Traditional credentials will continue to hold value, but I believe they will be considered in light of a candidate's perceived ability in 'learning how to learn.'" Gottschalk, the sociologist at the University of Nevada, is also of the same mind. While he thinks that employers will continue to prefer a four-year college graduate over an online student, there will be an increasing number of jobs for which the latter might be perfectly suitable or even better. "In any case, this preference will also probably fade over time."

Mary Chayko, a professor of communication and information at Rutgers University, has made the compelling argument that companies will embrace online educational credentials. "Employers will value applicants trained in diverse settings—traditional and nontraditional, face-to-face and digital—who can respond nimbly to constant change." In other words, the proliferation of online courses and credentials doesn't spell the end of traditional education. There's room for both, and employers will want to tap into both. The key point is that both the education system and the labor market are in flux. "Employers don't always know how to hire for today's workplace demands, and a certificate in a particular subject can be the difference between getting a job offer and being a runner-up," argues Lachance. She is confident that if employers accept online certificates, then online options will proliferate and their quality and differentiation will improve. We're only at the beginning of what will be a long process of transformation and development.

Perhaps the greatest obstacle to a future of multiple-career seekers lies with the government. For certain occupations, labor regulations don't make it easy for people to get accredited for a career switch soon enough to take advantage of opportunities as the economy changes. Moreover, there's a built-in animosity among organized labor and governments toward gig work. The government job bureaucracy itself, with its detailed levels and grades, seems to be completely at odds with a technologically driven economy in constant flux.

Governments are indeed the largest employers in virtually every country. The German IT giant SAP and the Institute for Government in the UK argue in a 2020 report that government work has been thoroughly transformed by technology, both in terms of back-office and in citizen-facing operations. The civil service in many countries around the world has gone through many reforms throughout the last hundred years, but is still wedded to the old principles of linear promotion paths and seniority pay, both grossly incongruent with the new demographic, economic, and technological realities of the twenty-first century. The consultancy Deloitte argues that "radical technological changes and new generational expectations about public service work, coupled with mission shifts across the government may challenge the traditional notion of 'public service' from lifelong agency employment to a more flexible federal career model." From the point of view of the end of the sequential model of life, a civil service that is more open, flexible, and porous—allowing for employees to rotate in and out of government more easily—is the hallmark for the future. A rigid state bureaucracy means that it will be hard for government departments and agencies to adapt to new trends, especially when it comes to retaining and attracting talent with the skill set required to be efficient and effective in this new environment.

THE (POTENTIAL) BENEFITS OF THE
MULTIGENERATIONAL WORKPLACE

Governments, businesses, and other types of organizations are slowly waking up to the benefits of digital education, career switching, and the potential benefits of a workplace in which several generations share the stage with the increase in life spans, health spans, and the desire to continue working beyond retirement age. Technology is further enhancing the trend by making it possible for people at more advanced ages to work from home and by enabling people to refresh their knowledge and thus prolong their active work life. "There is an increasing demand in the workforce today to add multigenerational diversity to the mix," writes University of North Carolina Kenan-Flagler Business School's Kip Kelly, who has conducted a thorough review of existing research on the topic. Having people from a broader age spectrum side by side in the workplace raises distinct human-resource and talent-management issues. The reason is that the multigenerational workplace provides an opportunity (and a challenge) to take advantage of the talents of each generation.

As Kelly sees it, based on multiple studies on the subject, the worldviews of these generations are different. The Greatest and Silent Generations and those who were kids during World War II "were raised in strong nuclear families where parenting was associated with discipline and strictness." They were also affected by the Great Depression. The baby boomers "have a strong work ethic, not because they view work as a privilege as [the Silent Generation does], but because they are motivated by rank, wealth, and prestige. They are extremely loyal to their employers, service- and goal-oriented, and competitive. They are also good team players." Thus, research indicates that they "prefer managers who seek consensus and treat them as equals." Generation X experienced in their youth and early adulthood the reverberations from the civil rights movement, Watergate, the energy crisis, the AIDS epidemic, and the fall of the Berlin Wall. Their mothers were employed outside of the household in much greater numbers than previous generations. "As a result, many experienced independence early in life and learned to thrive on change. They are independent, resilient, flexible, and adaptable." They prefer to hire people who are "straightforward, genuine, and 'hands-off' in their management approach."

Interestingly, a 2013 study by the consultancy Ernst & Young found that baby boomers and millennials both prefer to work with Generation Xers because of their drive to succeed tempered by a desire to collaborate. As children, millennials experienced 9/11, the rise in U.S. domestic terrorism, and the first noticeable effects of the climate crisis. Their key characteristic is their complete fluency in technology and their desire to be in touch and exchange information through social media. They thus expect more horizontal relationships and information flow than previous generations. They "want nothing to do with that hierarchy and reject traditional top-down communication." It's also the most diverse generation by race, ethnicity, national origin, and sexual orientation ever to be in the workplace, and the best educated ever, at least in terms of credentials. According to this research, they prefer managers with a lateral style, who believe in mentoring and coaching, and are goal-oriented yet collaborative. One can only guess at this point how Generation Z might behave in the workplace. Compared to millennials, they are even more technologically driven, diverse, and credentialed.

Research also found that while many of the intergenerational differences are real, they do not have to necessarily result in different values, attitudes, and behaviors in the workplace. Some of the differences are stereotypical and conceal the enormous degree of heterogeneity within each generation. Some of the differences attributed to each generation reflect age rather than context, an issue that we will explore further in chapter 9. Among the many benefits, one might include preventing "brain drain" from experienced employees leaving the company, widening the applicant pool by attracting potential employees of all ages, and creating a more creative workforce through diversity.

But, as we saw in chapter 1, even the most ardent supporters of the multigenerational workplace see the potential for conflict. In one study, intergenerational misunderstandings and conflict occupied 12 percent of the workweek. Perhaps the most interesting finding in this line of research is that employees from different generations tend to accuse each other of the same wrongdoings. Perhaps then the central issues have to do with misunderstandings due to stereotyping and with miscommunication. "Understanding and communication can help minimize any perceived generational gaps and focus employees on their shared values and expectations," concludes Kelly, striking an optimistic chord.

The good news is that the social skills that are increasingly being demanded by employers (see chapter 4) can also help overcome intergenerational conflict. "Social and emotional intelligence equip managers with skills to turn challenges of generational differences into positives," argue Caroline Ngonyo Njoroge and Rashad Yazdanifard, professors at the Limkokwing University of Creative Technology in Malaysia. Their main point is that the conventional wisdom is wrong in that generational differences do not necessarily result in differences in motivation and behavior. Besides, employees from different generations have common values and concerns. All generations yearn for a measure of job security and fulfillment. The key is for managers to use social and emotional intelligence "to positively impact employees' behaviors with outcomes such as job satisfaction, positive work attitudes, self-efficacy, and leadership potential and change management."

In their review of existing research, Eddy Ng and Emma Parry, from Bucknell University and Cranfield University in the UK, respectively, note that prevailing human resource policies and practices were put in place by baby boomers for baby boomers at a time when "organizations are striving to attract and retain the millennials while working to extend the careers of baby boomers." After reviewing over one hundred studies, they noticed that most researchers have not been able to separate the effects of age, period, and generation. That's an understatement, actually. A more accurate assessment would be that most research has failed at demonstrating that generational differences exist above and beyond those related to age and historical period, a shortcoming that we will revisit in chapter 9 when we discuss postgenerational marketing.

To make matters more complicated, generations develop asynchronously by country. For instance, the American baby boomers were born in the 1950s, but the number of children per woman peaked in the early 1960s in Southern Europe and in India, in the late 1960s in China, and in the late 1970s in sub-Saharan Africa. It is disheartening to realize that the bulk of existing research refers to North America and Western Europe. Ng and Parry conclude better research on the multigenerational workplace is needed instead of relying on "anecdotes and stereotypes from popular media."

The workplace is becoming radically different from what it used to be.

We've never seen so many generations working side by side, so many women employed outside of the household, so many childless employees in their thirties and forties, so many employees above the age of sixty, such a strong shift from traditional to secular and self-expressive values, and so much technological change. We need to connect the dots across these trends. Simply put, researchers on the multigenerational workplace have to consider the effects of current demographic, cultural, and technological shifts. To be fair, they do consider the latter, but simply to say that Gen Zers are more technologically savvy than millennials, millennials more so than Gen Xers, and so on. That amounts to scratching the surface of what's going on. We need to dig deeper to understand how the twilight of the sequential model of life is upending organizations and the labor market, and what its demise will mean for the multigenerational workplace instead of applying the same old social-psychological questionnaires, scales, experiments, and other research paraphernalia to try to understand a phenomenon that doesn't lend itself to traditional approaches and measures. Once again, we see researchers—and the managers who listen to them—attempting to solve the problem as opposed to dissolving it.

THINK "PERENNIALS"

As we saw in the book's opening pages, forward-looking companies like BMW are dissolving the problems associated with intergenerational differences, misunderstandings, and conflict by proactively reorganizing themselves to enable people of very different ages to work together. In 2013, financial services giant The Hartford launched a reverse mentoring program whereby millennial employees would coach other generations, especially executives, about digital technologies. Matched mentors and mentees meet frequently to explore mutual learning opportunities. Advice about technology flows in one direction, and business and career advice in the other. Brigitte Van Den Houte, vice president of human resources and global talent management at Pitney Bowes, the global shipping and e-commerce firm, has created mixed-age cross-functional teams of about fifteen employees who have equal influence over decisions regardless of age or seniority. "The old way of working no longer works," she says. At Steelcase, a file-cabinet manufacturer in Michigan, veterans and new employees form teams for mutual benefit. Indeed, the Pew Research Center documents that identification with generational labels has declined, especially among millennials, with just 40 percent who consider themselves part of that generation compared with 79 percent for baby boomers.

Consulting companies like Deloitte have begun to peddle the concept of the "Multigenerational Workforce." Most organizations rely on age and generation to organize their employees. "Forward-looking organizations are shifting their approach in an effort to better understand the workforce's attitudes and values, while harnessing technology to analyze and create new, more relevant insights into workers' needs and expectations," write consultants Erica Volini, Jeff Schwartz, and David Mallon in a client brief. "Organizations have an opportunity to design and implement workforce strategies and programs that are more targeted toward workers' individual attributes." The goal should be to enhance work satisfaction by helping people find meaning and feel that they are contributing to something larger than their job.

In other words, instead of endlessly debating generational differences and stereotypes in the workplace, companies should embrace the concept of *perennials,* a term coined in 2016 by Gina Pell, a serial entrepreneur. Perennials constitute "an ever-blooming group of people of all ages, stripes, and types who transcend stereotypes and make connections with each other and the world around them . . . they are not defined by their generation." Based on this concept, the Deloitte consultants argue that "rapid technological and organizational change means that workers must now reinvent themselves multiple times throughout their working lives," cultural expectations as to who should be the supervisor or the manager have changed, and a vast swath of the economy now consists of companies founded and run by very young people. Within organizations, they argue, these trends translate into a new reality in which interns in their sixties can work together with managers in their twenties.

This inversion of the traditional organizational hierarchy by age means that most of the assumptions built into human resource, talent, and career management are becoming obsolete. Under the sequential model of life, a career meant a linear progression from less to more status, prestige, responsibility, and pay. Deloitte's Global Human Capital Trends report shows that employees are no longer linking age or generation to expectations of advancement as much as they did in the past. "It's a sea change for employers, causing reversals of authority," says my Wharton colleague Peter Cappelli. "Suddenly 20- and 30-year-olds are working with people their parents' and grandparents' ages who are subordinates or peers, not superiors as they used to be."

Not surprisingly, tech companies seem to be at the forefront of this growing trend. "Our people team is composed of people who range in age from their 20s to their 50s, and we've all built this process together," says Diana Preziosi, senior human resources manager at Notarize, a platform that facilitates online transactions. "The value is the combination of different perspectives enabling us to think about all of our team at Notarize, rather than just one narrow perspective deciding what is best for the team." Jordan Weisman, CEO of Project Archer, an augmented reality company, notes that "in designing the 'future,' we constantly find ourselves pulling from related experiences in the past." At his company, "older team members might introduce references from 'The Jetsons,' while younger ones introduce something amazing from a K-pop band on TikTok. The learning is universal across the age spectrum and the combination of cultural and temporal experiences is generating some amazing work." Jordan Feinberg, talent acquisition specialist at GR0, the LA-based digital marketing agency, recounts, "We've found that creating mini pods within our structure, even within departments themselves, allows for a more open and collaborative environment where different generations can build trust in each other." For instance, their search-engine optimization (SEO) department is broken down into smaller units, each of them consisting of people from different generations.

But larger companies are not necessarily disadvantaged when it comes to shedding age and generations as meaningful categories, as the cases of BMW, The Hartford, and Pitney Bowes show. Lindsey Pollak relied on the experience of large and established companies as diverse as AT&T, GE, BNY Mellon, and Estée Lauder for her 2019 book, *The Remix: How to Lead and*

Succeed in the Multigenerational Workplace, which provides a step-by-step guide for dealing with the new demographic realities. She urges managers and employees alike "to embrace the fundamental fact that none of us, of any generation, will survive if we remain static and rigid." Adaptability, flexibility, open-mindedness, and refusing to take old assumptions as given are essential for effective organizations and fulfilling careers. "We are incredibly fortunate to live in an era with more opportunities, choices, and diversity than ever before. This is often scary and confusing, but isn't it also exciting?"

Seen from the perspective of the unraveling of the sequential model, the future looks promising. The multigenerational workplace is just one manifestation of the potentially positive consequences of such a momentous transformation. The others include the phasing out of retirement as we know it, offering people of all ages a wider range of options; the undermining of traditional inheritance practices, with the concomitant reduction in economic inequality; the reinvigoration of the feminist movement, which will make the world a better place; a postgenerational consumer market in which no segment defined by age is overlooked; and, more broadly, the postgenerational society. Stay tuned to the chapters that follow.

6

REIMAGINING RETIREMENT

There's one thing I always wanted to do
before I quit . . . retire!
—Groucho Marx (1890–1977)

"I've chatted with many of you about your plans once full-time work stops for you. And so I've asked some of you to join me up here and tell everyone what you told me," says Don Ezra, an author, blogger, and former pensions executive. He decided to interview people in groups to probe their plans and their feelings about retirement in preparation for his own. One of his interviewees commented that "I'm not yet 40, so that's a long way into the future, for me. But I admit I'm already worried about retirement. I'd like to retire young. It's the freedom—not having to be somewhere every day, not even having to answer to anyone—go to the gym, run errands, whatever," he explained with gusto. "There are happinesses associated with working, but for me, working is just a means to an end. I'm not sure I want to work for the sake of working." That instrumental approach to work—a means to an end—is very widespread because we have not thought carefully about infusing every job with meaning. As a side effect, we have come to reify retirement as an aspiration and a liberation.

"Well, my husband and I are a little bit older than 40! We're hoping to retire in the near future," a second interviewee noted. "Much as we love each other, we need social interaction. We can only be with each other a certain amount of time before we need to be with other people!" The fear of being socially disconnected, even when a loving partner is beside you, is another common thought besetting people when they ponder the pluses and minuses of retirement. "We hope we'll have a good relationship with our kids and the partners they choose, but that's not within our control." Parental retirement can actually add to the stress of young couples as they seek to have their own independence, to live their own lives. "What will we actually do? We want to avoid cold winters—maybe vacation together with another family (like my brother's family). Volunteering. My husband coaches sports. Me with the church. A hospice too, now that I've seen a friend who needed one. Some fundraising for good causes." Retirees tend to emphasize how much they crave intergenerational relationships. "And be grandparents! Please! Spoil our grandchildren! Seriously, help our children if they need us to help with raising grandchildren." That would be if any grandchildren are born before too late.

Making too many plans about spending time with children and grandchildren can be hard. "Where will we live? Our house is too big. Live near our grandchildren? There's no guarantee our son will stay where he is," added another interviewee. "So we're tentatively planning to go back to the town where we came from—our family origins—but we'll have to re-establish close relations with them."

"I'm Toni, and we retired a few years ago. Toby retired a few years ago. I'm a teacher and I retired before him. Then we moved to M [something between a small town and a farming community]. And that's it, really!" Toni has a self-deprecating attitude about life and is simply happy to go with the flow. "My brother-in-law jokes that we wake up with nothing to do, and by the end of the day half of it is still undone!" To kill time and feel useful, they volunteer for various causes. "We drive old people around, we read to them, we help organize events. The list is never-ending, if you really want to find something to do," says Toby. "And then of course our grandchildren! We always loved visiting them, and after Toby retired we could be even closer," says Toni. "And their parents are happy having us here, because we get along and it lets both of them work. So between the babysitting and taking them to school and bringing them back home—yes, we're really busy!"

Don asks, "Anything else?" Toni gets excited. "Actually, a lot more! Our social life extends to the church and a book club and other local social groups. We read a lot. We enjoy our old music. We even go to dances! All in all, it's really busy. But as I said, there's nothing different there that makes us role models for anyone. It works for us." When asked if their new life in retirement took shape right away, they adamantly respond that it did not. "It took a little while, actually. It's a close community. We felt a bit like outsiders at first, but the church and the book club helped. And of course through our grandchildren and their school activities. We and the other parents and grandparents really connected through them."

The difficulty most people have making sense of the decision to retire, and their experience after transitioning out of full-time work, suggests that retirement is one of the most oversold aspects of modern life. "I think retirement should be avoided as much as possible," says Eric Brotman, a retirement financial planner. "It (usually) can't be undone . . . It's dangerous to your health . . . It's dangerous to your wealth." Although retirement can be reversed, at least partially, and there's no evidence it's harmful to people's health or wealth, Brotman has a point: we have elevated retirement to a pedestal and, in many countries, enshrined it as a constitutional right. Let's look at the evidence on the virtues and the costs of retirement.

Among the various implications of retirement, its impact on health is a hotly debated issue among researchers. Any transition in life generates stress, as it takes time for the body and the mind to adjust. Retirement can result in social isolation and inactivity, both of which can seriously undermine physical and mental health. Lack of money may increase anxiety. But most research either finds no impact of retirement on health status or a mildly positive impact. Differences between blue- and white-collar workers are negligible, but retirees from lower socioeconomic status groups tend to benefit more from retirement. The most recent review of existing research concluded that there was no "association between early retirement, compared with continued work participation, and mortality." While "on-time retirement, compared with working beyond retirement, was associated with a higher risk of mortality," the correlation disappeared in studies in which health status prior to retirement was taken into consideration, as it should be. In sum, the fact and the timing of retirement do not seem to have a systematic effect on health and ultimate mortality.

A similar picture emerges in the case of the effect of retirement on financial wealth. It is beyond the obvious to state that retirement slows down, and potentially reverses, the process of wealth accumulation, with people using their savings and the right to a pension to pay for their living expenses. The danger lies in making overly optimistic assumptions about spending levels and investment returns after retirement. And on top of that, mishaps do occur, such as unanticipated healthcare expenses or family emergencies. But my point is that the sequential model of life places too much pressure on workers to save for retirement and on governments to deliver on promises made when the age structure of the population made classic pension systems financially viable.

According to the 2021 Transamerica Retirement Survey, the number one fear among Americans of different generations is outliving savings, with 42 percent of respondents, closely followed by declining health that requires long-term care, and a reduction in or elimination of Social Security in the future. The truly revealing part of the survey is that outliving savings is the number one fear not just among baby boomers and Generation Xers but among millennials as well (tied for first place with declining health), although they are still decades away from retirement. Even for the much younger Generation Z workers, outliving savings in retirement is the second-biggest fear after providing for the family's basic needs. Thus, financial pressures regarding retirement seem to afflict even the youngest generations of workers. The fear is not triggered by retirement; it becomes salient early in adult life. And it is astonishing to see that it trumps other issues like cognitive decline, losing one's independence, feeling alone, having affordable housing, and being laid off. Tellingly, a very small proportion of young workers report having no retirement fears: 6 percent of Generation Zers and 8 percent of millennials.

And retirement doesn't always lead to the enjoyment of more quality time. According to the Bureau of Labor Statistics, Americans age sixty-five and above who do not work have more time available for leisure. But instead of spending significantly more time reading or socializing, they mostly increase the amount of time they spend watching TV, from 2.9 hours daily among those working to 4.6 hours for those who do not. Thus, it's not travel or exercising that people turn to in retirement. The consequences can be dire.

Researchers at University College London in the UK analyzed data from the English Longitudinal Study of Ageing (ELSA) on 3,662 adults age fifty and older. "The analysis revealed that those who watched TV for 3.5 hours or more per day had an average decline of 8–10% in word- and language-related memory over the 6 years the study covered." People who watched less TV experienced half as much of a decline. "Television has been described as a unique cultural activity in that it combines strong, rapidly changing fragmentary dense sensory stimuli on the one hand with passivity from the viewer on the other." Given that the amount of time to allocate to activities is limited, the loss stems not just from the negative effect of "alert-passive" TV viewing but also from not engaging in cognitively beneficial activities such as reading, playing, visiting a museum, talking to friends and family, or traveling.

Beyond TV, seniors are spending more time in front of screens more generally, including smartphones, tablets, and computers. In 2019, the Pew Research Center reported that over a period of ten years, Americans age sixty and above spent more time on screens and less socializing and reading. Although the conventional wisdom suggests that millennials and Generation Zers spend a considerable amount of time using electronic gadgets, a Nielsen survey found that American seniors are now spending nearly ten hours per day in front of screens, 12 percent more than people in the thirty-five-to-forty-nine age group and a whopping 33 percent more than those in the eighteen-to-thirty-four age group.

"It's important to recognize the difference between good screen time and bad screen time," argues John Marick, CEO of Consumer Cellular, a wireless reseller focused on the needs of the fifty-plus age market segment. "When you are deploying tech just as a psychological pacifier or for distraction or because you're bored, that can take you to bad places." The AARP, while recognizing the problem, also points out that there are good uses of screen time among older adults, including watching a TED Talk, reading a newspaper, watching a nature documentary, recording a video with stories for the grandchildren, and visiting places online. And perhaps digital devices can help break with the whole concept of retirement by enabling flexible work practices.

The reification of retirement, and the fears and not-so-good aspects of it, speak volumes to the necessity for society to switch gears, to challenge the sequence of stages in life that places so much angst on people from the earliest days of our working experience. What are the alternatives? Will governments and companies help? May technology come to the rescue?

THE WINDS OF CHANGE

"Today I have worked, played, shopped, and swiped online," reports the new archetype of the American grandparent. Before the decade of the 2020s is over, there will be more gig workers and online shoppers above the age of sixty than below the age of thirty. That's because in the postgenerational society, we'll have a much larger number of people above sixty than below thirty, and technology will change the lifestyle of everyone regardless of age. "We don't stop playing because we grow old," said the playwright George Bernard Shaw. "We grow old because we stop playing." Even before the pandemic struck, a significant proportion of people age sixty and older were taking advantage of new technology to play, learn, work, and shop more comfortably and efficiently. While inequalities in access to the internet persist, home confinement and social distancing compelled the most recalcitrant to use digital platforms for the first time—and many of them found it useful and fun. We are at a point in history in which age matters much less than it once did when it comes to embracing new ways of getting things done and of enjoying life.

And as our active longevity increases, we will also see more and more people rethinking retirement. The 2015 movie *The Intern* is a witty take on how that might look. In the film, Robert De Niro plays seventy-year-old widower Ben Whittaker, who complains about the unbearable dullness of retirement. "How do I spend the rest of my days? You name it. Golf. Books. Movies. Pinochle. Tried yoga, learned to cook, bought some plants, took classes in Mandarin [*in Mandarin*]. Believe me, I've tried everything [*back in English*]." Finally, he joins a Brooklyn online fashion start-up under a new program to attract senior talent, led by founder and CEO Jules Ostin (Anne Hathaway), and eventually becomes her closest advisor and confidant—and a much happier man.

It's certainly true that people in many manual and physical occupations cannot perform their jobs indefinitely. Airline pilots, for example, are legally mandated to retire at sixty-five, an age limit that Congress had raised in 2009 by five years. Jobs that entail heavy, and in some cases dangerous, physical labor—from agriculture and mining to construction, manufacturing, policing, and firefighting—may not be safely performed beyond a certain age. But that doesn't mean those workers have to retire if given a chance by their employers to rotate into less physically demanding jobs or to go back to school. Other occupations, including teaching and intellectual work, aren't subject to stringent age constraints. "Old age treats freelance writers pretty gently," observed John Updike. It's certainly easier for professors like myself to keep going indefinitely.

In much of Europe, the mandatory retirement age oscillates between sixty and sixty-seven, even though most people remain perfectly capable of making contributions to the economy as workers. Despite frequent efforts to bill it as age discrimination, the courts have rejected the argument, and most governments fear that removing age limits might increase unemployment. To make matters worse, in Austria, Bulgaria, Croatia, the Czech Republic, Italy, Lithuania, Poland, Romania, and Slovenia, women's mandatory retirement age is lower than men's by as much as five years, even though on average European women live nearly seven years *longer* than men!

The situation is even more problematic in China, where the retirement age was set at sixty for all men, fifty-five for women in government jobs, and fifty for blue-collar female workers. As a result, the average age at retirement is fifty-four, about ten years lower than in the richest countries in the world. Clearly, the increase in life expectancy and the decline in fertility, even after the abandonment of the one-child policy, call for an increase in the age of retirement. But the government finds itself in an impossible situation. Raising the age of retirement can be counterproductive because so many young couples in China rely on their retired parents for childcare. In fact, one study found that the probability of having a child increased by more than 60 percent after a parent retired. Chinese policymakers are thus facing a dramatic catch-22.

Although governments don't change the mandatory retirement age frequently, people's actual decisions as to the age of retirement have evolved quickly. The average *effective* retirement age among men in Europe and the U.S. declined until the late 1990s, driven by generous pensions and early-retirement incentives in declining industries. After the turn of the twenty-first century, the situation started to change markedly. Rising inequality, a decline in personal savings, and the impact of the global financial crisis of 2008 compelled people to work until later in life. In 2018, American men and women retired an average of 3.1 and 2.8 years later than in 2000, respectively (see table 6.1). In the European Union, the overall increase in the effective retirement age has been less pronounced in the eastern and southern member countries (including France), with Central and Northern Europe approximating the American trend. In the UK, the trend has been closer to France's than to Germany's. Meanwhile, Canadian women have increased their retirement age faster than men. But the largest increases worldwide are in Australia, New Zealand, rich East Asian countries like South Korea, and parts of the Middle East (e.g., Turkey). Meanwhile, in many emerging markets, the opposite trend is underway, with the average effective retirement age continuing to decline in Mexico and in India, and stagnate in Brazil and Chile. While table 6.1 does not include data for China, the effective age of retirement is also dropping there.

We thus see a bifurcation in the world. While both the life span and the health span continue to rise in every country, over time, people are retiring later in the more developed regions but earlier in many emerging markets. The reason has little to do with differences in economic performance. Rather, the seemingly disparate trends since the turn of the twenty-first century are driven by what happened in the 1970s and '80s. Average effective retirement ages dropped too rapidly in Europe, the U.S., Canada,

TABLE 6.1: AVERAGE EFFECTIVE AGE OF RETIREMENT

	Men				Women				Change 2000 to 2018	
	1970	1980	2000	2018	1970	1980	2000	2018	Men	Women
United States	68.4	66.4	64.8	67.9	67.9	66.3	63.7	66.5	3.1	2.8
European Union - 27	68.4	65.1	61.5	64.0	65.8	62.9	59.7	62.4	2.5	2.7
France	67.9	63.6	59.0	60.8	68.8	63.9	58.6	60.8	1.8	2.2
Germany	66.5	63.1	61.0	64.0	64.2	60.9	60.3	63.6	3.0	3.3
Italy	64.9	61.9	60.4	63.3	61.8	61.9	58.4	61.5	2.9	3.1
Poland	73.6	68.0	61.6	62.8	72.2	65.1	59.2	60.6	1.2	1.4
Spain	69.4	64.8	61.6	62.1	69.0	66.6	61.8	61.3	0.5	-0.5
Sweden	67.9	65.3	63.7	66.4	66.6	64.0	62.4	65.4	2.7	3.0
UK	67.7	66.0	62.5	64.7	65.7	62.6	60.9	63.6	2.2	2.7
Canada	66.0	65.1	62.7	65.5	66.3	63.9	60.8	64.0	2.8	3.2
Australia	67.4	64.1	62.0	65.3	65.2	60.0	59.6	64.3	3.3	4.7
New Zealand	69.6	66.3	64.3	69.8	69.0	63.8	59.9	66.4	5.5	6.5
Brazil	72.1	69.7	66.7	66.6	73.6	73.3	62.8	63.3	-0.1	0.5
Mexico	..	78.6	74.5	71.3	..	78.7	69.6	66.5	-3.2	-3.1
Chile	70.8	69.2	69.9	70.0	65.9	67.0	67.4	66.7	0.1	-0.7
Israel	..	..	66.3	69.4	..	..	64.1	66.0	3.1	1.9
Turkey	68.6	68.3	61.6	66.3	57.4	64.8	57.0	64.9	4.7	7.9
Japan	72.8	71.0	70.1	70.8	68.4	66.6	66.2	69.1	0.7	2.9
South Korea	65.7	68.4	67.0	72.3	63.1	64.4	65.8	72.3	5.3	6.5
China	..	..	66.5		..	..	59.0		..	..
India	..	..	72.0	69.8	..	..	70.6	62.3	-2.2	-8.3

Source: OECD

Australia, and New Zealand and are now converging with the emerging markets from below. Meanwhile, several emerging markets are converging with the developed countries from above. The two exceptions to this general pattern are Japan and South Korea, where the effective retirement age never dipped much but is nonetheless on the rise nowadays.

It seems reasonable to say that if people are already retiring somewhat later, there is an opportunity to seize the moment and come up with new ways to ensure they can work for as long as they wish or they need to. As we saw in chapter 2, and specifically in table 2.1, there is ample wiggle room for people to retire later without completely exhausting their remaining years of health span, roughly ten years for men and twelve for women counting from their midsixties. Thus, people can continue working beyond the usual retirement age *and* still enjoy several years of retirement in good health. Postponing retirement, after all, benefits society and the economy by reducing the potential for intergenerational conflict over who pays for pensions and healthcare. Moreover, we could ride the wave of the increasing effective age of retirement to address loneliness, restructure the labor market, make the economy more dynamic, and create opportunities for intergenerational collaboration.

GUESS WHICH AGE GROUP ACCOUNTS FOR MOST NET JOB GROWTH

"Total U.S. employment grew by 11,767,000, or 8.5%, in the 20 years ending in December 2020," reported the Federal Reserve Bank of St. Louis in 2021. "All that growth—11,879,000, or 101% of the total—was due to increased employment of people age 60 and older. Meanwhile, the net employment change over the past two decades of people ages 16–59 was -112,000." Although there are 2.4 times more Americans ages sixteen to fifty-nine than above sixty, the latter group is growing eight times faster. Moreover, fewer young people are employed, but more people above sixty continue to be employed or retire and find postretirement employment. "The aging of the population and diverging employment rates across age groups together resulted in a sharp skewing of employment growth toward older workers during the last two decades." The St. Louis Fed's report asserts that two trends are certainly continuing: greater numbers of people above age sixty and a larger proportion of them employed.

At the root of this job growth is a new conception of life, work, and age. The first step is to create a new mindset around aging. "The traditional view of life was that we'd peak in the middle of our lives, retire, and go into decline," argues Jo Ann Jenkins, CEO of AARP, the largest retiree advocacy organization in the United States. "People are embracing age as a period of continued growth." The trouble with the existing system of retirement is that it makes people rely on some combination of Social Security, employer pensions, and personal savings or assets as opposed to empowering them to be in control of the last two decades of their lives. "Instead of just seeing dependent retirees, we're beginning to see a new type of experienced, accomplished workforce. Instead of seeing expensive costs, we're witnessing an exploding consumer market that is bolstering our economy. Instead of seeing a growing pool of dependents, we're seeing the growth of multigenerational communities with new and different strengths." Jenkins is precisely proposing to blur the boundaries between education, work, and retirement. "A key part of that retirement model that most of us have grown up with is freedom from work. Today, a key part of extended middle age is the freedom to work."

Finding employment beyond age sixty, however, continues to be challenging for many people. "One factor limiting older workers' job opportunities undoubtedly is employer discrimination," argue Katharine Abraham, of the University of Maryland, and Susan Houseman, of the W. E. Upjohn Institute for Employment Research. "Responding to an AARP survey conducted in 2017, 61 percent of workers age 45 and older said they had experienced or observed age discrimination in the workplace." Experimental studies in which researchers send matched identical résumés, save for the age of the applicant, reveal the extent of the discrimination. In one study, the interview rates were more than 40 percent higher for the thirty-five-to-forty-five age group than for those in the fifty-to-sixty-two age group. This pattern holds for different jobs and occupations, regardless of the skill level or educational requirement.

So, what exactly are the new opportunities that might help us overcome the limitations of the sequential model of life when it comes to what used to be our retirement years?

POSTRETIREMENT WORK

Nearly one in three officially retired Americans work for pay. The proportion is similar in many other countries outside Europe. In an extensive review of research on postretirement workers, Sherry Sullivan and Akram Al Ariss found that financial need is a main motive for finding employment after retiring, but level of education is also correlated with higher rates of postretirement work. Shortages in certain professional occupations make it easier for those workers to find part- or full-time employment. "Retirees with higher levels of education were significantly more likely to engage in paid postretirement employment, or a combination of paid employment and unpaid volunteer work, than those with less education."

Psychology plays a role as well. "Those who perceived work as fulfilling social . . . and personal . . . needs were more likely to engage in paid postretirement employment." Psychological considerations are also behind doing philanthropic work or launching a business. "Those who perceived work as fulfilling generative needs (e.g., work offers chance to pass knowledge to others and contribute to society) were more likely to engage in unpaid caregiving or volunteer activities." Other researchers found that partial retirees focused on independence and personal fulfillment tend to be self-employed, while those who want to contribute to society or to have something physical and mental to do are more likely to be employed.

This psychological evidence strongly suggests that postretirement work is not merely the result of financial miscalculations or poor planning—the realization after retiring that pension and savings may not be enough—but the outcome of a more complex combination of missing work and even planning. According to research based on the U.S. Health and Retirement Study, over 80 percent of those who work during retirement fully expected to do so. "Information known prior to retirement predicts subsequent unretirement nearly as well as ex-ante and ex-post information combined," argues Nicole Maestas, an economist at Harvard Medical School. "For the minority of unretirees who deviated from their pre-retirement expectation of not working, there is little evidence that financial shocks played a significant role." Rather, she argues, people make postretirement work decisions after they leave the labor force. "If anything, the data point to preference shocks—some individuals apparently found retirement less satisfying than anticipated." At the end of the day, the postretirement work decision is driven primarily by "unfulfilled work expectations" instead of by "unfulfilled leisure expectations." In other words, retirees who pursue work are unsatisfied about not the leisurely aspects of retirement but the displeasure from not working.

In any event, Maestas calculated that nearly 40 percent of all retirees, and as many as 53 percent of those who retire early, eventually go back to work. Postretirement work does have different characteristics than preretirement work. People who work after retiring are paid significantly less, and employer-provided healthcare is not as common. Postretirement workers avoid jobs with high physical demands, and they tend to leave manufacturing in favor of service-sector opportunities.

Perhaps the most interesting aspect of the different kinds of transitions that postretirement workers go through involves whether they shift directly from full-time work to retired but working part-time, or from full-time work to fully retired and then back to some level of work. In this second case, the sequential model of life is completely upended, as the worker moves back and forth between stages. Maestas found in her research that people who, in principle, have an easier time finding a job after retirement prefer to partially retire. By contrast, those who encounter more difficulties or need to learn new skills first retire and then start on a postretirement job. In the future, one may expect people who retire to use the extra time on their hands to go back into full-time learning mode, explore new occupations, and pursue one that fits their needs and preferences. In fact, Maestas also found that "those who unretire are more likely to have changed occupations than those who transitioned directly to partial retirement." This means that within the highest age groups, the sequential model of life may be giving way to more complex shifts from work to retirement, from retirement to learning, and from learning back to work.

TECHNOLOGY AND WORK FOR SENIORS

Consider how technology is changing what work tasks we do as human beings. Jane Falkingham, a gerontologist at the University of Southampton, argues that manual hard labor is increasingly being performed by machines or robots. "It's changing the nature of work, which will facilitate people working longer as well."

Advocates of age diversity and inclusion in the workplace believe that technology erases the disadvantages of aging and unleashes the potential of a multigenerational workplace. "Older employees in your team have a lot of value to give. They can look at tasks from a different perspective to your younger team members. They are also excellent mentors to the new generation," argues Lisa Michaels, a freelance writer, editor, and marketing consultant. For her, simple, easy-to-use software solutions based on AI can help people in their sixties and beyond adapt to changes in workplace technology and reduce errors in repetitive tasks, and thus help these workers focus on what they can do best. "Getting intelligent machines to complete repetitive tasks for older employees means that they can spend more time on creative, meaningful tasks." She strikingly proposes to use the Internet of Things (IoT)—all those connected devices and sensors—in a way that "a younger worker could access information directly from an older worker with more experience. In a mentoring situation, IoT can help mentors deliver guidance even when they're not physically present to train younger employees." She envisions situations in which "if something goes wrong for the trainee, the older employee would be able to step in and take control of the situation." She also proposes that data analytics might help track the impact of different work styles and perspectives in a multigenerational workplace.

But the most tantalizing opportunities lie in the new technologies for remote work and learning. To the extent that retirement is all about not having to be on a fixed schedule, including the commute to the job, then remote work may well come to represent the best opportunity for people beyond the age of sixty to work flexibly and joyfully, and for companies and the economy to benefit from their experience. Likewise, remote learning can help with the transition to postretirement work and with switching jobs and careers.

The AARP sees several big opportunities in remote work for older workers. As companies ponder where to strike the balance between remote and office work, the expectation is that blended work "will almost certainly prove to be a huge boon for millions of older employees in the months and years to come." The regimented five-day-per-week, eight-hour-per-day work schedule, with the associated stress and tiredness from commuting, is a leading reason for people to desire early retirement.

Remote work has the ostensible disadvantage of eliminating social interactions at the office, but it removes a major point of dissatisfaction. Even before the pandemic, flexible work options were becoming increasingly popular. In 2019, FlexJobs reported that 75 percent of workers wished to switch to a more flexible arrangement on consideration of work-life balance (75 percent), family (45 percent), time savings (42 percent), and commute stress (41 percent). "The potential savings associated with a surge in telecommuting are staggering," says Catherine Collinson, CEO and president of the Transamerica Center for Retirement Studies. "I'm most excited about the windfall of commute-avoidance time we can reinvest in our health, employability and retirement planning." Phyllis Moen, a sociology professor at the University of Minnesota, has found that when employees have flex-work options available to them, they feel "less stressed, more energized and more satisfied with their jobs." She also found that companies benefit because employees experience less burnout and are less likely to quit or retire.

It turns out that seniors may be the best suited for remote work. According to Chris Farrell, author of *Purpose and a Paycheck: Finding Meaning, Money, and Happiness in the Second Half of Life,* they have already internalized a work ethic after decades of employment and are increasingly adept with digital technologies, especially after the pandemic. "Our [corporate] clients tell us they are more comfortable allowing older workers to work remotely and have a flexible work arrangement because of their work ethic and experience," argues Sharon Emek, founder of Work At Home Vintage Experts (WAHVE).

The UK's Office for National Statistics reported in 2021 that workers performing their jobs remotely were expected to retire later. "More home working options increases the match between older workers' preferences and the available employment opportunities," argues Jonathan Boys, a labor economist at the Chartered Institute of Personnel and Development. "It can extend working lives and is a positive outcome from the big home working experiment." Even before the pandemic, employees above the age of fifty were asking for more flexibility, including remote work from the home.

While remote work has already become a major alternative to the traditional model, gig work, a technology-enabled form of freelancing, is growing quickly. Sharing apps and digital task platforms, in particular, have led to a blurring of the traditional boundary between the active and passive population, ushering in a series of new hybrid categories of part-time and freelance work. Some estimates by Gallup and Statista indicate that one in three American workers are engaged in the gig economy as their primary or secondary occupation and that gig work is expanding three times faster than the U.S. workforce. In the UK, one in seven adults have earned money from doing gig work, although more than half have a traditional job. Other studies estimate that one in ten UK workers completed platform-mediated tasks at least once a week.

The gig economy has the potential of utterly transforming life for seniors, enabling them to socialize and to earn some money on the side without having to compromise on their leisure time. "The freelance payment platform Hyperwallet just found in new research that 12% of 2,000 female gig workers it surveyed were ages 51–70," reports Elaine Pofeldt in a recent *Forbes* piece. According to Michael Ting, Head of Financial Networks at Hyperwallet, companies are reluctant to employ seniors because of the high salaries they would command given their superior experience, but they do not hesitate to retain them as freelancers, for the exact same reason.

The important point here is that seniors may well become the most assiduous gig workers. Wonolo, a platform where companies find short-term workers, reports that baby boomers did the most gigs, earned the most money, and obtained the highest ratings. "I think traditionally, people think of the gig workers as millennials," said Beatrice Pang, vice president of strategy and finance at Wonolo. "We actually always knew that they are much broader. Our workers range from 18 years old to over 80 years old." Baby boomers from the San Francisco Bay Area on Wonolo were making on average $1,003 a month, compared to $949 for Generation Xers, $777 for millennials, and $616 for Generation Zers.

"Boomers also do some of the most physical gigs," notes Pang. "You would think that they're picking the administrative, customer service work that doesn't require the physical work, but they actually do a lot of physical work like fulfillment warehousing and general labor." It's simply a myth that only knowledge workers with high levels of education and relatively high incomes are the ones who can take advantage of the gig economy. But is retirement a level playing field? Or are there deep disparities in retirement experiences and outcomes?

INEQUALITY IN RETIREMENT

The tale of the haves and the have-nots has become a standard narrative of the twenty-first century. Unfortunately, inequality percolates throughout the entire age structure, and it reaches alarming levels during retirement. The sequential model of life seems, in the end, to produce three main types of people: those who can afford to retire comfortably, those who retire but struggle to get by, and those who cannot afford to retire. Income inequality tends to result in much larger disparities in wealth, and thus in very different possibilities when it comes to retirement. Let's not forget that in the U.S., about 80 percent of the net worth is owned by people above the age of sixty. In most other countries in the world, the proportion oscillates between 50 and 60 percent. This staggering concentration of wealth is not evenly distributed, with 20 to 30 percent of seniors accounting for over 90 percent of the accumulated wealth.

Lower-income, less educated people without stable jobs have not paid enough in social security taxes to qualify for a pension that will afford them a good standard of living in retirement. Most of them did not have access to an employer-sponsored pension plan and could not save enough. Single women (especially single mothers) and racial minorities of limited means find themselves in even more precarious conditions because they are less likely to be homeowners and thus deprived from the opportunity to build equity. African Americans and Latinx people have, on average, slightly less than half the retirement wealth of mainstream whites. Once in retirement, members of those two groups are nearly twice as likely to lack sufficient income to cover basic necessities, according to the Elder Index of the University of Massachusetts Boston.

The pandemic has only exacerbated these disparities. "Those with great jobs, expensive homes and lots of savings are going to be better off. Their jobs survived. They no longer have to commute. Their home equity has ballooned. Their mortgage costs have plunged. Their 401(k) plans are up, up, up," writes Brett Arends in the financial website MarketWatch in late 2021. The new era of rising prices and interest rates beginning in 2022 may also end up benefitting homeowners relative to renters because real assets are at least a partial hedge against inflation, and renters may not be able to afford a mortgage and thus have to absorb increasing rent levels. The bifurcating fortunes of people heading toward retirement, and in retirement, have become so stark that it is utterly impossible to talk about the prospects for retirees, or about the retirement experience, without making it clear whether we're talking about the haves or the have-nots. The sequential model of life, built on the premise that eventually everyone gets to retire with a decent pension, has simply failed to deliver on such a universalistic promise. How can a multigenerational society dissolve the problem?

RETIREMENT IN THE
POSTGENERATIONAL SOCIETY

More than a century after the inception of retirement as a stage in life, the tensions, frictions, and cracks in the system are becoming readily apparent. Increases in life expectancy are pushing national social security schemes to the brink of bankruptcy, and research strongly suggests that retirees suffer from loneliness, boredom, and even health risks. Moreover, the inequalities in accessing a good retirement have become too obvious and widespread to brush aside. Retirement needs to be reimagined, not merely fixed.

The long-term approach must incorporate a reorganization of the entire life cycle, not just of the last two or three decades of life. That's why so many countries and politicians have floundered in their attempts to address the underlying issues—they typically look at only the tail end of the problem. Such a reorganization needs to embrace the notion that we can, and should, be engaged in learning, working, and leisure throughout our lives, under a more flexible framework.

If instead of compartmentalizing learning, work, and leisure by age we enable people to choose the mix of activities they desire at each stage of life, we might be able as a society to help people achieve financial security, fulfillment, and equity. Why not offer scholarships or financing for people of all ages who want to learn a new trade or skill? Why not enable men and women to enter and exit the workforce at various points so that they can raise a family, refresh their knowledge, or take time off? Companies need predictability and a commitment on the part of their employees, but perhaps they can create flexibility for themselves and for their employees by using the gig economy more efficiently to meet their staffing needs.

The traditional approach to labor and employee management as practiced by so many human-resource departments at companies, and supported by labor unions and other special interest groups, can continue to coexist with new forms of organizing work that enable people to shift back and forth between learning and work, and at the same time enjoy leisure. The point here is not to impose a new model of life that some will perceive as unpredictable and precarious but to give people an option between the classic way of organizing the employment relationship and a new, innovative, flexible, and technology-enabled format, one in which people of the so-called retirement age can be full participants if they wish.

Skepticism, resistance, even hostility to a more flexible system in which retirement is not necessarily the final destination will be widespread, in spite of the increasing number of seniors who engage in postretirement work and who crave the opportunity to contribute, to engage, to remain active. A true postgenerational society cannot pigeonhole each generation into a functional role, from the playground and the school to the workplace and the couch opposite the TV. Those shackles need to go.

In more ways than one, many of the frictions threatening to undermine intergenerational harmony have to do with retirement, state pensions, and healthcare funded through taxes on younger workers. Another source of discontent refers to what happens in terms of intergenerational wealth transfers when people pass away. As people live and work longer, what might happen to inheritances? Are we shifting to a world in which younger retirees will inherit from older retirees? What are the implications for the overall degree of wealth inequality? Will these changes promote or undercut the postgenerational society? I will consider these questions next.

7

INHERITING AT ONE HUNDRED

Mr Podsnap was well to do, and stood very high in
Mr Podsnap's opinion. Beginning with a good inheritance,
he had married a good inheritance, and had thriven
exceedingly in the Marine Insurance way, and was
quite satisfied.
—Charles Dickens (1812–1870), *Our Mutual Friend*

The legendary philanthropist and socialite Brooke Astor lived to age 105. When she passed away in 2007, a fierce battle ensued over her $100 million fortune. Her only son from her first marriage, Tony Marshall, and his son Philip Cryan Marshall had been feuding over the inheritance, with the grandson accusing his father of taking advantage of the grandmother's frail mental state. In one of the most sensational trials in New York's storied family litigation history, Tony was convicted in 2009 on two charges of grand larceny. The 89-year-old served just eight weeks of the one-to-three year sentence due to poor health. He died the following year.

"Longevity has a way of upending estate planning," writes Amy Feldman in *Barron's*, a magazine about wealth and personal finances. The postgenerational society poses several challenges to inheritance traditions. Historically, most parents would pass away when their children were in their forties or fifties, but nowadays the norm is the sixties or seventies. In just a couple of decades, it will be more like eighties and nineties. "People haven't given thought to it, and it's going to create a lot of issues," notes Adam von Poblitz, the global head of wealth advisory services at Citi Private Bank.

Inheriting in an increasingly postgenerational world will change life for millions of Americans, Europeans, and Asians, where wealth accumulation has proceeded at a fast pace in recent decades. "Why Millennials Should Not Rely on an Inheritance" is the title of a 2020 blog on the website of life insurance giant MassMutual. Not that long ago, experts were predicting a "great wealth transfer" from baby boomers to their children and grandchildren. Some estimates ran as high as trillions of dollars, mainly because of the concentration of wealth at the top of the age distribution. Remember that in the United States, 80 percent of the net worth is owned by people above the age of sixty.

In Europe, the concentration of wealth toward the upper end of the age distribution has led the French government to worry about a "widening generational wealth gap." A study in the UK found that "home ownership at the age of 30 for those born in the 80s is around 40%, whereas for those born in the 70s it was almost 60% at the same age. For those born in the 50s and 60s, at age 30 it was well north of 60%." That's a wide yawn.

Further down the road, increasing longevity could not only postpone inheritances but also make them smaller as people exhaust their retirement nest egg. According to the Federal Reserve, the average inheritance in the U.S. is $707,000, but because the numbers are so skewed toward mega-fortunes, the reality is that most are much smaller. In fact, the median is only $69,000, meaning that half of all inheritances are below that sum. And a majority of Americans do not inherit any significant sum, especially disadvantaged minorities. Compare those amounts to the average annual cost of a private room in a nursing home, which surpassed $100,000 for the first time in 2019. Perhaps the multigenerational housing option we discussed in chapter 3 will become more attractive if millennials want to inherit anything.

"Most of my clients today are saying that their goal is to take care of themselves," says Annalee Leonard, who runs her own investment advisory firm in Pensacola, Florida. "And if that means there is no money left, so be it."

The feeling that rising life expectancy may shrink inheritance amounts must be tempered by the fact that there are fewer heirs due to the decline in fertility. The ultimate balance between these two opposing forces is yet unknown. What are the implications of longevity and an active lifestyle for intergenerational wealth transfers? Will younger generations have to work harder to own a home? Will the growth in wealth inequality slow down as estates become smaller and people inherit at an older age? Or will the reverse be true as wealth accumulation continues to grow and there are fewer heirs given the decline in fertility? And how will women be affected, given that they live five years longer than men, on average?

IT ALL STARTED IN BABYLON

Hunter-gatherer societies were very different from our own. Anthropologists have documented that inheritance of personal belongings such as utensils or weapons was rare, and in many cases those instruments—and even the hut—would be destroyed to keep the spirit of the deceased at bay. Settled societies since the Stone Age turned to the practice of burying belongings along with the corpse, a practice also used on a grander scale in ancient Egypt and Mesoamerica. In other cultures, especially in North America, belongings were shared among relatives or friends.

Forms of inheritance recognizable from today's perspective emerged from the ancient Judaic and Babylonian traditions around five thousand to six thousand years ago. From then on, different cultures adopted systems of inheritance frequently privileging some descendants over others. Thus, we find patrilineal or matrilineal systems, preference for the first (primogeniture) or the last child (ultimogeniture), and partible inheritance practices, whereby each child gets an equal share.

At the time when state educational and pensions systems came into being during the second half of the nineteenth century, the concept of the nuclear family as a legal entity became firmly entrenched in civil law (see chapter 3), and various inheritance rules came into being to reinforce family integrity and financial stability within the framework of the sequential model of life. At a time when most parents had more than two children, inheritance played a role in reproducing patterns of inequality, although inheriting per se did not fully guarantee the same standard of living as that of the parents. Moreover, countries levied taxes on estates and inheritances to raise revenue and moderate wealth disparities.

INHERITANCE EXPECTATIONS AND OUTCOMES

Fast-forward to the present. "Estate planning and inheritance are inherently emotional and often uncomfortable topics of conversation," notes Marcy Keckler, vice president for financial advice strategy at Ameriprise Financial, "but addressing them head on as a family can prevent a lot of uncertainty and tension down the road." Having regular conversations about money seems to lead to better planning and to realistic expectations about inheritances. According to an analysis by investment company Charles Schwab, "On average, young adults expect to retire at 60 years of age, seven years earlier than full Social Security benefit eligibility for their age bracket," and "more than half (53 percent) believe their parents will leave them an inheritance, versus the average 21 percent of people who actually received an inheritance of any kind." The problem with unwarranted financial optimism is that it leads people to save less and carry more debt.

In the UK, for example, adults on average expect to get an inheritance of about 132,000 pounds (approximately $145,000 as of late 2022), when according to government statistics the average amount passed down by parents is 30,000 pounds. People ages eighteen to thirty-four are even more optimistic, assessing their inheritance at 151,000 pounds. Many millennials plan to use their inheritance to purchase a new house, but only 7 percent actually do so. "People are living longer than ever, so relying on an inheritance to get on the housing ladder is a risky strategy as you may get less, and much later than planned," said John Porteous, from Charles Stanley, the advisory company that conducted the survey. "In reality, most people save and invest to get on the housing ladder."

Overly optimistic inheritance expectations seem to be the rule across the developed countries. "Counting on a lottery win is disastrous financial planning, but nearly half of Canadians are banking on another kind of windfall when they look to their financial future," writes Gail Johnson in *The Globe and Mail*. "Forty-four per cent are expecting an inheritance." More than four in five Canadians say they are missing their financial objectives due to the high cost of living, overspending, and a heavy debt burden. "Comments like 'spoiled,' 'entitled,' or 'lazy' are just some of the words I hear people using to describe young adults, often millennial, receiving money from parents," notes Shannon Lee Simmons, a financial planner in Toronto. "Most times, if I meet with a person who is receiving monetary gifts from parents, there is extreme guilt." Canadian financial planners say that parents are the ones doing all the planning, while their children continue to make dubious decisions about personal finances. "The parents typically ask about how to structure the gift, when to give, how much to give, and what to do with the money once it's given," says Carlo Palazzo, another Toronto-based financial planner. "It's mostly the parents coming forward and doing the planning for the kids," and telling them that the inheritance should go toward a down payment on a home.

"Over time and across societies there has been a commonly accepted norm that leaving wealth to children is a good thing to do," writes Mary Tomlinson, a research fellow at the Swinburne Institute for Social Research in Melbourne, Australia. "But only recently has the prospect of inheritance become an actual expectation." Baby boomers own about half of the housing stock in most developed countries like Australia, and as real estate prices ballooned in many markets, so did inheritance expectations, further inflated by housing unaffordability and high debt among younger generations. In neighboring New Zealand, some financial advisors differentiate themselves from the pack by talking plainly about how "life is way too short to delay having fun," "there's a 50% chance your kids will blow it," and "your children won't remember 'the stuff.'" Joseph Darby, CEO of Milestone Direct Limited in Auckland, concludes that "it's best to spend the inheritance before lawyers become the only winners."

In fact, among American baby boomers, "roughly half of all money inherited is saved and the other half spent or lost investing," concludes Jay Zagorsky, a professor at the Ohio State University. These findings compare to 65 percent savings for very wealthy heirs and 15 percent for the average lottery winner. It makes sense that heirs save more than lottery winners given that they can at least do some planning in anticipation of the windfall.

An interesting twist on inheritance expectations is the intergenerational contract historically prevalent in Japan, whereby children are legally entitled to the inheritance, but in exchange for taking care of their parents. Minae Mizumura's popular 2017 novel, *Inheritance from Mother,* puts the issue in the crudest possible way. The fictional Mitsuki Hirayama, a teacher and translator of French, simply asks, "Mother, when are you ever going to die?" She cannot count on her sister or unfaithful husband to take care of her. "Japanese women lived longer every year, lingering like specters," says the author. "Mitsuki pictured women in cities and rural areas across Japan, their faces shadowed with fatigue, longing in secret for their mother's death. Such women wanted freedom not just from their mother, but also from the trauma of seeing the cruelty of old age up close." The book ends on a positive note, as Mitsuki pushes the reset button after her mother's death, using the inheritance to begin a new life.

The traditional Japanese intergenerational contract has shifted since the 1970s for legal, economic, and demographic reasons. Children's legal obligation to attend to the welfare of their parents was abolished in the 1970s (although a strong social norm remains), the long postwar economic boom and high savings rate has led to rapid wealth accumulation, and the number of heirs has declined. "The levels of inheritance appear to be higher among the younger cohorts," writes Misa Izuhara, a professor at the University of Bristol, "reflecting perhaps a general increase in home ownership among their parents' generation and the decrease in fertility rates." As a result of these trends, the Japanese experience the last few years of life is shifting from a long-standing situation in which "the vast majority of the Japanese used to spend their entire life living with extended family members, and approximately one half of older people still live with their adult children today." In the 1990s, wealth accumulation in Japan meant that parents started to have market-based options available to them rather than relying on children for their care, but that too has come to an end with the stagnation of the economy.

In China, by contrast, both wealth accumulation and the decline in fertility have accelerated since the turn of the twenty-first century and will continue to do so for at least another two decades. "I was born in 1980, the year China implemented the one-child policy: I don't have siblings, and neither do my peers," writes Yun Sheng, a contributing editor for the *Shanghai Review of Books*. "We are the chubby (pampered) babies surrounded by parents and grandparents in posters and cartoons." But "little emperors" like Yun were spoiled in the traditional sense, given the attention and pressure to perform well at school. "Growing up wasn't a lot of fun, but we didn't have much to complain about either." Most of his peers were the first to go to university in their families. Members of his generation have good jobs, but find it hard to own a large apartment or house. They have trouble saving for the future. "My generation may not have as much wealth as the previous one but we're materialistic and hedonistic. We splash out on whatever pleases us, possibly as a reaction to the pressure we're under."

Yun's description, however, is only accurate to the extent that people have not yet inherited from their parents. "The one-child policy also created a doubling-up effect of wealth, created during China's economic growth or accumulated by the parents, which is eventually inherited by their only child," writes Christina Zhou, an online producer in ABC's Asia Pacific Newsroom, who was born in China and migrated with her parents to Australia. "This is especially profound in families where the mother and father are themselves only children, and their offspring marries another offspring also from a family where the parents are only children." Thus, she continues, "the next generation ends up inheriting all wealth from both sides of the family."

Given the diversity of historical traditions and the cross-cutting economic and demographic trends, what should people expect to happen in the future when it comes to inheritance? Is the expectation of a windfall justified? Let's do the numbers.

THE INHERITANCE MULTIPLIER

The numbers reveal that inheritances are indeed becoming larger, especially in China. We've already come across the two fundamental reasons for that. The first is wealth accumulation, one of the cardinal trends of our time. The amount of wealth per capita, adjusted for inflation, gives us a sense of whether there's more money to be inherited. The second has to do with the decline in fertility. If each successive generation has fewer babies than the preceding one, then the number of heirs declines and the average inheritance per sibling increases.

Table 7.1 provides the first-ever approximation to the wealth and fertility trends that will multiply the value of inheritances many times over during the next two or three decades. Column A shows the wealth inheritance multiplier, which captures how much average individual wealth has grown between 1995 and 2020. Emerging markets lead the pack thanks to rapid economic growth (China, India, Vietnam), although some developed markets like Sweden have also fared well. By contrast, Southern Europe, Latin America, the U.S., and especially Japan have not seen as much growth in average individual wealth. In column B, we find the fertility inheritance multiplier, which is higher if fertility has already dropped or is expected to do so, which would increase the average share of each heir over successive generations. On this count, we find the biggest declines, and hence the largest multipliers, in South Korea, Thailand, Brazil, Mexico, China, and Turkey. At the other end of the spectrum, in most of Europe and Japan, the multiplier is very low because fertility has been much lower than in emerging markets for quite some time.

Column C shows the result of multiplying the wealth and the fertility figures, which roughly indicate how much more money per heir there will be in the future compared to today. China and South Korea stand out because they have large wealth *and* fertility multipliers, followed by India and

TABLE 7.1: INHERITANCE MULTIPLIERS FOR SELECTED COUNTRIES

Country:	A × Wealth Inheritance Multiplier	B = Fertility Inheritance Multiplier	C × Combined Inheritance Multiplier	D = Life Expectancy Factor	E Adjusted Inheritance Multiplier
China	6.9	3.4	23.5	0.5	11.7
Vietnam	3.2	3.0	9.6	0.7	6.7
South Korea	2.6	5.1	13.3	0.5	6.6
India	3.4	2.9	9.9	0.5	4.9
Thailand	1.9	4.3	8.2	0.6	4.9
Canada	2.4	2.5	6.0	0.8	4.8
Lithuania	3.4	1.5	5.1	0.8	4.1
Sweden	4.2	1.2	5.0	0.8	4.0
Poland	2.4	2.2	5.3	0.8	4.2
Mexico	1.7	3.6	6.1	0.6	3.7
New Zealand	2.1	2.1	4.4	0.8	3.5
Turkey	2.1	3.4	7.1	0.5	3.6
Australia	2.0	1.9	3.8	0.8	3.0
Brazil	1.3	3.8	4.9	0.6	3.0
USA	1.8	1.9	3.4	0.8	2.7
Russia	2.2	1.5	3.3	0.8	2.6
South Africa	1.3	2.8	3.6	0.7	2.5
Spain	1.6	1.8	2.9	0.8	2.3
Egypt	2.0	2.3	4.6	0.5	2.3
France	1.9	1.5	2.9	0.8	2.3
Romania	1.7	1.6	2.7	0.8	2.2
Nigeria	2.2	1.4	3.1	0.6	1.8
UK	1.6	1.4	2.2	0.8	1.8
Germany	1.6	1.4	2.2	0.8	1.8
Argentina	1.5	1.5	2.3	0.8	1.8
Italy	1.2	1.8	2.2	0.8	1.7
Japan	0.9	1.7	1.5	0.7	1.1

Sources: UN Population Division and World Inequality Database.

Fertility inheritance multiplier = Ratio of Total Fertility Rate in 1950–1965 over 2020–2040, using medium variant.

Wealth inheritance multiplier = Ratio of Wealth per person in 2021 over 1995, adjusted for inflation.

Combined inheritance multiplier = Fertility inheritance multiplier multiplied by Wealth inheritance multiplier.

Life expectancy factor = Ratio of Life expectancy (in years) in 1950–1955 over 2035–2040.

Adjusted inheritance multiplier = Combined inheritance multiplier multiplied by the Life expectancy factor.

Vietnam. By contrast, heirs in Japan are definitely out of luck, as the country has about the lowest combined inheritance multiplier in the world because of the decline in wealth since the 1990s, and fertility had already declined by then.

The calculation shown in column C is misleading, however. The third and last aspect we need to take into consideration is life expectancy. If parents live longer, they may use more of their savings in retirement and thus leave behind a smaller inheritance for their children to enjoy. Column D shows changes in life expectancy for people born from the 1950s to the 2030s. The smaller the life expectancy factor, the greater the expected life span will be over time, a sign that individual inheritances may not be as big on average as the wealth and fertility indicators seemed to suggest. Thus, if we multiply column C and column D, we adjust the inheritance multiplier to arrive (finally!) at a number that simultaneously takes into consideration changes in wealth, fertility, and life expectancy. Clearly, being an heir in China, Vietnam, South Korea, India, Thailand, and Canada will be a good thing for some time to come. Heirs in the U.S. and most European countries will see a bit of an improvement, but not something that would be life-changing. Japanese heirs will be the worst off. Americans are essentially inheriting more, later. "Inheritances used to go more toward mid-career, mid-life expenses like kids," says Lincoln Plews, coauthor of a Capital One research paper on the subject. "And now they're likely going more toward concerns of people in their 50s, which is saving for retirement."

The importance that inheritance is acquiring has permeated popular culture in countries like South Korea. *Shining Inheritance, The Heirs, Great Inheritance,* and *A Hundred Years' Inheritance* are among the most popular TV dramas about family trials and tribulations in a country obsessed by intergenerational dynamics. The erstwhile Hermit Kingdom has stunned the world on two counts. It has made the transition from Third World to First in a mere two generations, and it has seen the most precipitous decline in fertility of any society in the world, from a high of 6.3 babies per woman in the late 1950s to just under 0.9 in 2022. Rapid wealth creation and accumulation combined with fewer potential heirs is a recipe for intergenerational wealth transfers on an unprecedented scale, even if parents live longer and need to use more savings to make it through retirement.

INHERITANCE, INEQUALITY, AND TAXATION

"It is our civic duty and responsibility to pay all taxes," read part of a statement by the Samsung family, which controls one of the largest technology companies in the world as well as a host of other subsidiaries active in every branch of the South Korean economy, from automobiles, appliances, and clothing to construction, insurance, and healthcare. They were making the headlines globally in April of 2021 for the estimated $11 billion inheritance tax bill triggered by the passing of Lee Kun-hee, the son of the conglomerate's founder. Mr. Lee's greatest achievement was to catapult Samsung Electronics to become the world's largest maker of smartphones, topping Apple and Huawei. The family had been embroiled in controversy, including tax dodging, dubious corporate maneuvers, and political bribing scandals. The amount of tax due, equivalent to half of the deceased's estate, was so large that it imperiled the family's ability to hold on to its control of the storied corporation and its other affiliates, proposing to pay it in part by donating an art collection worth billions and numerous resources to worthy causes. "Ordinary people like me can't fathom how much it is," said Park Soon-mi, a stay-at-home mother in Seoul. "It's good for the chairman to leave so much money in taxes and make such big donations for the society." The Samsung tax saga is not the only instance of how wealth and privilege in South Korea have captured the world's imagination. The sardonic, gripping film *Parasite* (2019), which won four Oscars, including Best Picture and Best Director, has been referred to as the best film of the twenty-first century (so far). It focuses on the worrying rise of inequality in Korea. Ironically, it made quite a few people rich after grossing $258 million worldwide on a budget of a mere $15.5 million.

Not all countries in the world tax the intergenerational transfer of wealth. South Korea taxes it at 50 percent, and in some cases at an even higher rate. In the U.S., where both the federal government and the states impose a levy on estates, the detractors call it a "death tax." According to a study by the Organisation for Economic Co-operation and Development, the first inheritance tax was adopted in Austria in 1759. France and a few other European countries followed suit in the 1790s, the UK in 1894, the U.S. in 1916, and Japan and South Korea in 1950. Despite how controversial it has become, revenue from inheritance, estate, or gift taxation doesn't represent more than 1.5 percent of total fiscal revenue in any country around the world. At a time when the size of inheritances is growing in so many countries and inequality is rampant, does it make sense to tax inheritances to level the playing field? Are there any unintended consequences?

In Europe and the U.S., after decades of peace, economic growth, and lower taxation, the share that inheritance represents of total wealth has climbed steadily since the 1980s. This trend has been documented in several studies by the French economist Thomas Piketty, author of the bestselling *Capital in the Twenty-First Century* (2013). If inherited capital is contributing a greater share of wealth accumulation as time goes by, and wealth growth outstrips income growth, then we see inequality rising, something that creates economic, social, and political tensions.

As it turns out, however, careful research based on 168,000 estates and bequests in Sweden by Mikael Elinder and Daniel Waldenström found that inheritances reduce wealth inequality. The reason is straightforward. "Even though richer heirs inherit larger amounts, the relative importance of the inheritance is larger for less wealthy heirs, who inherit more relative to their pre-inheritance wealth," they write. "This is in part driven by the fact that heirs do not inherit debts, which makes the distribution of inheritances more equal than the distribution of wealth among the heirs." The truly thought-provoking implication here is that inheritance taxes have the effect of increasing inequality, *unless* the tax revenue is transferred to the more disadvantaged economic segments of society.

But it's hard to see how the large amounts of money to be inherited over the next few years by a relatively small number of people can possibly lead to a better distribution of wealth. "Forbes reports $30 trillion over 'many years,' PNC says $59 trillion by 2061, CNBC mentions $68 trillion over 25 years, and the *New York Times* confirms the variety of these assessments but puts it at around $15 trillion over the next decade," writes Meredith Haggerty, a senior editor at Vox. Some estimates indicate that the top 1 percent will receive one-third of the inherited wealth, and that's after they attended better schools, better colleges, and had access to more lucrative labor market opportunities. Even then, Edward Wolff, a professor at NYU and author of *Inherited Wealth in America,* also argues that inheritances have an equalizing effect, echoing the argument of the Swedish scholars that intergenerational wealth transfers are proportionally more important for middle- and low-income people. America, however, is not Sweden, and only one in five households receive an inheritance. Still, writes Haggerty, "the wealth transfer, in increments of $20,000 or $30,000, has the potential to make a select few stable for the first time, to shore up some people on the shrinking island of the middle class." Capital One's analysis on the subject corroborates this view by estimating that most estates to be bequeathed in the U.S. over the next decades will benefit the middle class and lower-income households.

The "great wealth transfer" to millennials may just enable some of them to overcome the fact that they have fallen behind in average wealth accumulation relative to previous generations. According to the Federal Reserve Bank of St. Louis, "The typical older millennial family was 34% poorer than we would have expected," mainly due to lower homeownership rates. Just under half of American millennials own their dwelling, and thus the other half is not participating in the recent surge in housing prices and the associated wealth accumulation. A similar effect occurs because participation in the stock market is not universal among the younger generations. As a result, highly educated millennials will fare better than working-class millennials, except for those carrying high levels of student debt.

While the debate rages, one thing is clear. Not every millennial can expect a large inheritance—or any inheritance at all. That's why Piketty proposes the government provides for an "inheritance for all" at age twenty-five in the amount of 120,000 euros (about $120,000). "Inequality of property creates huge inequality in life opportunities. Some people have to pay rent their entire life. Some people receive rent their entire life," he argued in an interview. "Some people can create firms or inherit from the family's firm. Some people are never able to create firms because they don't have even a little bit of capital to begin with." Detractors of the death tax make the exact opposite argument, indicating that inheritance taxation undermines family businesses, entrepreneurship, and job creation. And thus the controversy continues.

REMARRYING DISRUPTS INHERITANCES

Longer life spans are also increasing the chances that married people might divorce or become widows. That dynamic in and of itself doesn't necessarily affect inheritances. But if people remarry, then the implications can be extensive—and messy. About 21 percent of marriages in the U.S. are between two people who were previously married before divorcing or being widowed, and another 20 percent involve one newlywed who had been married before. The proportions are higher for people above the age of fifty-five. "Only 29% of previously married adults ages 18 to 24 (admittedly a small group) had remarried in 2013, compared with 67% of those ages 55 to 64," writes Gretchen Livingston in a Pew Research Center study. "But the likelihood of having remarried has dropped sharply for those younger than 35," with only 42 percent of them remarrying in 2013, compared to 72 percent in 1960. "Some suggest that longer lifespans have contributed to increasing divorce at older ages as people realize they have many more years to live and want to find fulfillment in that extra time. The same factor may be contributing to increases in remarriage among older adults."

In addition, it used to be the case that divorced men would seek to remarry at rates double those for divorced women. But now the difference by gender has more than halved, driven primarily by the decisions made by white women. In other words, we're going from a world in which people above the age of sixty used to be widowed at some point to another in which people in that demographic divorce and remarry.

Inheritances will be affected by a combination of three trends: longer life spans, wealth accumulation at advanced ages, and remarrying. "The older you are when you remarry, the more likely it is that you're bringing assets into the marriage—retirement savings, life insurance policies, brokerage accounts, real estate and the like," notes Sarah O'Brien, a personal finance reporter with CNBC. That is if people choose to remarry. "A common reason older partners choose to remain single is that they want to leave their property to their children," says Lina Guillen, an attorney and author (no relationship to the author). "Children may have expectations for a coming inheritance. Things can get sensitive when a new spouse comes along."

Consider the Anastasios, interviewed by Tammy La Gorce for a 2018 *New York Times* story on remarrying at advanced ages. They exchanged vows at age eighty-four (he) and seventy-seven (she). Her youngest daughter wanted to know, "Supposing you die, who's going to get your house?" He did not think that such concerns should deter them from getting married. "We were always treated like a married couple," he recounts. "And we started to think, the only reason we're not married is to satisfy [her] daughter." To avoid problems, many remarried couples sign prenup agreements and wills that ensure their children get the inheritance they were expecting. "We told our kids right off the bat, what we're doing is joyful, and we don't want to be crass about it, but your inheritance is not going to be affected," said another newlywed man interviewed for the same story.

One of the most sensational cases of remarriage inheritance woes ever involved Spain's Duchess of Alba, who remarried in 2011 for the second time at age eighty-five. Cayetana tied the knot with Alfonso Díez, a civil servant and businessman twenty-four years her junior, after denying for years that they would become husband and wife. She held at the time so many titles—seven duchies, one count-duchy, twenty marquessates, twenty-two earldoms, one viscountcy, and one lordship—that she ranked ahead of Queen Elizabeth II in the pecking order of nobility. She was also a distant relative of Winston Churchill's. The newlyweds signed documents to protect her children's inheritance. Nonetheless, at her death in 2014, they waged a rancorous battle over various assets in her estate, resulting in Alfonso's acceptance of a cash payment of a mere one million euros and some objects of sentimental value, thus excluding palaces, jewels, and works of art.

In the postgenerational society, expect messy inheritance situations as life expectancy soars, remarrying at advanced ages becomes more frequent, and wealth accumulation proceeds at a rapid pace, even if the sums involved do not nearly approach those of the Duchess of Alba.

WOMEN, WEALTH, AND INHERITANCE

"Women are getting richer," reads the first sentence of a Barclays wealth report. "Women now control 32% of the world's wealth, according to Boston Consulting Group (BCG)." "Women as the Next Wave of Growth in U.S. Wealth Management" is the title of a recent McKinsey article. "How Women Are Redefining Wealth, Giving and Legacy Planning," RBC Wealth Management explains. These are among the myriad headlines of recent studies on a fundamental process of our time: women are accumulating wealth faster than men. Women's access to education—and hence good jobs—has expanded in many parts of the world. While discrimination in promotions and in pay persists, women's economic status is generally improving. That's not to say that all women are getting rich; certain categories of women experience serious hardships and setbacks in life, including teenage mothers, single mothers, divorced women, and women with less than a high school education.

Another reason why women are accumulating wealth faster than men in so many countries is that they live longer, and hence tend to inherit from their spouses or partners. There are in the world 1.3 women for each man above the age of sixty, 1.6 above the age of sixty, and 2.3 above the age of eighty. The ratios are more skewed in parts of the world with older populations, such as East Asia, Europe, and the Americas (see table 7.1). In countries such as Russia, Lithuania, South Korea, South Africa, Turkey, Argentina, and Japan, there are more than 3 women for each man above the age of eighty. This is due to a combination of reasons, including high rates of male mortality beginning at age forty and, in cases such as South Korea, extraordinarily high life expectancy among women. At the other end of the spectrum, in India and Nigeria, the ratio is just 1.3 for ages eighty and above. In many rich countries—Canada, Sweden, the United States, the UK, Australia, and New Zealand—the ratio is relatively low at age sixty and above, but it grows quickly to over 2 women for each man at age eighty and above. France, Italy, Germany, and Spain have slightly more imbalanced ratios. All in all, the gender imbalance at advanced ages simply makes it easier for women to account for a greater share of wealth—at least for the remainder of their lives—if they can inherit from their other half.

Women's rights to property and inheritance have fluctuated across time and space. Up until very recently—in some countries just forty years ago—women were not allowed to handle money independently of their husbands, brothers, or parents. In some parts of the world, women still don't enjoy the same economic and contractual rights as men. But this wasn't the case in all cultures and civilizations. Perhaps we should learn from ancient Egypt. "From our earliest preserved records in the Old Kingdom on, the formal legal status of Egyptian women (whether unmarried, married, divorced or widowed) was nearly identical with that of Egyptian men," writes Janet H. Johnson, a professor at the University of Chicago. "Women were able to acquire, to own, and to dispose of property (both real and personal) in their own name. They could enter into contracts in their own name." While Jewish law during the biblical era privileged sons over daughters, in the absence of the former, women enjoyed full inheritance rights. Women's property and inheritance rights were more limited in ancient Hinduism and classical Greece, but the Romans enabled freeborn women's economic rights. Contrary to the stereotype, Islamic law enshrined the right of women to property and to inheritance, although privileging sons over daughters.

The Middle Ages began with women being able to own and inherit (as under Anglo-Saxon and Norse laws and traditions), but ended by depriving women of the most basic economic rights, unless they were widows. With only a few, isolated exceptions in Europe and North America, women had to wait until the French Revolution and its aftermath to enjoy equal inheritance rights, although the joy was cut short by the restoration of the monarchy. In 1850, Iceland claimed the title of being the first country to legally enshrine equal inheritance rights during the contemporary period. It took the U.S. and the UK until 1922 to make that move. Equal pay for equal work was still four decades away, and actual nondiscrimination is still a work in progress. According to the World Bank, as of 2021, women did not enjoy equal property and inheritance rights to men in 41 countries, located mostly in Africa, the Middle East, and Asia. In the 149 countries that guarantee such equal rights, the key question becomes how fast women are accumulating wealth and how much they are likely to bequeath.

According to the Survey of Consumer Finances, American women own a third of total family financial assets. By 2030, women may own a larger amount than men. When it comes to managing their money, women are more likely to seek professional advice, be concerned about outliving their assets, focus on real-life goals like health and well-being, and avoid risks in investments when compared to men. But while women seek more advice than men on financial matters in general, surveys in the UK indicate that they do not plan for the inheritance they will leave behind, which results in higher rates of taxation for similar amounts of assets. "Out of those who are liable to pay inheritance tax, women's net estates are worth 1.3 billion pounds more than men's," notes Dawn Mealing, head of advice policy and development at Fidelity International. "Yet, almost half have done no financial planning to make sure this wealth is gifted the way they want." This seems especially worrisome since women face ever bigger decisions regarding inheritances because more of them "are responsible for both theirs and their partner's wishes."

In the context of the postgenerational society, it is important to consider how women's wealth accumulation may change inheritance practices. Women care more about providing for others, especially in terms of education, well-being, and healthcare. They also are more inclined to obtain comprehensive insurance. Given these preferences, will women who live to advanced ages skip the generation of their children in their wills given that they are already settled in life and bequeath their assets to their grandchildren, who might be more in need of them?

"When it comes to passing money through generations of the family, it's long been the case that when older generations die, their children receive whatever is left behind," observes Tanita Jamil, a consultant at St. James's Place Wealth Management. "But, with older generations increasingly expected to live into their 80s and even 90s, recent years have produced a shift—and one that poses a real challenge for women in the so-called 'sandwich generation.'" These are mothers who are raising their children and at the same time caring for aging parents. In the UK, more than six in ten sandwich-generation members are women. According to the Office for National Statistics, the average age group inheriting is fifty-five-to-sixty-four-year-olds. When the inheritance arrives just as people are preparing for retirement, the question becomes who is in more need of it, the children or the grandchildren? Between 2015 and 2019, about 19 billion pounds were inherited by British grandchildren, compared to 23 billion by the children. In addition, more than half of people inheriting at age fifty and above chose to pass the money on to their children and grandchildren. This trend will likely accelerate as women account for a larger share of wealth, especially above the age of sixty.

But do better economic and wealth prospects for women mean they're better off? Not necessarily. In fact, women at all ages take on levels of responsibility for the care of others that are not commensurate with the way in which they are rewarded. They tend to allocate more of their time, income, and wealth toward the education and health of family members. They continue to be discriminated against on the job. In other words, it is somewhat misleading to associate wealth accumulation with equity and well-being. After all, the cards continue to be stacked against women in many walks of life. Can a fundamental restructuring of the sequential model of life lead to better outcomes for women? That's the subject of the chapter that follows.

8

A GAME CHANGER FOR WOMEN

Freeing yourself was one thing, claiming ownership
of that freed self was another.
—Toni Morrison (1931–2019)

"I put off trying to have a baby until I felt my career was in just the right place for me to take a step back for a year," writes Canadian journalist Carley Fortune, the executive editor of Refinery29, a website for women, who had previously worked for some of her country's largest dailies. "My work was everything to me—my main source of pride and my creative outlet—it gave [me] my identity as well as some of my most valued relationships. I didn't want to let go of that to have a kid, and I didn't want to be passed over for bigger and better (and better-paying) opportunities when I was on leave." She used to change jobs frequently, which made matters worse because everything else in her life had to be put on hold so that she could impress her new boss. "I never felt like I could step away. Until, eventually, I did."

Why do we put women on a spot like that? Why do we ask them to choose between having a baby and having a career? Is there a better way to organize life and careers? Can women find a way of being treated fairly when it comes to their experience in the labor market? Can a postgenerational approach help?

The backdrop to the stress and inequity experienced by so many women in the labor market and the corporate ladder is the pressure that society places on them to make up their minds about work and family. Back in 1978, *Washington Post* columnist Richard Cohen wrote a famous opinion piece in which he coined the term *biological clock,* as it applies to the trials and tribulations of career women of reproductive age. "Composite woman (actually, several women at different times) is coming to lunch. There she is entering the restaurant. She's the pretty one. Dark hair. Medium height. Nicely dressed. Now she is taking off her coat. Nice figure." After such a misogynistic prelude, the piece turned to the heart of the issue. "It is wonderful being her age, which is something between 27 and 35," he continues, "and the fact of the matter, in case you should wonder, is that there is a new man in her life." He asks what's wrong after she looks down. "Off the record?" She hesitates for a moment and then lets it come out. "I want to have a baby." Regardless of marital status, "what there is always, though, is a feeling that the clock is ticking. A decision will have to be made. A decision that will stick forever." The stakes involved for the two human beings having this conversation are so dramatically different. There are so many things the man does not need to worry about, ever. "Like the ticking of the biological clock."

Trouble is that the imagery of the clock can be used to reinforce sexist conceptions, writes Moira Weigel, who teaches communication at Northeastern University. Back in the late 1970s, in the wake of the second feminist movement, the pill, and the legalization of abortion, "the spate of stories about the biological clock . . . focused on individuals," not on organizations, she writes. "The media glamourised professional women who decided to have children while pursuing demanding careers, and warned women who put off having children that they would regret their diffidence later." She added that the possibility of women not wishing to be mothers was something only rarely considered.

It's clear that the growing phenomenon of women pursuing a professional career clashed head-on with the sequential model of life. The deterministic concept of the biological clock implied a double standard whereby the responsibility for raising a family was laid on the woman almost entirely, effectively reinforcing notions of patriarchy, and instilling in her a sense of guilt if she didn't make time for having children and even if she postponed having them. And there was no mention at the time of the male clock, based on the myth that men remain capable of having children forever, although they are at fault in half the cases of couples who seek fertility treatments. "The role of the biological clock has been to make it seem only natural—indeed inevitable—that the burdens of reproducing the world fall almost entirely on women," Weigel concludes. "There are moral as well as practical implications to this idea: if you do not plan your life just right, you deserve to end up desperate and alone."

As much as the rhetoric of the biological clock can have the effect of not letting women make the decisions they want to make and become who they want to be, the clock itself does overlap almost perfectly with the period in life prescribed by the sequential model during which people are supposed to excel at studying and at working if they want to get ahead professionally. The chain of play-study-work-retire, with precise and inflexible timing built into it, was designed for men more than a hundred years ago. At that time, only (a few) men could hope to study beyond basic schooling, have a job with benefits outside of the household, and receive a pension in retirement (women would get one as widows, not as workers). The model worked for many decades, but only because most women were denied educational opportunities and discouraged from working outside of the household. It was only after an increasing number of women could learn a profession and have a career that we could get a glimpse of the extent to which the sequential model was out of whack with women's aspirations and realities.

If during the 1960s women fought a crucial battle over individual rights in their long struggle for equity and parity, the abolition of the sequential model of life could represent another game changer, if only we could do just that. Historically, the sequential model has benefited men because they do not need to interrupt their careers to start a family. Many women, by contrast, wrestle with the extent to which the sequence of play-study-work-retire is at odds with their yearnings and preferences given that most promotions at companies or within the government bureaucracy take place when employees are in their thirties and forties, precisely when many professional women wish to have and raise children. What's worse, in an unequal world in which mothers take on a disproportionate share of household tasks, even when employed, men can focus on their careers while women struggle to get ahead—or, worse, see no other option but to take time off to attend to their children. No surprise that when schools remained closed during the coronavirus pandemic, a whopping 2.5 million American women quit their jobs to focus on household tasks and help their children with online learning.

"The traditional working pattern of education, full-time career and retirement is based on the typical working lives of men," wrote Sharon Mavin of Newcastle University Business School in 2001. "There is no single typical working pattern for modern women," she further notes. "It is clear that, while male career models remain and women are the ones to step off the fast track to meet family responsibilities, they will continue to be at a competitive disadvantage in career advancement." It's as simple—and damning—as that.

According to careful longitudinal research by demographers Patrick Ishizuka and Kelly Musick, American "women in pre-birth occupations with higher shares working 40 or more hours per week and higher wage premiums to longer work hours are significantly less likely to be employed post-birth." Among the most inflexible occupations, we find middle- and high-level managerial positions in business or in professional service firms (consulting, auditing, etc.), in which "being there" and maintaining personal relationships are key to good performance, promotion, and pay. Although some other occupations provide working mothers with a measure of flexibility, the general pattern is that the traditional (male) model of career advancement assumes an uninterrupted trajectory, with promotions happening at predictable points in time. Corporate restructurings, technological change, and remote work may in the future create a variety of alternative career pathways, but we shall see below that it's unclear if women will benefit from those opportunities as much as men. In the meantime, women continue to get the short end of the stick in terms of having to make compromises on their family life, suffering from high levels of stress, going through career interruptions, and forgoing opportunities for promotion and career advancement. The system simply works better for men than for women. Much better indeed.

POSTPONING THE FIRST CHILD

Perhaps the most ostensible consequences of the difficulties that women need to navigate when pursuing their career and family dreams are demographic in nature. Women's greater access to educational and job opportunities now than in the past has resulted in the postponement of having children and in a decrease in the number of children. The two are closely interrelated. In most developed countries, the mean age of the mother at her first childbirth increased by between three and five years since 1970. The first child is now born when the mother is in her early thirties in South Korea, Italy, Spain, Japan, and the Netherlands. In the rest of Europe, it's above twenty-nine years. In the U.S., it's twenty-seven (see table 8.1).

Those averages, however, conceal a great divide by education and place of residence. For highly educated American women living in urban areas, and especially along the two coasts, the mean age is in the midthirties, but for those with less than a high school education living in rural areas, the mean age can be as low as twenty. Those are two different worlds in one. According to Heather Rackin, a sociologist at Louisiana State

TABLE 8.1: MEAN AGE OF MOTHER AT FIRST CHILDBIRTH

Country:	1990	2000	2010	2020
South Korea	..	27.7	30.1	32.3
Italy	26.9	..	..	31.4
Spain	26.8	29.1	29.8	31.2
Japan	27.0	28.0	29.9	30.7
Netherlands	..	28.6	29.2	30.2
Germany	..	..	28.9	29.9
Denmark	26.4	27.8	..	29.8
Sweden	26.3	27.9	28.9	29.7
UK	25.5	26.5	27.7	29.1
France	..	27.8	..	28.9
Poland	..	24.5	26.5	27.9
Israel	..	25.7	27.2	27.7
USA	24.2	24.9	25.4	27.1
Romania	..	23.6	25.5	27.1
Canada	25.9	27.1	28.4	..

Source: OECD Family Database.

University, "Lower-socioeconomic-status people might not have as many opportunity costs—and motherhood has these benefits of emotional fulfillment, status in their community and a path to becoming an adult."

There are many factors behind the increase in the age at first childbirth among women with more than a high school education. Existing research has identified "the rise of effective contraception, increases in women's education and labor market participation, value changes, gender equity, partnership changes, housing conditions, economic uncertainty and the absence of supportive family policies." But the key point is that these factors reinforce each other. Cultural changes have led to women's access to education and jobs, which in turn increases contraceptive acceptance and use and leads to further lifestyle changes and nontraditional living arrangements. Uncertainty and rising living costs only add to the trend. We'll analyze what policies might improve the situation later in this chapter. But first, let's examine how this whirlwind of change affects women who work and have a family.

STRESS À LA CARTE

"Women with children will know all too well the tension between being a hands-on mum and managing a busy job," says Dr. Judith Mohring of Priory Wellbeing Centre in London. "But it's not just mothers who feel they fail to live up to an imaginary feminine ideal. Women have so many arenas in which they can compete: how we look, the quality of our friendships, and, of course, the work we produce." That's the recipe for the primordial soup in which stress and burnout grow. "Sometimes it can feel that there are just too many ways to fail. And that's when self-doubt, low self-esteem and self-criticism can come to the fore."

One way of visualizing the problem is to frame it in terms of time pressure. Women with a day job are also on the "evening shift" at home, where they average twice as much time dealing with household tasks as men. But the situation at work itself is oftentimes more stressful for women than for men. A comprehensive Canadian study concluded that women experience more stress at work because they have less decision latitude, are often overqualified for the job, and are less likely to get a promotion. These three aspects reinforce each other to produce stress.

During the pandemic, navigating work and family was no picnic for women. If there ever was a double-edged sword for women, that's remote work. Increased childcare and schooling at home created what Marianne Cooper, a sociologist at Stanford University, called a perfect storm. A McKinsey / Lean In survey found that one in four women was considering slowing down their careers or dropping out of the labor force. Pressure on working mothers just doubled. "I also worry that my performance is being judged because I'm caring for my children," said one woman interviewed for the study. "If I step away from my virtual desk and I miss a call, are they going to wonder where I am? I feel that I need to always be on and ready to respond instantly to whatever comes in. And if that's not happening, then that's going to reflect poorly on my performance." Studies have found that, during the pandemic, women enjoyed much less uninterrupted work time at home than men. To make matters worse, a Qualtrics/theBoardlist survey conducted in July 2020 identified that, during this period of widespread remote work, men were being promoted at a rate three times greater than women.

The real issue, of course, is not the pandemic but the unequal division of labor in the household. "Rather than telling women they need to get back into the office, we need to be asking why this unpaid work isn't shared more evenly between women and men," says Dr. Mary-Ann Stephenson, director of the Women's Budget Group in the UK. Pandemic or not, women and men experience the effects of parenthood on their jobs in sharply divergent ways. The quantification of that difference is actually shocking.

THE MOTHERHOOD PENALTY AND THE
FATHERHOOD BONUS

"I had a pending promotion that was actively stalled once I announced I was pregnant," remembers Allison (a pseudonym) in an interview with *New York* magazine. "They ended up giving me the additional work and respon-sibilities, but held off on the title change and raise." The problems started even before giving birth. "From pregnancy on, I wasn't brought to as many outside meetings, to any situation where I'd be representing the organization. I think the male senior staff members just weren't comfortable with a pregnant woman being the face of the organization." Predictably, mothers go out of their way to show that they are hard workers. "I also found that management really watched mothers carefully for being absent or late, so I was always careful to arrive early and stay late." Given this evidence, there's only one possible conclusion. "We have a real problem in the way that we treat and value motherhood."

The Modern Family Index, published annually by Bright Horizons, shows that two-thirds of Americans believe mothers are more likely to be passed up for a new job than fathers and that career opportunities frequently go to less qualified employees instead of working mothers. Stunningly—or perhaps not—working mothers get a 4 percent pay *cut* for each child, whereas fathers enjoy an average 6 percent *increase,* much of which has to do with different promotion rates over time, according to a study by sociologist Michelle Budig. "Employers read fathers as more stable and committed to their work; they have a family to provide for, so they're less likely to be flaky," she observes. "That is the opposite of how parenthood by women is interpreted by employers." The way in which we have used age to organize and time careers and promotions reflects a patriarchal bias, which is deeply embedded in the sequential model of life and the concept of the nuclear family.

After taking age, experience, and education into consideration, "most of the remaining gender inequality in earnings is due to children," concluded a team of three Princeton economists who used a comprehensive data set on salaries and careers in Denmark. "The arrival of children creates a gender gap in earnings of around 20% in the long run, driven in roughly equal proportions by labor force participation, hours of work, and wage rates." The truth of the matter is that most women change their pattern of work after giving birth, but men rarely do, and if they do, they make only minor adjustments.

Some parts of Europe present a stark contrast to the U.S. The motherhood penalty turns into a premium as state pension systems compensate for career interruptions. But that's only the case in Eastern Europe and in Scandinavia. In the rest of Europe, the penalty persists. "The motherhood penalty in retirement income is significantly lower if universal pension benefits, which guarantee an income independent of the individual's working history, exist in a country," concludes Katja Möhring, a researcher at the University of Mannheim in Germany. Still, the gender pension gap is as large as 30–50 percent of men's level in half of European countries, including the five largest economies (Germany, France, the UK, Italy, and Spain), and between 10 and 30 percent in most of the other half.

More broadly, the gender gap in monthly earnings after accounting for hours worked and worker characteristics is widest in Brazil, Indonesia, Mexico, Portugal, and South Korea. The same five countries are also the worst in terms of hourly earnings. In all twenty-eight Organisation for Economic Co-operation and Development (OECD) countries in the study, the gender differences in pay that remain "unexplained" (mostly attributable to discrimination) are larger than those that can be explained by reference to hours worked and worker characteristics. The gender gap increases with age and after women have children. Research has found, however, that women with children narrow down most of the gap relative to childless women by the time they turn fifty years of age. "Motherhood is 'costly' to women's careers," concluded Joan Kahn and her colleagues. "Children reduce women's labor force participation, but this effect is strongest when women are younger, and is eliminated by the 40s and 50s. Mothers also seem able to regain ground in terms of occupational status," and the wage penalty persists only for women with three or more children. Thus, working mothers recover relative to women without children, but they do not close the gap with men. Many go back to work because they need the money while others do so because of the guilt of not providing their daughters with a role model. "I fully intend to go back to work," said a stay-at-home mother interviewed for *The Atlantic*. "I feel I'm letting my girls down by not working." That's yet another pressure that working mothers endure.

THE CONTROVERSY OVER THE MOMMY TRACK

"In Big Law, there are two tracks for women: You either don't have a family, or do have a family and have au pairs and help out the wazoo, work insane hours, and never see your family. Or you get mommy-tracked, which means you have less desirable projects and go part-time," notes Sally (a pseud-onym). "Going part-time means you have a significant pay cut for a very marginal decrease in the number of hours you're expected to work. It's not at all in proportion to the reduction to actual effort." Another issue is what happens once you get off the mommy track. "After I came back from mater-nity leave, everyone was ostensibly supportive, but I did really struggle to get my workload back," remembers Sally.

The mommy track has been controversial since it was first proposed as such in 1989 by Felice Schwartz, president of the nonprofit organization Catalyst. "The cost of employing women in management is greater than the cost of employing men," read the first line of her widely discussed *Harvard Business Review* article. "This is a jarring statement, partly because it is true, but mostly because it is something people are reluctant to talk about." As evidence of this "fact," she pointed to women who take maternity leave never to return to the job or who decide to take a break from their career for other reasons. She urged corporations to abandon their male-centered career con-ceptions to ensure that talented women's human capital wouldn't go to waste and to recognize that there were two kinds of women, "career-primary" women and "career-and-family" women. For the former, her recommen-dation was to "clear artificial barriers from their path to the top," while for the latter—in her view the majority—she suggested "rates of advancement and pay [that] will be appropriately lower" in exchange for "flexibility." She advised companies to "conduct a cost-benefit analysis of the return on your investment in high-performing women . . . If women's value to your com-pany is greater than the cost to recruit, train, and develop them—and of course I believe it will be—then you will want to do everything you can to retain them." Thus what came to be called the *mommy track* was born. A bitter controversy ensued.

The supporters of Schwartz's basic insight applauded its realism and prac-ticality, while her detractors expressed outrage at the proposal to relegate women to slower career paths with lower pay. "It's tragic because it reinforces the idea, which is so strong in our country, that you can either have a family or a career, but not both, if you're a woman," protested Patricia Schroeder, a

Democratic congressperson from Colorado. "Of course the business people love it, because it's what they don't feel free to say, and here's a woman saying it for them." Schwartz dug in, countering that "the fact is that at this point in time women do take a larger part of the responsibility for child-rearing." Fran Rodgers, president of Work/Family Directions, found it "disturbing" to see how Schwartz tried to fit "women into the existing culture, instead of finding ways to change that culture. And this idea of dividing women into two groups, but completely ignoring the diversity among men, is just horrifying." Richard Heckert, chairman of both DuPont and Schwartz's Catalyst, observed that she "seems to say that family is still a women's problem and the way to fix it is to find women not having children."

Three decades later, some companies have returned to the idea with apparently good results. In 2015, Vodafone announced that it would offer sixteen weeks of paid maternity leave and an optional thirty-hour week at full pay for six months. Meanwhile, IBM offered employees a reduced work-week at a prorated salary level for up to five years. Economists point out that the problem with offering flexible work arrangements, even when offered to both men and women, sends a signal to the employer that the employee is not willing to sacrifice everything on the altar of job performance and career advancement. The problem lies in that this "signaling game" can become an explicit criterion for not granting promotions and pay increases or, even worse, an implicit, unconscious bias. Most importantly, there is no evidence that women who take maternity leave are less committed to work or less willing to prioritize work. Requiring all mothers *and* fathers to take leave would in principle eliminate the value of the signal, although the contrast between parents and childless employees would still be salient. While most countries in the world have a national paid maternity leave policy (one exception is the U.S.), it also applies to fathers in less than half. In practice, far more mothers take leave than fathers, and that's why economists propose to give very strong monetary incentives for both parents to take advantage of a paid leave.

The fundamental problem with the mommy track, maternal leave, paternal leave, and other forms of flexibility, while effective at reducing the mother's age at first birth and facilitating her return to the labor force, is that they are aimed at solving the problem, not dissolving it. In the knowledge economy, educational requirements have increased. Many men and women don't finish their education until their late twenties, and it takes several years thereafter to establish oneself professionally, get promoted, and find one's footing on the corporate ladder. It's the sequential model of life that creates a problem because both men and women would prefer to start a family early on, but postpone it to pursue their career dreams. And yet, as complicated as navigating the timing of the sequence of stages has become under normal circumstances, the problem pales by comparison with the predicament of women who have a baby in their teens or who singlehandedly raise their children.

THE UNNECESSARY PLIGHT OF TEENAGE
AND SINGLE MOTHERS

"I was the talk of the whole school. It was the most *embarrassing time* of my whole life," remembers Stassi. "I was, I had a lot of pointing, whispers when I walked down the hallway, you know: 'that's the girl that's pregnant with twins, that's the girl with twins,' and I heard someone say, 'oh, her life is over.'" She persevered, finished high school, was accepted into a major research university to pursue a degree in social work, but she gave birth in August, just before the semester started, and went instead to a community college. She dropped out before graduating, and went on welfare. She used the money to pay for childcare and attend a trade school, where she found other teenage mothers among the students and the instructors.

That's what I would call a *derailment,* a horror story about how the sequential model of life offers few alternatives, if any. If there's a group of women for whom the play-study-work-retire sequence does not work, it's teenage mothers. Given the structure of the educational system and the labor market, having a baby in adolescence can have devastating consequences. Although live births to teenage mothers in the United States are down by more than half since the early 1990s, about 160,000 women ages fifteen to nineteen deliver a baby each year, the highest number among comparably rich countries. Nearly 3 percent of African American, American Indian, Native Hawaiian, and Latinx women give birth in their teens. Among non-Hispanic white women, the rate is 1 percent. The problem lies not in having a baby, which can be a fulfilling experience, but rather in that only half of teenage mothers graduate from high school, compared to 90 percent for the rest of women. To make matters worse, their children "are more likely to have lower school achievement and to drop out of high school, have more health problems, be incarcerated at some time during adolescence, give birth as a teenager, and face unemployment as a young adult," according to the Centers for Disease Control and Prevention.

There are teenage mothers who manage to get ahead. Erica Alfaro became pregnant at age fifteen. Her boyfriend dumped her. She worked the tomato fields along with her mother. She dropped out of high school and enrolled in a homeschool program. It took longer than usual, but hard work eventually enabled her to consider a college education. She was twenty-seven at her graduation ceremony from California State University San Marcos, with a degree in psychology. She displayed a sign that read, "We did it Luisito! 2%" in reference to her son and to the fact that only 2 percent of teenage mothers graduate from college by the time they turn thirty, which means that virtually all of them forgo the average 85 percent wage premium that college graduates enjoy in the American labor market over high school graduates.

How can a rich and technologically advanced society tolerate such a low college graduation rate among teenage moms? If we want teenage mothers to succeed in the knowledge economy, we need a more flexible model of life that enables them to finish high school and pursue some postsecondary education (if they wish to do so) later in life along with generations of younger people who did not reel from having their educational plans disrupted, postponed, or derailed. They just need a different timing and rhythm to seize the opportunities that life offers. And that's exactly what the sequential model of life all too frequently denies them. It's simply another example of inequality of opportunity.

While the proportion of teenage mothers has dropped by more than

60 percent in the U.S., it continues to be very high in the developing world. "Globally, an estimated 15% of young women give birth before age 18," notes a study by UNICEF, the United Nations' children's agency, which "can derail girls' otherwise healthy development into adulthood and have negative impacts on their education, livelihoods and health." The trouble is that the proportion can be as high as 30 or 40 percent among teenage women living in rural areas. What's different about teenage motherhood in the developing world is that "many girls who are pregnant are pressured or forced to drop out of school, which can impact their educational and employment prospects and opportunities." Other, more severe consequences include "reduced status in the home and community, stigmatization, rejection and violence by family members, peers and partners, and early and forced marriage." In addition, major health sequels include "obstetric fistula, eclampsia, puerperal endometritis and systemic infections." As in the developed world, teenage pregnancy rates have fallen, albeit much more slowly.

Poverty is often the trigger to a teenage pregnancy. "Sometimes you may need some money, but when your parents cannot raise it and a boy comes providing for everything," says one adolescent Ugandan mother. "When he wants you to pay back, what can you use to pay back his money if not sex since you are not working?" A seventeen-year-old in Ghana recalls that "I was in school and I had to pay my exam fees. . . . I needed money. Then this boy expressed interest in me. He helped me on more than two occasions, which landed me with a pregnancy." Teachers and school administrators throughout sub-Saharan Africa say that keeping girls in school at little or no cost to them and teaching them useful skills like jewelry making or bookkeeping would help them become more independent in addition to offering sound and clear advice on sexual relationships.

While developing countries lead the world in teenage motherhood, the U.S. takes the top of the podium when it comes to children living with a single parent, usually their mother. Nearly a third of the eight million American households headed by a single mother live in poverty, are jobless the entire year, and face food insecurity. Around half of American single mothers never married, nearly a third are divorced, and 20 percent are either separated or widowed. The wage gap with comparable men is much greater for single mothers, especially if they are Black or Latinx. The median income for families headed by a single mother was $48,000 in 2019, compared to $102,000 (more than twice as much) for married couples. That's mainly because single mothers have little left for educational expenses after allocating over half of their income on housing and a third on childcare. They're also less likely to be homeowners. Single mothers, in other words, are worse off because they did not follow the traditional linear path from getting educated to being promoted at work and accumulating enough home equity and savings for retirement. They simply missed several trains, leaving them with few or no opportunities to catch up.

LIBERATING WOMEN FROM THE TYRANNY
OF THE SEQUENTIAL MODEL

The way we have organized parenthood and careers has generated a litany of seemingly intractable problems. The tyranny of the biological clock, whether abused to perpetuate the patriarchy or not, does in practice shape the decisions made by many women. Meanwhile, postponing having babies until certain professional goals are achieved has contributed to a precipitous decline in fertility and a pensions crisis, something that we shouldn't blame on women but rather on the age-regimented nature of the education system, the labor market, and the corporate promotion ladder. When mothers don't work outside of the household, they feel guilty for not providing their children with the "right" role model. And if they continue, or return, to work, they suffer from stress and also from the guilt of not dedicating enough time to take care of their children. Women continue to suffer from a motherhood penalty in addition to other forms of discrimination at work and from the indignities and trauma (or worse) associated with sexual harassment. Mommy-track patches to the problem, unless carefully implemented, can lead to decelerated careers and subpar pay. While education allows women to pursue a professional career, its absence can seriously limit the job opportunities available to teenage mothers. And the list excludes domestic violence, which is more likely to persist over time and have more serious consequences if women feel trapped in a relationship or lack alternatives.

The sequential model seems to leave behind—or push aside—many mothers who would like to enjoy their job life to the same extent as other women and men do. Dropping out of high school due to a teen pregnancy, being a single mother after a divorce or separation, or simply not following the usual steps in sequence lands them in a disadvantaged position relative to other women and to many men. The sequence of play-study-work-retire leaves very little wiggle room for women to pursue motherhood and a career simultaneously. If they have children too early, they get penalized or fall seriously behind in terms of education and career opportunities. Any mishap along the way—an untimely pregnancy, a separation, a divorce, a child with serious health or learning problems, a pandemic that keeps children at home—can create enormous difficulties, setting the mothers back in the labor market, slowing their rate of promotion, or forcing them to exit the labor force altogether.

Having (fewer) children at a later age does bring some benefits, such as greater financial and emotional stability. The decline in fertility that postponement generates has prompted governments to implement a patchwork of policies to reverse the trend. A common policy intervention is to offer parents direct cash payments in the form of a baby bonus or family allowances. In a systematic review of research on the effectiveness of these policies, scholars find mixed evidence and are reluctant to establish a positive effect on the number of children that parents have. The same goes for indirect transfers, such as child credits, healthcare access, housing policies, and the like. Given that allowing parental leaves and providing on-site childcare or subsidies are effective at facilitating the mother's return to the labor force and reducing the age at first childbirth, a potential path is to take further steps toward making work arrangements more flexible.

It would be a stretch for me to argue that abandoning the sequential model of life would solve all the issues affecting women's experience as workers and mothers, either in the case of highly educated professional women who become mothers in their thirties and those who do so in their teens.

But we should by now be keenly aware that solving the problems is no match for dissolving them, especially when for many women it means choosing between interrupting their careers and postponing or forgoing educational opportunities.

In a postgenerational society, we should be able to let people of different ages pursue their education and their careers together. If women had more options as to when to study, work, seek a promotion, and have the children they desire to have, they'd be in a much better position to navigate the constraints imposed on them by biology, modern life, and men's dismal record at contributing to household tasks. We would also be able to offer a new array of opportunities to teenage and single mothers. But that assumes the availability of the resources necessary to design their own, personalized sequence of stages in life, moving back and forth between study and work multiple times.

The fact that on average women live longer than men (about five years in the U.S. and globally, with the difference being as low as three and as high as seven, depending on the country) multiplies the advantages that women could obtain from the abandonment of the age-based, staged model. Women stand to gain more than men if society were to embrace a multigenerational workplace in which promotions are as likely to happen at age fifty or fifty-five as at age thirty or forty. A longer life span provides for more opportunities to pursue different jobs and careers. In addition, women remain in good physical and mental shape far longer than men. If women could be promoted at similar rates to men—not just in their thirties and forties but also well into their fifties and even sixties—much of the motherhood penalty might vanish.

Women, however, can't unilaterally change how jobs, careers, and promotions play out without their employers' collaboration or government regulations and labor laws that are conducive to multiple professional pathways. For progress toward gender parity to happen, for women to be able to break out of the straitjacket of the sequential model of life, a third wave of the movement for women's rights might be needed, one that fundamentally changes the educational system and the allocation of labor to various jobs and positions.

One may get a glimpse of the best way to dissolve the problem by look-ing at the efforts by many women to make and remake their careers after they become mothers. Sociologists Andrew Hostetler, Stephen Sweet, and Phyl-lis Moen found that women with the heaviest work and family demands are more likely to go back to school, perhaps because of the combination of the need to earn money and greater resilience. Research in countries as diverse as the U.S., the UK, Jamaica, and South Africa shows that many teenage mothers are eager to continue in school or to return to it after having their babies, but financial constraints and lack of institutional and family support tend to frustrate their attempts. "I decided to come back to school because I realized without education you are nothing," notes Sue, a South African teenage mother. "I want to have a better future [for] myself and my child." The desire to do well in life is there, but the culture of orderly and sequential achievement in life stands in the way.

"A lot of times I wish I could be a normal teenager—still attending school," says a fifteen-year-old mother who lives in Texas. "But for me, there's a lot to look forward to. It's not all about having a normal teenagehood, it's about having a different one." If society and the culture continue to define as "normal" all of those things that everyone should do at a certain age (as in the expression *age-appropriate*), it will be hard for many women to overcome even small deviations from the linear path from play and study to work and retirement. The postgenerational society must be built on multiple path-ways, on different ways of being a teenager, an adult, a student, a worker, a retiree.

Women successfully fought for equal political rights at the turn of the twentieth century and for equal civil and economic rights during the 1960s. But neither achievement eliminated the tyranny that the sequential model of life represents for women. The ideal future world is one in which both men and women can take as many breaks from work to raise kids or study as needed without losing ground professionally. It's a tall order, but that's the direction in which employment practices may shift due to not only eq-uity considerations but also rising life expectancy, technological change, and talent scarcity. Triggered initially by the pandemic-driven withdrawal of men and, especially, women from the labor force, the dearth of workers may help reduce the underrepresentation of minority groups and women as employers seek to fill job vacancies. The good news is that a postgenerational approach to careers would be beneficial to companies as well, especially in terms of talent attraction and retention in the labor market, and also in their quest to gain share in consumer markets, as we shall see next.

9

THE POSTGENERATIONAL CONSUMER MARKET

Marketing is a battle of perceptions, not products.
—Al Ries (1926–2022)

"My three children who are all born after 2001 are all classified in the 'Generation Z' age group," writes Australian marketer Jane Hillsdon. "Aged 9, 12 and 14, they all use social media. And while there is only a couple of years between them all, they all use social media very differently." Jane's observation may strike many people as being every other parent's favorite topic of conversation—talking about the differences among their children. But her comment highlights that, from early on in life, we take divergent paths. "It's incredibly important that as marketers, we have a deep understanding and empathy of the nuances present within each generation," she argues. "If you assume that two people will respond to the same content or can be reached on the same channel just because they fall into a certain generation, your marketing will miss the mark." It seems as if at some point marketers stopped being curious about their subjects, preferring instead to focus on attributes like age or gender, which often lead to stereotyping and bias. "Do not infer generic information about a particular generation upon them," she warns. "Find out what their values are, exactly which media channels they use and why they use them. What's important to them, who influences them, what frustrations do they have?"

When we envisioned the postgenerational workplace of the future in chapter 5, we concluded that generational thinking can lead us seriously astray. Assuming that people are better at this or that because they belong to a certain age group is no substitute for understanding the potential in each human being. The danger of stereotyping people by reference to their age is at least as grave when it comes to the consumer market, especially at a time when conceptions of "young" and "old" are increasingly rejected as biased, discriminatory, or fallacious. After all, successfully selling stuff to consumers requires making some assumptions about their needs, wants, and lifestyles.

Ever since marketing became an academic discipline about a century ago, marketers have debated the best way to target their efforts by using a technique known as *segmentation*. The easiest way to segment the market is by geography, which at the time essentially involved the distinction between rural and urban markets. Demographic characteristics also became essential to segmentation from the very beginning, especially age, gender, education, family size, income, and so on. A seemingly more sophisticated approach involved focusing on personality traits and lifestyle, which became very popular in the corporate world after the massive use of psychological testing during World War II. Soon thereafter, marketers started to focus on behavioral aspects such as purchasing, use, and brand loyalty. And then came the digital marketing revolution driven by social media and artificial intelligence, which enabled marketers to algorithmically target their messages, though still subject to stereotypes and biases.

One perilous, and frequently misguided, approach to marketing has survived throughout these different phases. It's the idea that generations matter, that being born during a particular period (oftentimes a decade or two) exerts a lasting imprinting effect on people's lives and lifestyles. At first sight, it seems logical. It's not the same to be a teenager in a suburb of New York in the 1950s and in the 2020s. But does that mean there's something we can call the baby-boom generation and Gen Z? Can we assume that all boomers shared similar experiences and thus behave in basically the same way relative to people from other generations? Do people evolve or even change drastically over the life cycle regardless of the context in which they were born?

But as important as the debate over the usefulness of the concept of generation might be, there's another side to the controversy that is becoming even more relevant in the wake of the emergence of the postgenerational marketplace. For the past few decades, marketers have tended to assume that their attention should be placed on "young" consumers in their twenties and thirties, for several very good reasons. First and foremost, it was the largest segment of the market from a purely numerical point of view given higher fertility and lower average life expectancy than nowadays. Second, in a context of rising educational levels, expansion of the middle class, and rising incomes, younger consumers as a group also had high, if not the highest, total purchasing power. And third, young people tended to be the most sophisticated, discerning, and demanding consumers, always chasing the latest fad and the most exhilarating experience. Young consumers thus became the yardstick to measure the future potential of new products and services, especially after the internet, smartphones, and social media took the world by storm. Marketers nearly unanimously bought into the idea that it was essential for brands to capture the imagination of the young, since they were not just the trailblazers but also the consumers with the highest "lifetime value," given that they had decades of spending ahead of them.

This worldview is coming crashing down due to demographic and technological change. The center of gravity of consumption is steadily shifting toward the group of people above the age of sixty due to their larger numbers, savings, and purchasing power compared to other generations. In addition, their lifestyle is no longer that of an "old" person because they can enjoy being in good physical and mental shape for a longer time (see chapter 2). In the past, marketers used to obsess about each new generation of consumers for about a decade or so—and then shift their attention to the next generation. "For many years, knowing how to market to Millennials was the hot ticket for most marketers," writes Sonya Matejko in *Forbes*. "Today, advertisers are wrapping their heads around how to reach their younger counterparts, Gen Z." The assumption has been that today's teenagers are tomorrow's trendsetters. How does a truly postgenerational market change this dynamic? Are we about to witness a revolution in marketing?

The key point to grasp is that people are increasingly defying generational labels. Monoparental and multigenerational households are becoming more frequent, and the nuclear family is no longer the norm. Fathers are taking parental leave. Year after year, more people are going back to school to update, refresh, or switch careers. The pandemic has invited everyone to embrace technology regardless of age or education. Online courses are increasingly popular and accessible. Retirees are returning to work . . . "This variation inside generations creates a challenge for marketers," Matejko warns. "How do you market to changing peer groups?" The fallout from this apparent inability of marketers to change with the times includes accusations of stereotyping, bias, and ageism. Something is indeed rotten in the kingdom of marketing.

GENERATIONAL STEREOTYPES, BIAS, AND FUZZINESS

Where did the avocado-on-toast millennial stereotype come from? Many members of that generation ask themselves why it is that they have been labeled as lovers of the fruit of the *Persea americana*. The cliché is so pervasive and loosely used that virtually nobody who invokes it has a clue as to its origin. To make a long story short, it's all because of a throwaway line in a 2017 interview on Australian TV that went viral in the most millennial of all ways. The interviewee, self-made billionaire Tim Gurner, mentioned that "when I was trying to buy my first home, I wasn't trying to buy smashed avocado for $19 and four coffees at $4 each." Ever since, the expression has been used to accuse millennials of being lazy, egocentric, entitled, and spendthrift.

We humans can't resist categorization, and with it comes stereotyping at best and bias at worst. During a talk at a millennial marketing conference in 2016, comedian Adam Conover argued that "generations don't exist. We made them up. The entire idea is unscientific, condescending and stupid . . . Let's drop the pandering and generalisms and treat them like people." He noted that experts, pundits, journalists, and marketers recycle the same clichés time and again, simply applying them to the youngest generation around in an endless pattern of repetition.

Thus, a 1968 *Life* cover lambasted baby boomers for their living in affluence. Eight years later, *New York* magazine published a blistering piece by no less than Tom Wolfe about the new era that grown-up baby boomers had ushered in. "We are now—in the Me Decade—seeing the upward roll (and not yet the crest, by any means) of the third great religious wave in American history, one that historians will very likely term the Third Great Awakening," he wrote. "Like the others it has begun in a flood of ecstasy, achieved through LSD and other psychedelics, orgy, dancing (the New Sufi and the Hare Krishna), meditation, and psychic frenzy (the marathon encounter)." For Wolfe, it all goes to hell with "'Let's talk about Me' . . . with the most delicious look inward; with considerable narcissism, in short," which logically leads to the thought of "I only have one life to live" empowered by the "unprecedented post–World War II American development: the luxury, enjoyed by so many millions of middling folk, of dwelling upon the self." Wolfe famously ended the essay with "the beat that goes . . . Me . . . Me . . . Me . . . Me . . ."

Similarly, a 1985 *Newsweek* cover story referred to Generation X as "entitled," not willing "to work for a living," and "laid back, late blooming or just lost?" And in 2013, *Time* infamously argued that "in the U.S., millennials are the children of baby boomers, who are also known as the Me Generation, who then produced the Me Me Me Generation," purely a group of lazy, entitled, materialistic narcissists who still live with their parents, prefer to take selfies, have thousands of followers but only a few friends—and love avocado on toast.

It's the exact same accusation of selfishness and entitlement over and over, levied against each and every post–World War II generation!

This is unfortunately a well-known pattern. Psychologists Stéphane Francioli and Michael North have produced systematic evidence of disparagement of younger generations by previous ones for lacking in values, motivation, and thrift. Whether by age or generation, misunderstanding and discrimination continues to be rampant. It's stereotypical, unfair, unsubstantiated, and unhelpful. And it represents a stark reminder that generations cannot be taken too seriously as constructs—especially when it comes to marketing. It's simply bad business.

For starters, comparing the attitudes and behaviors of different generations is tricky. The Pew Research Center, one of the finest survey research institutions in the world, recognizes that researchers often confound age, period, and cohort effects. Age is merely the position of each individual in the life cycle. *Period effects* involve events that change all generations equally, while *cohort effects* are events or trends that affect one generation differently from another. Some researchers have noted "the impossibility of separating age, period, and cohort effects." As if the problem weren't intractable already, there's several other complications messing up the analysis of generations that render the task practically unworkable. Among the most relevant factors are the increasing ethnic diversity of the younger generations in Europe and North America, the postponement of marriage, and the rise in life expectancy. Given that marriage changes people's consumption profile, the trend has direct implications for marketing. More broadly, marriage postponement and greater life expectancy essentially rescales the age dimension altogether, with life-changing events taking place at chronological points in people's lives different from in the past.

The other obvious issue with generational analysis is where to draw the line between generations. The American baby boomers may be those born between 1946 and 1964, but in other countries, the peak in fertility took place in the late 1960s or in the 1970s. And why is it that the millennial generation is normally defined as those born between 1981 and 1997? Using data on American high school seniors each year between 1976 and 2014, sociologists Stacy Campbell, Jean Twenge, and W. Keith Campbell documented that generational differences in work values and workplace preferences change gradually with age, not abruptly between generations. Thus, there are no obvious year-of-birth cutoff points one may use to demarcate generations. For example, "early GenX'ers are higher in social values than later GenX'ers, and late GenX'ers and early Millennials look fairly similar." In other words, little or nothing changes suddenly at the boundary between two generations. There are no structural breaks separating them. "Generations might be best conceptualized as fuzzy social constructs," the researchers concluded. Fuzzy in the sense that they're overgeneralized, inaccurate, deceptive categories. Use them for marketing—or any other purpose—at your own risk.

Given the problems and complexities associated with the concept and measurement of generations, why do so many companies and organizations continue to use it? Cort Rudolph, Rachel Rauvola, and Hannes Zacher argue that "generationally based practice is built upon the rather shaky foundations of this science, putting organizations and their constituents at risk—not only of wasted money, resources, and time, but of propagating misplaced ideas based on a weak, arguably non-existent evidence base." The concept, they note, has become useful as a tool for sensemaking, imperfect as it may be. Along with everyone else, marketers were stunned at some of the early differences that millennials displayed in their preferences and behaviors regarding not only consumption but also work and leisure. There was at the time no better way of explaining them than by creating a new generational category. Thus, generations exist as "social constructions," as concoctions we come up with when we feel at a loss to explain something new. As such, constructions have real effects because when people "define a situation as real, it is real in its consequences," as the famous sociologist Robert K. Merton once put it. Psychologists concur with sociologists in that "an efficient, albeit often flawed, strategy to facilitate sensemaking is the construction and adoption of stereotypes . . . understood in terms of . . . overgeneralization of others." In sum, using a generational category is fraught with perils, can lead to bias, and is intrinsically misleading and flawed.

FROM AGEISM TO THE AGELESS CONSUMER

"I walked into the Everlane concept store in preparation for an upcoming meeting at their corporate office," remembers Tamar Miller, the founder and CEO of Bells & Becks, a women's luxury footwear brand. "As I looked around trying to find an outfit, a feeling of alienation came over me. From the perky twenty-something sales associate that looked at me askance when I walked in, to the array of androgynous, box-looking, nondescript apparel, it was clear that I didn't belong." Everlane was founded in 2010 in San Francisco as a primarily online clothing retailer, and thus is not a traditional, outdated brand but rather an industry disruptor. Consumer brands—whether established or new—seem to be allergic to age. "Unless brands are specifically made for the older age group," argues Carolyn Odgers, business director at Carat Ireland, a media and marketing agency, "they don't want to be associated with older people, because it might mean that younger people—who have a perceived longer lifetime value, but are not nearly as brand loyal—are put off by the product because someone with gray hair buys it."

Ageism is a rampant problem in marketing. Stereotyping and outright discrimination based on age isn't an innocent by-product but a core element of segmentation. "Ageism in the world of PR, advertising and marketing not only produces slanted messaging, but it's also bad for business," says Patti Temple Rocks, formerly of ICF Next, a marketing agency in Fairfax, Virginia. "We're fixated with youth in business. We often conflate 'young' with higher levels of creativity and technological aptitude, while 'older' equals technologically inept, out of touch and, as many ads imply, 'basically dead.'" The diagnosis is widely shared among industry experts. "What we have traditionally done is attach fresh, vibrant, new and change with youth," says Vicki Maguire, chief creative officer at Havas, the French advertising and public relations firm. "Quite frankly, that's bollocks, but we are a very short-sighted and navel-gazing industry, and that is to our detriment," an assessment that's only a mild exaggeration.

Part of the problem lies in that in the U.S. more than half of those employed in advertising, public relations, and marketing are under forty years of age, and 80 percent are younger than fifty-five. The rush by agencies and companies to hire young talent versed in digital social media has only made matters worse. Rocks recalls a client meeting to plan the launch of a menopausal drug. "I looked around and thought, 'unless everyone is having deep conversations with their mom, no one here has a clue what this is like.'" People above the age of fifty-five reportedly account for more than half of new car sales. "Close your eyes and picture the last car commercial you saw," she says. "Was the customer 55 or older?"

Few brands have yet realized that the category of "ageless consumers"—defined as those who no longer act their age in the sense that they no longer conform to the stereotypes of "old" and "young"—is growing by leaps and bounds. Companies peddling personal care and prestige beauty products have been among the first to realize its potential. L'Oréal, the French beauty group, "wants to show the world that age is not an issue and women are beautiful at every stage of their lives," writes Georganna Simpson in *Campaign,* an advertising magazine. "It wants to challenge stereotypes and positively shape our perception of age, fostering a community where everyone embraces growing older." In 2019, L'Oréal partnered with the British edition of *Vogue* to launch their "Non-Issue" campaign, featuring Jane Fonda, Helen Mirren, Isabelle Adjani, and Val Garland, among other ageless celebrities. Women "feel left behind by the beauty and fashion industries because of their age," Edward Enninful, editor of British *Vogue,* wrote. "Now is our moment to challenge the industry, together." The campaign spread like wildfire throughout social media. "It was a privilege to work with [these] iconic brands," says Ginevra Capece Galeota, global accounts executive at Facebook. "We were able to fuse traditional media with our innovative technology to show through quality content that age is a non-issue." As it should be.

An early pioneer in the ageless trend, the Estée Lauder Companies advertised in 2021 the position of executive director for ageless innovation to "enable the brands and R&D to create greater value with the Ageless Consumer based upon demographic/cultural intelligence, identified technology, subcategory, product and execution opportunities." Their goal is to spread throughout the entire organization and its various brands the idea that age is no longer a defining factor in marketing.

But companies in industries other than prestige beauty are lagging seriously behind. For decades, most of the fashion industry has deliberately ignored women beyond their thirties. "The majority of women over 40 that we heard from don't feel included or represented by the fashion marketing they see on social media," argues Miller. According to marketing research, fashion brands have traditionally considered that having "old" people wandering inside their stores would tarnish their brand image among "young" consumers. It's just such an awful thought.

Modern product design and marketing emerged at a time when each successive generation of people was larger than the preceding one. The baby boom of the 1950s transformed American society and American business. The middle class became the backbone of the economy. Everything seemed to revolve around "young" and "middle-aged" consumers from the baby-boom generation, simply because they constituted the largest segment of the market in terms of spending power. According to the Boston Consulting Group, by 2030, about 40 percent of the total consumer spending growth will be by people above the age of sixty. The proportion is even higher in Japan (60 percent) and Germany (70 percent), due to their more skewed age distribution. Given that people above that age remain in good physical and mental shape longer (see chapter 2), the ageless consumer is just one of many transformations in the world of marketing and brands.

The concentration of wealth at the top of the age distribution we saw in chapter 7 will make the ageless consumer the most attractive segment of the market moving forward. Thus Everlane and other clothing retailers will not only have to welcome and attract customers across generations but recognize that they need older people to buy their products and services. The demographic trend couldn't be clearer: beginning with Japan and China, and with Europe and the United States following shortly in their wake, the largest segment of the consumer market by 2030 will be people in their sixth decade and older. By 2030, China will have 105 million more people above 60 than in 2022, for a total of 370 million, India 45 million, and the

United States 13 million. Even poor countries like Bangladesh and Indonesia will see increases of 50 percent or more of people in that demographic. The challenge for companies and brands will be to cater to the needs and preferences of not just two or three but seven or eight different generations. Still, many marketers have a distorted picture of spending by age group. Jeff Weiss, founder of Age of Majority, did a survey of marketing consultants. "We found that marketers, on average, thought that millennials comprise 39% of all consumer spending, when it's actually only 18%." The misconceptions and plain mistakes are so pervasive that it seems as if most marketers have lost their footing by squelching in the mud of stereotyping and bias.

"Life stage and age have been decoupling over the past generation, with milestones like education, marriage, kids, career, and retirement becoming unmoored from traditional age constraints," writes Jeff Beer in *Fast Company*. Still, marketing consultants and account managers are told by their bosses to acquire new customers, and those tend to be young in age irrespective of their life situation. According to Dipanjan Chatterjee, a Forrester analyst, there's a "mindset among many brands where marketers are rewarded for acquisition after which the customer gets passed on to some other part of the organization." Thus, incentives within companies need to be aligned with the idea of the ageless consumer. According to research by the AARP, many advertising agencies have no experience whatsoever with older consumers.

Academia fares no better than agencies and the brands they promote when it comes to ageism. In a review of 128 peer-reviewed studies of the behavior of "old" consumers published between 1980 and 2014, Robert Zniva and Wolfgang Weitzl found that the research "is still dominated by investigations using chronological age," with scant consideration given to how people age and whether their lifestyle changes at some point. In fact, they found only one study that did not use chronological age as the main explanatory variable, and only a third used an alternative measure to age to ascertain if the results might be affected by the choice of indicator. Most importantly, they found that most research fails to use longitudinal data collected over time as people age, mainly because it would make the research "expensive and time-consuming."

INTERGENERATIONAL INFLUENCE

"I was the iPhone of my time," declares Lydia Riera (played by *West Side Story* legend Rita Moreno), advising granddaughter Elena to "use your phone and chapsmat somebody" to find a suitable escort for her *quinceañera* party. In episode after episode of this Netflix hit, *One Day at a Time,* the grandmother proves to be an influencer shaping everybody else's decisions in this multi-generational household, especially when it comes to personal relationships and spending money. Other sitcoms show that the most influential person in a multigenerational setting may be a middle-aged mom, as in Netflix's *Family Reunion,* or dad, as in ABC's *Black-ish.*

One of the most significant trends for the future relates to intergenerational influencing. "From Facebook to YouTube and TikTok, we've seen an increase in boomers and Gen X influencers on social media platforms lately," argues Nicla Bartoli, cofounder of the Influencer Marketing Factory. They're called the *granfluencers.* During the 2021 holiday shopping season, well-known companies such as Amazon, Nike, and Lululemon, along with up-and-coming fashion designers like Altuzarra, Fenty, Jacquemus, and Rachel Comey, used senior influencers to advance their brands. "Like typical influencers, granfluencers cover a wide range of topics, often dominate a specific niche, participate in paid campaigns, and share their lives openly on the internet to thousands, even millions of followers," writes a blogger in the Social Standard, an online trade publication. They encourage their followers to celebrate age diversity and to avoid prejudging and rushing to unwarranted conclusions. "Brands who have jumped in and started to use granfluencers in their marketing strategies are adding elements of wisdom, reality, and life experience to their brand image." And most importantly, they engage younger people very effectively, in a prime example of multigenerational appeal.

"Stealing Your Man Since 1928" is Helen Ruth Elam's most memorable, and circulated, saying (she was born that year). Better known as Baddiewinkle, she became an Instagram sensation at age eighty-five, after music star Rihanna started following her. She's reached 2.5 million followers. Agencies have used her image to launch their websites, and she has promoted numerous shows, Netflix series, and products. There are many rankings of the top ten granfluencers in the world. Some examples include Hamako Mori (age ninety), a Japanese woman who's been playing video games since her fifties, is known as "Gamer Grandma." Her YouTube channel has nearly half a million subscribers. "It looked like so much fun, and I thought, it's not fair if only children played it." Guinness recognized her as the world's "oldest gaming YouTuber." South Korea's Park Mak-rye (age seventy-three), a longtime small restaurant owner, became a YouTube and Instagram sensation at age sixty-nine, and boasts nearly 2 million social media followers. She focuses on food, cosmetics, and travel posts. The late Narayana Reddy was dubbed "Grandpa Kitchen." He posted his first cooking video on YouTube at age seventy-one and had 6.1 million subscribers when he passed away two years later. Today, the channel has over 9 million. The videos would show him cooking large amounts of inexpensive food for his local community in southern India. Doña Angela is a Mexican cook who shows how to prepare traditional recipes to an audience of 3.4 million YouTube subscribers and 5 million Facebook followers.

Consider the 'grandmillennial' home décor trend that has cropped up in recent years, which encompasses millennial-age consumers who, according to House Beautiful, "have an affinity for design trends considered by mainstream culture to be 'stuffy' or 'outdated,' like wallpaper, ruffles and wicker," writes Kait Shea in *Event Marketer,* an online magazine. The fact is that granfluencers are becoming tastemakers and trendsetters for younger generations. The phenomenon is especially strong in China. At age ninety, Jiang Minci has millions of mostly millennial followers. She simply shared several video episodes of her life, including her arranged marriage, flight, and work as a railway engineer. Simply put, granfluencers have become lifestyle icons.

TikTok, a platform meant for teenagers and young adults, has started to encourage the interaction among grandparents and grandchildren to promote intergenerational understanding. For example, Joe Allington, known as @grandadjoe1933, an eighty-seven-year-old who has two million followers, began posting after he became popular in his granddaughter's videos. "I was completely shocked at the number of people from every corner of the world who watch me on TikTok," he commented. "But I don't do it for the fame. I do it for the tremendous fun with my granddaughter." Jenny Krupa, eighty-eight, and her grandson Skylar Krupa, twenty, make TikTok videos together at a farm in Alberta, Canada. "I'm 88 and probably have more followers than you," she boasts. (She has more than a million, placing her in the top 1 percent.)

Besides granfluencers and their huge future potential, marketers are scrambling to understand who is the main influencer—the person making or influencing purchase decisions—at a time when so many generations interact with one another. The answer appears not to be straightforward, as the roles of grandparents and grandchildren, for example, vary dramatically depending on social class, race, ethnicity, and religious background.

"Because of ease of access to information, a 50-year-old Gen X parent is just as likely to influence their 20-year-old Gen Z child as the child is to influence the parent," says Vic Drabicky, founder and CEO of January Digital, a consultancy. "Therefore, brands must consider how their marketing strategies play into this dynamic." The problem he poses is not trivial, and it requires a sophisticated marketing approach. "For effective generational marketing— and to build an engine in which consumers of all ages feel ingrained—brands need to find the similarities that tie generations together." Watching sitcoms might actually offer clues. "Most often, those include a common sense of humor or a shared emotional mindset," he argues. Karla Martin, managing director at Deloitte, agrees. "While all trends aren't for everyone, you see more younger women borrowing pieces from their mother's closet, and then mothers are looking to younger generations to pick a trendy piece that updates her look." It's not just intergenerational influence but also use.

Some brands have taken note of these trends and are now developing ways to increase these types of multigenerational posts. "We want grandparents to enjoy TikTok with their grandchildren," says an executive at the company. Grandparents and grandchildren are making videos together in an increasing number of accounts on the platform, a trend that started during the lockdown phase of the pandemic. Such multigenerational digital experiences help reduce loneliness and bonding, and create memories "you will have for generations to come," according to Rebekah Miller, who makes videos with her grandfather and has nearly half a million followers. "I was shocked honestly, I never thought this would happen." One of them had over one million views. "Whoa, that's a lot of people," her grandpa said.

In addition, the growth in "multigenerational households will throw brand purchase decisions off balance," argues Scott McKenzie, global head of Nielsen's intelligence unit, part of the global market research firm, since sixty million Americans now live under the same roof with people of three or more generations. "Now more than ever, children are exposed to the purchasing habits of older caretakers, which could have long-term effects on their own mindsets as consumers," argues Sharon Vinderine, the founder of Parent Tested Parent Approved in Canada. "Consequently, brand loyalty, price sensitivity and the perception of value may shift as children watch and mimic the habits of this new group of direct influencers." Increasingly, the consumer behavior of children and young adults is being driven by both their parents and their grandparents, who now live longer. And this is actually happening whether they all live in the same dwelling or not.

Another recent multigenerational dynamic refers to the kind of "collaborative consumption" involved in platforms such as Uber and Airbnb. At a time when most assets (homes, cars) are owned by people above the age of forty-five but most users of such ride-hailing and accommodation-sharing services are below that age, two-sided platforms create unique opportunities for multigenerational interaction. And the list goes on.

PERENNIALS AND POSTGENERATIONAL MARKETING

"More and more marketers are starting to talk about 'perennials,' consumers whose behavior is dictated less by their age than by their beliefs," argues Deloitte's Martin. (Remember that the term was coined by serial entrepreneur Gina Pell, as we saw in chapter 5.) The important point here is that postgenerational dynamics are themselves setting new trends. "These perennial consumers are trying new things and, as a result, they tend to be less concerned with what they are 'supposed' to wear. Instead, it is all about finding a look that feels authentic for them." In the postgenerational era, perennials will replace the fuzzy, stereotyped concept of generation. "Tory Burch . . . didn't start her company and say, 'I am building a brand for women from 18 to 70, now let's go design for it,'" says Drabicky. "Instead, they focused on impeccable, timeless design, quality product, listening to customers and being true to who they were versus trying to adapt to be for everyone." The New York–based retailer has more than three hundred stores worldwide and e-commerce websites in seven languages. The founder recommends looking for an "emotional connection to brand regardless of age, and a heightened willingness to take risks and test new products, media platforms, designs and so forth." Martin concurs in that "there is no one-size-fits-all for postgenerational success," as is generally the case in business.

Brands are starting to get the idea of postgenerational marketing. In 2015, Céline turned Joan Didion into its poster girl. In 2016, Nike launched a new installment of its "Unlimited Youth" campaign featuring the "Iron Nun," played by eighty-six-year-old Ironman triathlete Sister Madonna Buder. "There are a lot of times when I had to think about failures and not reaching the goals I may have set for myself," she says in the video. "Then I realized the only failure is not to try because your effort in itself is a success." *Advertising Week* selected it as its Ad of the Day.

According to industry experts, Nike seemed to accomplish the impossible by combining humor with an uplifting message on a sensitive issue. Both ads clearly struck a nerve, "driving heavy doses of words reflecting admiration . . . as well as words that indicate humor . . . tugging at the heartstrings . . . and keeping attention." Ace Metrix reported that the ad resonated well with a wide range of viewers, scoring very high on likability and attention. "Love the nun and the message that you're never too old," said one millennial viewer. "I loved the repartee between the nun and the announcer. It made the ad feel more real and life like rather than an actual advertisement," noted another. "I love the way this is shot and the main character shown. I can completely relate to this," commented a third millennial. "I am invested in being very active and trying to be that active when I am in my old age. Nikes are the most comfortable shoe I've had for running." The ad also captured the imagination of slightly younger viewers. "This is a fantastic ad! I love the Sister and her determination . . . much more energy than I have . . . lol!" Gen Zers also succumbed to the campaign's charms. "It is inspiring and entertaining to watch and learn about the Iron Nun."

A year later, in 2017, Mercedes-Benz unveiled its "Grow Up" campaign with themes such as getting a job and being a good parent. The goal was to appeal to millennials without eroding the brand's position with the preceding generations. It emphasized design and technology but without compromising on quality, reliability, and safety. "Our brief was to create a content-driven campaign for the compact cars of Mercedes-Benz. Instead of marketing these five cars with separate campaigns, we decided to bring them together under a new brand platform for the first time," says Veit Moeller, creative director at Antoni, the German ad agency. "It was also the first time that we felt we could target a younger demographic, being that the compact cars in many ways are the gateway to the brand." Their approach was to define "a universal insight that felt true not only to the brand's heritage, but also to the next generation of Mercedes-Benz drivers." In a way, they found a formula for expanding their potential customer base.

Also in 2017, CoverGirl introduced its "I Am What I Make Up," starring Issa Rae (then age thirty-two) and Maye Musk (sixty-nine), among other personalities, for the launch of a series of new product lines, including a foundation that came in forty different shades and was thus suitable for different skin tones. "It was exciting to work on this CoverGirl campaign, as it's a reflection of today's cultural climate—one that's positive, inclusive and empowers women to express their own ideas about beauty," said Sam Caine, from MPC's New York studio. The campaign was meant to "celebrate and liberate the diversity of beauty," noted Laurent Kleitman, president of Coty Consumer Beauty. "Beauty should make people happy, when we champion individuality and self-expression."

These examples illustrate the various paths that brands may take to embrace the postgenerational market. "I could see two strategies: Either you go more inclusive, don't define by age, but look at values and similarities between your audience, because there are plenty of things a boomer and a millennial have in common," notes Sarah Rabia, global director of cultural strategy at the American division of advertising agency TBWA Worldwide. "Or you get laser-focused on this audience, but with a tone that's upbeat, modern, and progressive." Marketers frequently mention that when people are asked to describe how they would like to age, they tend to say in a post-generational setting, enjoying the overlaps and the diversity of different age groups.

"It's also important to note that in most cases, people didn't set out to be postgenerational," observes Drabicky, "it organically happened." The moment for marketers is fortuitous given that shifting demographics coincide with the algorithmic revolution in marketing. Consumers "expect to have an ongoing dialogue with the brand, to feel like they have input into product and to feel like they are part of a community," argues Martin. "From a brand marketing perspective, that means that you need to have a lot of touchpoints with consumers and those touchpoints need to feel customized to every de-mographic. The product is, in many cases, the same, but the messaging needs to be tailored. "While it is critical that the overall message of the brand is rooted in its distinct set of emotional and functional benefits, it is possible to articulate that message with distinct nuances to different generations," says Pierre Dupreelle, a partner at Boston Consulting Group. "With the micro-targeting possible through sophisticated digital marketing and per-sonalization, brands are able to highlight key drivers of cultural credibility to younger consumers through media or channels that will reach younger consumers without alienating older generations." McCann, the global ad agency, recommends segmenting by attitude to identify groups such as age-less adventurers, communal caretakers, actualizing adults, youth chasers, and future fearers, among others. "We now have readily available, intimate details of consumers' lives, including their hobbies, friends, job interests, and vacation plans," notes Jessica Kriegel, an organizational development con-sultant for Oracle. "Companies can target consumers based on much more specific and accurate information, rather than on outdated and unsupported stereotypes . . . A generation is too broad a category." Not only broad, in fact, but also fuzzy and potentially misleading.

The opposite strategy to fine-grained algorithmic segmentation and targeting—a more inclusive approach—can also work, supported as well by digital marketing. "I was recently chatting with the owner of a bagel shop in my neighborhood, and she told me her daughter had introduced her to Third-Love's bras," recounts Heidi Zak, cofounder and co-CEO of the women's fashion brand. "She then told me that her mom had just started buying bras from us, as well. That's three generations who are using the product, which is very cool to hear from a customer." For her, the trick is to simply ignore age and focus on how the product can appeal to the widest possible group of customers. "We wanted to have a bra for all women, and while that certainly included all ages, we were more concerned with being size-inclusive at the time . . . marketing a product to several generations doesn't require multiple strategies."

In fact, Zak didn't realize they were using young models in their ads although a large proportion of their loyal customers were over the age of forty, until one of them brought it to her attention. "You don't have to pursue an older demographic relentlessly by using specific messaging just for them. It's more about creating a brand that focuses on inclusivity and diversity as a whole." ThirdLove's Instagram and Facebook feeds now include images of women of various ages and body shapes. "Posts of our older models on social media have high engagement—and that doesn't exclusively come from older generations. Younger women often comment or message our customer service team to say how much they love seeing those posts." The goal, according to Zak, is to build authentic and inclusive brands, to become "a brand with a universal message that people of all ages can get behind." That's a good recipe for any business.

A growing number of agencies are embracing diversity to overcome ageism in marketing. "Bring together your most open and willing employees, young and old, and see what happens," says Ollie Scott, founder of Unknown, a recruiting consulting firm. "Cognitive diversity is our special way of staying alive and it reaps results that prove that it is ageism in the marketing business that needs to be retired." Duncan Tickell, chief revenue officer of Immediate Media, concurs. "When it comes to brand marketing, we've long espoused the value of our mature audiences—our research has shown that over-40s are tech savvy media consumers . . . We call them Generation Wealth and recognize they have been overlooked for too long by many brands that mistakenly see younger generations as the priority." For her part, Annalie Killian, vice president of strategic partnerships at Sparks & Honey, observes that "more than 500% of budgets are targeted at millennials; yet consumers 55+ spend more than double the 18–34s." She proposes to "replace this obsession with youth with strategy informed by cultural insights to firstly, fully humanize the value and values of consumers at every age, and secondly, mirror the intersection of multiple generations living, working and playing side by side." And that essentially entails abandoning long-held assumptions about market segmentation based on age.

Whether marketing is analog or digital, the key is to find and exploit the points of contact across generations. "For effective generational marketing—and to build a big tent in which all people feel vested—brand managers need to find the various threads that tie the generations together," argues Matthew Schwartz in the blog of the Association of National Advertisers. "Otherwise, most marketers will twist themselves into pretzels trying to be all things to all age groups, and waste precious dollars in the process." Progressive Insurance, for instance, came up in 2017 with a campaign called "Parentmorphosis," which appealed to people of all ages. It basically reminded people that we all become our parents, with a healthy humoristic touch. One of the ads showed a young wife morphing into her father with all the manly mannerisms and an interest in golf. "Do you think we own stock in the electric company?" she says while vehemently switching off a lamp. Each spot ends with the announcement that "Progressive can't protect you from becoming your parents, but we can protect your home and auto."

"When it comes to marketing preferences, the amount of common ground among generations might be surprising," says Stacia Goddard, senior VP for strategy and consulting at Data Axle. "Across the board, consumers want personalized communications and experiences from brands they have relationships with and are loyal to." They found that between 77 and 88 percent of baby boomers, millennials, Gen Zers, and Gen Xers shared this desire. Even when it comes to channel preferences, the overlap is stunning. Everyone lists email as the preferred way to communicate with companies, with the only exception of Generation Z, which prefer social media. The only big difference has to do with influencers, which are preferred by younger folk. "While overall each generation's buying habits, media preferences and desire to engage with brands varies, it is important to note that generations are not segments, and even segments are too broad today."

Marketers have a long way to go before they fully embrace a postgenerational approach to their trade. It's just one more example of the extent to which our mindset needs to change in response to such epochal transformations as the increase in both the life span and the health span, the return to work of many retirees, the rise of alternative family arrangements, the new roles and realities of women in society, and the availability of novel tools for digital marketing. We are no longer in a compartmentalized world in which people of a certain age live, study, work, play, and shop only with people of the same age and do so following age-specific patterns of influence and behavior. In this context, what might a truly postgenerational society and economy look like?

10

TOWARD A POSTGENERATIONAL SOCIETY OF PERENNIALS

The difficulty lies not so much in developing new ideas
as in escaping from old ones.
—John Maynard Keynes (1883–1946)

In 2013, Yuichiro Miura, a Japanese eighty-year-old who had undergone four heart surgeries and recovered from a fractured pelvis, reached the summit of Everest for the third time in his life. He called his daughter from the top of the world using a satellite phone simply to say, "I never imagined I could make it to the top of Mount Everest at age eighty. This is the world's best feeling, although I'm totally exhausted." He had planned his third climb meticulously. "I told myself that I would not give up," he remembers. "Even when I wanted to give up or wavered along the way, I always shook it off and kept climbing upward." His feat challenged the conventional wisdom about age and resiliency. Even with supplemental oxygen, you can only stay on the summit of Mount Everest, where the air is three times thinner than at sea level, for about a half hour. "However," Miura remembers, "I found myself staying an hour to admire and photograph the view. To be able to spend an hour on Mount Everest, the highest point on Earth, was the most extravagant experience I've ever had."

Only a handful of elite mountaineers have climbed Everest solo. Given his age, Miura's feat was the result of a multigenerational effort by a large team, including his son Gota. One might argue that climbing Everest requires the energy and stamina of people in their thirties, the climbing experience and good judgment of those in their forties, and the mental fortitude of people in their fifties and beyond. Miura's team included a Japanese climbing leader in his early fifties, Miura's forty-three-year-old son, a cameraman in his thirties, thirteen climbing Sherpas ranging in age between twenty-six and forty-four years, five Japanese in support roles at base camp whose ages were not reported, and five kitchen Sherpas ages fourteen to eighteen. There are limits to what human beings can achieve, but the constraints become less daunting if generations collaborate with one another, contributing their unique strengths as the team seeks to overcome the various obstacles along the way, from the icefalls above base camp to the dangerous avalanches at twenty-thousand-foot altitude and the treacherous last few steps just below the summit. In addition, generations in this expedition played different roles, learning from one another and preparing themselves for future expeditions.

Miura is a splendid example of the perennial. His inspiring feat doesn't mean that we should all take to high-risk endeavors like summiting icy, windswept mountains. His many accomplishments serve to challenge the way we traditionally think about the life course. But perhaps the subtlest takeaway is that, in sharp contrast to Miura's Everest expedition, the sequential model prescribes that living, learning, working, and consuming takes place mostly among members of the same generation—or two at most. The crisis of this conception of life has been long in the making. "It is utterly false and cruelly arbitrary to put all the play and learning into childhood, all the work into middle age, and all the regrets into old age," observed Margaret Mead, the cultural anthropologist and bestselling author of *Coming of Age in Samoa,* first published in 1928. Four decades later, in the early 1970s, one of the most visionary management consultants of all time, Peter Drucker, optimistically proclaimed that "we now accept the fact that learning is a lifelong process of keeping abreast of change." Half a century after Drucker, we continue to expect that what we learn in school or college will last a lifetime, that we make a living in a single line of work, and that we enjoy a long retirement. Given how long we now live and the accelerating rate of technological change, the schooling-to-work-to-retirement model needs to be revisited.

For well over a century, one generation has played while another studies; one or two generations worked under the direction of another; and two generations are in retirement. Is that the best way of organizing life? Is it delivering prosperity and well-being? A litany of problems have come to afflict large segments of society, and they all stem, at least in part, from the straitjacket that the sequential model represents. We've covered in previous chapters many issues, including adolescent stress, delayed adulthood, teenage motherhood, declining fertility, lack of work/family balance, midlife crises, career dead ends, intergenerational conflicts, pension shortfalls, retiree loneliness, gender-based discrimination, economic inequality, and disgruntled consumers. These issues are devouring us as individuals and exposing entire communities and nations to unbearable levels of tension. Instead of resorting to patchwork policies, we can make each of those problems go away if we reorganize the way we live our lives, if we dissolve the problems rather than merely solving them. We need to overcome the rigidities of the Bismarckian sequential model by no longer defining ourselves and what we do in terms of age alone by adopting a perennial mindset.

THE PERENNIAL MINDSET AS METHOD

I mentioned in the introduction that this book wouldn't offer a specific solution for each of the enormous problems the sequential model of life has contributed to. As I wrote in the preceding chapters, the postgenerational revolution and the concomitant rise of the perennials—driven by demographic and technological transformations—is an invitation to assess who benefits from our present system and who doesn't. It's an exhortation to reflect on whether it's a way of living our lives that needs revisiting to unleash everyone's full potential through true equality of opportunity. I am keen on casting doubt on some taken-for-granted assumptions about playing, learning, working, and consuming—and you should be too. We need to break the mold inherited from a foregone era. The reality all around us has already moved beyond the strict, sequential model of life. But the problems persist, and some of them are getting worse. It's time to use this perennial methodology and the postgenerational approach to life to begin dissolving rather than merely solving problems, to gradually change the system guiding our lives so that new opportunities become available.

For starters, the method inspired in the notion of a postgenerational society of perennials has the potential of leveling the playing field by removing the stigmas attached to not progressing through the stages of life on a timely basis. For example, those who don't have a clear career plan as teenagers or who experience setbacks in life will enjoy a better chance of finding their own path when different generations live, study, work, and consume together. They will not stand out as misfits.

A perennial way of thinking also facilitates better outcomes in other domains and for people who have not suffered from life-changing crises or tragedies. For example, people are increasingly taking to reinvention, but the way professional careers are structured doesn't help. The workplace belongs to multiple generations, but we have not yet reaped the full potential of the complementarities that exist among the skills, expertise, and experience of different generations. Technology continues to render knowledge antiquated, but we still don't have a fluid way for people to move back and forth between study and work over the entire life span. And most marketers seem wedded to the notion that lifestyle brands are the province of the young, thus missing out on how different generations influence each other inside and outside the household.

IMAGINING A POSTGENERATIONAL SOCIETY OF PERENNIALS

"Seven in ten workers say they like working with generations other than their own, and the majority agree that both younger and older workers bring a set of positive benefits that enhance the workplace environment," concluded an

AARP study conducted in 2019. "In particular, workers value the give and take aspect in a multigenerational work environment." The potential benefits of the multigenerational workplace are manifold, according to Debra Whitman, AARP's chief public policy officer. "Work teams that comprise multiple generations perform better than those that do not . . . The multigenerational workforce improves workforce continuity, stability and retention of intellectual capital . . . Plus, an age-diverse workforce gives companies more insight into the marketplace, including the vast segment of older consumers." Those key advantages we identified in previous chapters.

But the benefits extend well beyond business and the economy. Age is both a biological reality and a social and political construction. Medicine and technology are redefining the life span and the health span, inviting us to recalibrate long-held social and political assumptions, perceptions, and expectations about what people can and can't do at different ages. Now we need to reinvent the way in which we live our lives.

Here's what a true postgenerational society of perennials would look like: One that invites a reorganization of how we live, learn, work, and consume. It means generations interacting because of more porous boundaries between school and work, mainly under a blended model that leverages technology for hybrid remote and in-person learning. It offers teenagers a less stressful path to carving out a niche for themselves, one in which they can reimagine their careers by going back to school several times without having to make fateful, lifelong decisions before they are ready to do so and under parental pressure. It enables parents (especially young mothers) to balance their work and family obligations, reducing the likelihood of having to choose between family and career by facilitating study, work, and family transitions at different ages without following a rigid schedule. It promises opportunities to those who otherwise would be left behind, including school dropouts and those facing career dead ends due to technological change or economic restructuring. And it provides the conditions for a more fulfilling and financially secure full or partial retirement.

Let's summarize the potential benefits of the postgenerational society of perennials before we turn to assessing what types of cultural, organizational, and policy changes need to happen to make progress. Relaxing or moving away from the sequential model of life would help:

- Reduce the stress many people feel while making transitions from one stage to another through more flexible timing and more pathways to advancement.
- Enable those left behind to recover from episodes of bad fortune or questionable decisions, through alternative, perhaps winding roads to a satisfying life.
- Unleash the full creative potential of workers of all ages by virtue of new workplace practices that balance cognitive ability and job experience.
- Facilitate people's lifelong learning to cope with disruptive technological change, or to reinvent oneself, by making education and knowledge more widely available.
- Level the playing field for parents in the corporate world and the labor market through more flexible career paths.
- Avoid some of the negative by-products of retirement, including loneliness, through schemes that help retirees work part-time if they wish.
- Strike a workable balance between the hard-won rewards of retirement and the aspirations of younger generations by overhauling pension systems and facilitating part-time employment or self-employment by retirees.
- Reduce sources of age bias and discrimination by educating everyone about the strengths and weaknesses inherent to each of us without unfairly stereotyping groups.
- Build a consumer market where all generations feel at ease by embracing inclusive approaches to marketing.

These are possibilities we should be pursuing in earnest, but we won't be able to make any progress unless cultural, organizational, and policy changes take place. It doesn't have to be massive or itself revolutionary. It can be measured and gradual. We can take our time, experiment, and adjust. Every incremental step we take toward the society of perennials will help.

CULTURAL CHANGE

"All the world's a stage," commences the famous soliloquy in William Shakespeare's *As You Like It*. "And all the men and women merely players." Jacques, overwhelmed by melancholy, recounts "their exits and their entrances" through the "seven ages," describing the predicament of the infant "mewling and puking," the "whining" schoolboy, the "sighing" lover, the soldier "bearded like the pard," the justice "in fair round belly," the "sixth age . . . with spectacles on nose and pouch on side," and, finally, the "second childishness . . . sans teeth, sans eyes, sans taste, sans everything."

Only Shakespeare could put it in such a vivid and blunt way.

The sequential model of life is deeply ingrained in the culture, as revealed by so many plays, novels, poems, films, and TV shows on the various stations of life, laying bare the trials and tribulations involved in the chain of life course transitions through infanthood, childhood, adolescence, adulthood, retirement, and so on. The popular imagination is replete with iconic representations of the various stages and the rites of passage from one to the next—including the consequences of not proceeding through each of them in sequence and on a timely basis, as we saw in chapters 2–4.

As a first step, the coming of the postgenerational society of perennials requires a change in mindset. Schools, universities, companies, government agencies, and the entire economy are organized around the classification of people into fixed age groups. This system has served the world well for over a century but is now itself showing the signs of age. As longevity, fitness, and technology continue to apply pressure on organizations and society, we must find new templates so that people of different generations can enjoy their longer, fitter lives to the fullest. The future holds increasing postgenerational ways of playing, living, learning, working, and consuming.

Culture is all about categories. Abandoning certain categories that constrain what people can and can't do is sorely needed because they define what is "age appropriate." Categories are especially harmful if they're turned into a classification system that is exclusive and exhaustive, meaning that each and every individual is in one, and only one, category at any given point in time. The sequential model classified people into generational categories according to age and activity, prescribing a linear path from cradle to grave for those who wanted to be successful in life. It became the foundation of how organizations of all sorts would deal with people, including nurseries, schools, universities, hospitals, government agencies, and companies, among others.

Doing away with categories may be difficult to achieve, but perhaps we can overcome the prejudices based on classifying people by age and generation. For example, the World Values Survey asked over eighty thousand respondents in fifty-seven countries between 2010 and 2014 if they find it suitable for a thirty-year-old and for a seventy-year-old to be appointed as their boss. Other questions asked if most people in their country view those above age seventy as "friendly," "competent," and "with respect." The survey included a few more point-blank questions asking if "older people are a burden on society," "older people get more than their fair share from the government," "old people have too much political influence," and, most importantly for our purposes, "companies that employ young people perform better than those that employ people of different ages."

In general, more than half said that they would feel comfortable with either a thirty-year-old boss or a seventy-year-old. What's really interesting is that people very much prefer a younger boss in Latin America, Russia, the former Soviet republics, and some Western European countries like the Netherlands, Spain, and Sweden. By contrast, in China, Germany, and Japan, people had a slight preference for a seventy-year-old boss. In the U.S. and South Korea, there was almost no difference in people's eyes.

The good news is that "being less educated, younger and male significantly increased the odds of an individual having high ageist attitudes," according to a thorough statistical analysis. I think it's good news because, as an educator, I can see a path toward achieving cultural change—that is, by educating young minds, especially men, about the benefits of the postgenerational society. Age and generational prejudices are more pronounced in lower-income countries in South Asia, the Middle East, and Africa, all regions of the world where populations are young and schooling can benefit greater numbers of people in the future. Thus, I remain optimistic. But cultural change can be stifled by organizational rules and procedures. Those must change as well.

ORGANIZATIONAL CHANGE

"I am sixty-nine years old, and that means I am unemployable," says Diane Huth, a San Antonio, Texas, resident. "I worked in corporate America for more than forty years with big-name companies in branding," just like legions of other professional men and women. "But I cannot get a job, the same job I rocked fifteen years ago. I cannot even get an interview for that job because of all the screening mechanisms. I'm just too old; nobody takes me seriously for a job at my age, even in things I had excelled at." At the other end of the age spectrum, young people complain they're not given enough responsibility at work, their job doesn't pay enough to buy a home, or they can't even get a stable job.

As in the case of cultural change, we're caught in the debate about age and generational discrimination, attempting to solve the problem rather than dissolving it. To be sure, we must address all forms of overt and implicit discrimination through legal, cultural, and organizational means. But we also need to ensure that we benefit from multigenerational learning, work, and leisure in all organizational settings, including educational institutions, businesses, and the government. Otherwise, we won't be able to minimize the snags of teenage depression, midlife crises, career dead ends, the pensions crisis, and so on.

The education sector has the most potential to make a difference in a postgenerational society of perennials. It can help with overcoming cultural biases and create new opportunities for people to move back and forth between school and work. "The illiterate of the 21st century will not be those who cannot read and write," argues the author and consultant Alvin Toffler, "but those who cannot learn, unlearn, and relearn." Demographic, economic, and technological transformations will force us to go through that cycle several times within our lifetime. Learning a new skill is becoming increasingly common not just through formal schooling beyond age twenty-five—in the U.S., more than one in three college students are above that age—but through the bewildering array of digital options to pick up a new skill, such as data analytics, public speaking, or sketching. Unlearning habits, procedures, and mindsets is essential to succeed in a new position within the same organization, let alone to switch to another employer or to an entirely new kind of occupation. Bankers turned activists constantly need to remind themselves that there is no internal rate of return to be easily calculated in community organizing. And relearning often involves refreshing old learnings. Many former students of mine say that they did not realize while in business school how important leadership skills are—until years down the road when they found themselves at the helm of an organization after years of working in more technical positions.

Enabling people to pursue nonlinear and multiple career paths facilitated by learning, unlearning, and relearning requires not just new educational opportunities but also employers willing to revisit their usual ways of selecting, attracting, rewarding, and retaining talent. This is a tall order because human-resource practices are highly bureaucratized, in both business and government. Making promotion ladders more flexible would be a good first step. Following the examples of companies that have created a postgenerational workplace on the factory shop floor and the marketing function, to name but two departments within the corporation, would be the ideal approach to overcoming the shortcomings of the sequential model of life. "With change going on everywhere, companies are facing wicked problems they have to solve in order to drive growth," says Gary Kopervas, senior vice president of brand strategy, story design, and innovation at 20nine, a brand agency in the Philadelphia suburbs. "We find that matching boomers, gen Xers, millennials and gen Zers together in a creative environment leads to richer and a wider spectrum of solution options . . . If creativity is the goal, creating a multi-generational environment can help fuel better solutions."

A truly postgenerational workforce will result from more companies of all sizes accepting online education credentials for hiring and promotions. Otherwise, employers will neglect the skills of an increasing number of capable students. For example, in the fall semester of 2019 (i.e., just before the pandemic), there were 3.4 million college students in the U.S. exclusively learning online, approximately 17.5 percent of the total. The percentage was only 13 percent at public universities, but 21.4 percent at private nonprofit colleges and universities, and a whopping 62.8 percent at private for-profits. Thus, we also need public universities to join the bandwagon and innovate.

Some companies are already realizing the potential of postgenerational marketing and the postgenerational workplace, as we've seen in previous chapters. But they are still few and far apart. It might only take a few big corporations to create a trend toward a truly postgenerational workplace. Nudging, regulation, and new policy initiatives may be needed, though, to get a larger number of companies of all sizes to join the bandwagon.

POLICY CHANGE

"I think that it is important [that] the whole society and the government in particular focus on creating a mutual understanding between younger and older people," said Olipcia, a seventy-four-year-old Haitian woman interviewed for the United Nations' *Global Report on Ageism*. But policymakers themselves also need to learn how to overcome their own ageist biases, which frequently translate into policies that stereotype, prejudge, and discriminate against people due to their age in the realms of education, work, housing, and healthcare, among other policy areas. The upper echelons of policymakers in the government bureaucracy tend to be of "middle age," neither young nor retired, although elected and nonelected politicians tend to be of a higher age.

The transition to the postgenerational society of perennials will certainly require legal adjustments to address discrimination against young adults and people over the age of sixty in employment, access to housing and healthcare, and legal proceedings. In the report, the United Nations found that age discrimination against both ends of the age spectrum is rampant in developed as well as developing countries. But the change required to advance a truly postgenerational society will need to go well beyond the legal to include cultural, organizational, and policy aspects, and it will have to go well beyond overcoming ageism to embracing a new way of organizing life that enhances the interactions among different generations. In fact, postgenerational contact and collaboration may also be the best way to overcome stereotypes, prejudices, and discrimination based on age.

In addition to uprooting discrimination, the postgenerational perennial mindset can be promoted by policies that improve access to education, both in terms of attitudinal change and more flexible career pathways. Governments could also consider reallocating resources to improve the health span while the life span continues to grow. To reap the benefits of the postgenerational classroom and workplace, one could be much bolder, adding the generational dimension to equity, diversity, and inclusion policies like affirmative action, as suggested by economist David Neumark in a recent piece for the Brookings Institution, a think tank. If rapid progress is the priority, perhaps quotas could be considered. What if all large companies had to reserve a certain proportion of jobs for high school dropouts, parents with young kids, or people with grandchildren? I can name several reasons why quotas could prove to be counterproductive and unfair. I could also give a similar number of reasons why they could be productive. In certain instances, I think the current system needs a shock, a reboot. Perhaps only quotas can provide such a fresh start. We've seen this work in boards of directors of business corporations, where without such requirements women and minorities would still be largely excluded from corporate governance. Why can't we give it a try in the wider organizational world?

Governments create nudges and incentives for all sorts of behaviors, including saving for retirement, economizing on energy use, having children, and so on. Given its many potential benefits, the time has come for such policies to promote generational interaction. Why not offer schools, universities, and companies positive incentives to make it easier for people to pursue nonlinear trajectories that help them adapt to changes in the economy and the labor market? Or to maximize the chances for interaction and collaboration among generations in the workplace? And how about ensuring the future viability of pension systems by making it easier for people to enjoy a mix of work and rest over most of their health span? We certainly need a large injection of imagination to shift from the linear path of the sequential model to a multiplicity of pathways enabling people to find their own life trajectory. And while technology has created the need for such flexibility by making knowledge obsolete faster, it may also be the savior by offering more differentiated educational and career options at a time when the demand for learning continues to skyrocket.

ACCELERATING THE POSTGENERATIONAL SOCIETY AND ECONOMY

The good news is that postgenerational ways of living, learning, working, and consuming are driven by powerful forces that are becoming stronger by the day. The perennial mindset is beginning to take hold. Declining fertility means smaller age cohorts in school and college—especially in East Asia, Europe, and North America—thus creating a huge incentive for traditional educational institutions to serve the needs of age groups other than those traditionally enrolled in them. Technological change is another great accelerator of postgenerational learning given that it makes people's knowledge and skills obsolete faster than in the past, thus inviting them to go back into learning mode along with others in different age groups. Rampant labor shortages in the wake of demographic changes, geopolitical tensions, and the coronavirus pandemic are already compelling companies and other employers to reconsider their biases toward employees beyond a certain age. Brands and marketers are now recalibrating their approach as the center of gravity of consumption shifts toward the upper groups in the age distribution. As schooling, working, and shopping become genuinely postgenerational so will leisure and entertainment, given that we tend to play with those we interact with at school and work. Thus, the coming of the society of perennials is being fueled by demographic swings, technological change, and momentous events like the coronavirus pandemic.

The pace toward a postgenerational society differs markedly depending on the aspect under consideration. Let's gauge multiple generations living together first. In the developed world, up to 20 percent of the population lives in a multigenerational household (see chapter 3). That proportion is growing. Much of the growth is still driven by necessity, but more people are now living with at least two other generations out of personal choice. In the emerging and developing countries, it is declining from a much higher level, driven by urbanization and new economic opportunities. Thus, when it comes to multigenerational living, we find a bifurcation in the world mostly along the lines of developed versus developing countries.

In stark contrast to postgenerational living, when it comes to multigenerational learning, our second key dimension, the entire world is moving toward greater numbers of people beyond their twenties seeking education, albeit from relatively low levels. The proportion of the population age thirty and above enrolled in postsecondary degree programs is greater than 10 percent only in Australia, Finland, and Turkey, and above 5 percent in Denmark, Iceland, Sweden, New Zealand, Hungary, and Brazil. In the United States, it's about 4 percent. As we saw in chapter 5, one in every four Chinese above the age of sixty are attending a special university for seniors. The challenge when it comes to traditional degree-seeking education will be not only to accommodate students of all ages but also to move away from a model in which different types of colleges and universities cater to the needs of students of different ages learning side by side in a truly postgenerational fashion.

Unlike in the traditional model, online postgenerational learning has exploded around the world and across age groups. In the twenty-seven countries of the European Union, the percentage of people above the age of thirty engaged in online education has risen from less than 10 percent in 2015 to more than 20 percent by 2021. In the United Kingdom, it's approaching 30 percent, and in the United States, it is at least as high. Companies have taken notice. According to KPMG, a consultancy, in 1995, only 4 percent of large and medium-size American companies were making online learning available to their employees. By 2022, the proportion was nearly 90 percent. An AARP survey of nearly six thousand executives across thirty-six of the member countries of the Organisation for Economic Co-operation and Development (OECD) conducted in 2019–2020, found that over 80 percent found information about lifelong learning, education, and training either very or somewhat useful. Just over 75 percent said that providing training and lifelong opportunities to employees at their company was very or somewhat likely. We already have large proportions of people above the age of thirty engaged in lifelong learning. The next step is to create an educational system for perennials, which essentially entails desegregating education by age group so as to unleash the benefits of true multigenerational learning.

The corporate sector has also begun to embrace the concept of the multigenerational workplace, under pressure as it is from an acute scarcity of talent. This is the third dimension of the society and economy of perennials. The same AARP survey found that age was a factor in 47 percent of the 64 percent whose companies had an equity, diversity, and inclusion policy. About 46 percent had looked into the potential advantages of having a multigenerational workforce. Of those, 70–80 percent were either very interested or somewhat interested in exploring the business value and strategic advantage of multigenerational workforces, the tools for benchmarking against other companies in this area, information on how to design a workplace that meets the needs of a multigenerational workforce, and practices and insights related to the management of multigenerational workforces and teams. They also expressed similar levels of interest in initiatives such as reentry or return-to-work programs, intergenerational employee resource groups, mixed-age teams, and phased retirement programs. Nearly 84 percent considered that creating a multigenerational workforce would be very valuable or somewhat valuable to their company's success.

Thus, executives seem to be very keen on the multigenerational workplace. But what about the workers? A survey of ten thousand employees in seven European countries conducted by the consultancy Deloitte in June 2020 revealed that only 6 percent thought their companies were equipped to lead and manage a multigenerational workforce. That's a huge gap that needs to be bridged.

The fourth dimension, multigenerational consumption, is on the increase because of multigenerational living, learning, and working. Brands are beginning to appeal to multiple generations both by emphasizing the commonalities among generations and leveraging the new trend of multi-generational joint consumption and perennial marketing. The unimaginable is actually happening. Media and streaming companies are creating multigenerational content, including the likes of the Discovery Channel, Fox Entertainment, CBS, Telemundo, TikTok, and Facebook. Beauty brands are now targeting the "19/99" age segment, which the Canadian company 19/99 says on its website is "designed for those who want to define their own beauty and aren't concerned about what is considered appropriate." As far as they are concerned, "there is no magic number. This is beauty for the retaliation age." As we saw in chapter 9, automobile companies are also joining the trend, as are such popular companies as Disney and LEGO.

It's encouraging to see that trends in living, learning, working, and consuming are mutually reinforcing and increasingly pointing in the direction of a postgenerational society and economy. Let's sum up some of the best ways to accelerate the evolution toward a postgenerational society of perennials:

- Leveling the legal playing field through the elimination of egregious forms of age discrimination, including those that limit access to education, employment, housing, and healthcare.
- Encouraging innovation and competition in the education sector to enable people to participate in lifelong learning and to make it possible for generations to learn together. This would include providing student financial aid for people of all ages.
- Reforming job performance evaluation and promotion schemes so that parents don't have to navigate complex trade-offs between family and work, including those already used by some companies and organizations (extended promotion clocks, paid time off, and so on).
- Adopting government policies that provide nudges, incentives, and funding for individuals and companies to make it easier to

move back and forth between school and work, thus encouraging organizations to maximize postgenerational interaction and collaboration.

- Persuading a greater number of companies and government agencies to experiment with postgenerational approaches to work, training, reskilling, and careers. They should also accept quality online education certificates when hiring and promoting. In this way, early corporate and government adopters can become the vanguard of change, the role models for other companies and organizations to emulate. Governments and forward-looking employers must champion the multigenerational society and economy by maximizing the opportunities for intergenerational awareness, learning, and collaboration.

But let's not get carried away by the potential benefits without considering some of the big risks involved in this transition. There are three important caveats in the postgenerational revolution and the adoption of a perennial mindset that we need to bear in mind. Perhaps the biggest issue involves access to the instruments and tools that will enable people to pursue multiple pathways in their lives, including education, technology, and financial security. Remaining vigilant about equal access to those resources is crucial for the benefits of the postgenerational society to spread widely. Perhaps proposals like a basic income could go a long way in terms of encouraging people to switch jobs and careers as they seek to catch new waves of economic and technological change.

Another concern is the possibility that reduced fertility and enhanced wealth accumulation in the knowledge economy, even with increased longevity, will send inheritances through the roof, with the ultimate result of exacerbating inequality. While the effects will be felt differently across the world (see chapter 7), further income and wealth disparities between the haves and the have-nots would seriously undermine the overall benefits of the postgenerational society, putting equality of opportunity at risk.

In the highly polarized cultural and political climate afflicting so many countries around the world, a speedy, drastic transition from a sequential model of life to another with many pathways and feedback loops may prove to be controversial. The reason lies in that proposing a change in how we live our lives will immediately trigger a wide array of responses, depending on one's cultural and political lens. At a time when the traditional concept of the nuclear family is no longer the norm, reactionary points of view might propose a return to archaic values and practices—including relegating women to traditional roles—something that is not just unworkable but also unacceptable to many groups in society. We must move forward while avoiding a backlash or exacerbating social and political fissures.

So let's be pragmatic. Let's minimize social strife and political extremism by thinking strategically about both incremental and radical change. Let's continue to discover the ways in which the sequential model of life is preventing people from realizing their full potential. Let's challenge the assumptions that are causing the most trouble, especially those about the compartmentalization of the stages of life. Let's launch pilot programs based on new ideas and possibilities both to prevent people from falling behind and to unleash each individual's potential in this age of demographic, economic, and technological transformations. Let's invite governments, companies, educational institutions, and other types of organizations to think about citizens, students, and workers as perennials, to be creative, to think outside the box, to become engines of change, to dissolve problems rather than simply solving them. Just a few of them can make a huge difference by experimenting with various aspects of postgenerational ways of living, learning, working, and consuming.

Paying attention to intergenerational sources of conflict over jobs, housing, taxes, healthcare, pensions, and sustainability while transitioning to a better-balanced, flexible society of perennials will be the hardest test of all. Large-scale transformations are never easy or frictionless. In fact, they are characterized by social and political disruption, upheaval, and dislocation. Expect no less this time around. Still, by jettisoning outdated assumptions and ways of doing, and with a hefty dose of imagination, we might be able to reorganize our lives in a way that creates a future landscape that's better for most people: for the high school dropout and for the A student with a master's degree; for the teenage mom, the professional woman, and the divorced woman seeking to reenter the labor market; and for those displaced from their jobs by technological change and for the knowledge workers. That's the inherent promise of adopting the perennial mindset, one that will change the meaning of so many terms that we have long used to pigeonhole people into rigid categories and life stages.

•

Vast demographic and technological transformations are gradually bringing about postgenerational ways of living, learning, working, and consuming. As a result, it's becoming increasingly possible to liberate scores of people from the constraints of the sequential model of life, leveling the playing field so that everyone has a chance at living a rewarding life. It's about time we adopted a perennial mindset to dissolve rather than solve problems. The society and the economy are no longer those of the late nineteenth century, when such a linear way of organizing our lives came into being to meet the requirements of industrialization. Now we find ourselves in a rapidly evolving postindustrial economy driven by knowledge and technology, requiring both organizations and people to be much faster and flexible at adapting to mercurial circumstances. To excel at this new, competitive game, we need to embrace the spirit of generations living, learning, working, and consuming together. The postgenerational revolution is already in the making, with more and more people becoming true perennials. We just need to escape from old conceptions and ride the wave of change.

ACKNOWLEDGMENTS

Writing a book amounts to embarking on a journey of personal discovery. With this book, I've made some progress in terms of understanding how I have evolved from one stage in life to the next. In fact, I wrote it as I switched gears in my career from being a professor to becoming a dean, while emerging from the pandemic, like most other people, puzzled about what the future might bring, and more aware than ever of the passage of time. The book questions the way we usually live our lives. It challenges some common assumptions. I was not aware of the implications of many of those commonly held beliefs until I started to talk about them with other people. As a professor, I owe much of what's in the book to feedback during my lectures on the topic. It's been thousands of students, executives, and other audiences whose questions and comments I've found most useful when it came to adding nuance and exploring side topics in the book.

I was fortunate to work with some of the most amazing people in the book world: Jane von Mehren of Aevitas Creative Management; my editor, Michael Flamini of St. Martin's Press; my team of publicists led by Paul Sliker; and Francis Hoch at Chartwell Speakers Bureau. Their commitment to excellence encouraged me to aim high and to work hard to deliver.

The actual writing of this book took place at home in Philadelphia and in Cambridge. I am most grateful to Mohamed El-Erian, president of Queens College, where I spent many evenings and weekends typing and retyping the manuscript. Benito Cachinero, José Manuel Campa, Carlos de la Cruz, Álvaro Cuervo, Julio García Cobos, Emilio Ontiveros, and Sandra Suárez gave me, as usual, innumerable tips and saved me from making numerous mistakes.

As with my previous books, my wife, Sandra, and my daughters, Daniela and Andrea, have seen me work on it and offered constant support. I dedicate this book to the three of them.

REFERENCES

All internet sources accessed on August 20, 2022.

PERENNIALS AND THE POSTGENERATIONAL SOCIETY IN FIGURES

"Life Expectancy in the USA, 1900–1998," https://u.demog.berkeley.edu/~andrew /1918/figure2.html; U.S.; United Nations, World Population Prospects 2022 (New York: United Nations, 2022); World Health Organization, Global Health Observatory, https://apps.who.int/gho/data/view.main.HALEXv; Bureau of the Census, "American Families and Living Arrangements: 2021," tables H1 and FG3, https: //www.census.gov/data/tables/2021/demo/families/cps-2021.html; "Financial Issues Top the List of Reasons U.S. Adults Live in Multigenerational Homes," Pew Research Center, March 24, 2022, https://www.pewresearch.org/fact-tank/2018/04 /05/a-record-64-million-americans-live-in-multigenerational-households/; OECD's

Education Database, https://data.oecd.org/education.htm; the data on online learning by age come from the Statista database; *Global Insights on a Multigenerational Workforce* (Washington, DC: AARP Research, August 2020); "The Rise of Intergenerational Influence?," Media Leader, March 2, 2021, https://the-media-leader.com /the-rise-of-intergenerational-influence/.

INTRODUCTION

The World Economic Forum's definition of "old age" appears in "What is Old Age?," April 21, 2015, https://www.weforum.org/agenda/2015/04/what-is-old-age/.

On BMW, see Christoph Loch, Fabian J. Sting, Nikolaus Bauer, and Helmut Mauermann, "The Globe: How BMW Is Defusing the Demographic Time Bomb," *Harvard Business Review,* https://hbr.org/2010/03/the-globe-how-bmw-is-defusing-the -demographic-time-bomb; Val Grubb, "Managing Four Generations in the Workplace," Val Grubb & Associates, October 18, 2015, https://valgrubbandassociates .com/managing-four-generations-in-the-workplace/; "The Future of Work: Changing Values in a Multi-Generational Workforce," GetSmarter, September 28, 2020, https: //www.getsmarter.com/blog/market-trends/the-future-of-work-changing-values-in -a-multi-generational-workforce/; Marti Konstant, "Multigenerational Workforce Requires Culture Shift," Marti Konstant's website, 2022.

On multiple generations in the workplace, see Brendan Shaw, "Five Generations in the Workplace," Shawview Consulting, June 7, 2019, https://www.shawview.com/post /2019/06/07/an-historical-moment-five-generations-in-the-workplace; Jeff Desjardins, "How Different Generations Approach Work," Visual Capitalist, May 30, 2019, https://www.visualcapitalist.com/generations-approach-workplace/; Michael Vincent, "The Benefits of Having Multiple Generations in the One Workplace," ABC News Australia, March 6, 2019, https://mobile.abc.net.au/news/2019–03–06/benefits-of -having-multi-generations-in-the-one-workplace/10873564.

On using different parts of the brain to solve problems, see Katherine Ellen Foley, "Scientifically, This Is the Best Age for You to Lead," Quartz, May 9, 2019, https://qz .com/work/1614701/the-best-age-to-lead-is-probably-in-your-50s/.

1. THE FOUR STATIONS IN LIFE

On the history of compulsory education, see Peter Gray, "A Brief History of Education," *Psychology Today,* August 20, 2008, https://www.psychologytoday.com/us/blog /freedom-learn/200808/brief-history-education; Francisco O. Ramirez and John Boli, "The Political Construction of Mass Schooling," *Sociology of Education* 60, no. 1 (January 1987): 2–17.

The German teacher and the punishments inflicted on pupils is cited in James Mulhern, *A History of Education: A Social Interpretation,* 2nd ed. (New York: Ronald Press, 1959), 383.

On industrialization and schooling, see E. P. Thompson, "Time, Work-Discipline, and Industrial Capitalism," *Past & Present* 38 (December 1967): 56–97. The Turner quote is on page 84. Charles Perrow, "A Society of Organizations," *Theory & Society* 20, no. 6 (December 1991): 725–762.

The workplace novels are discussed in Joanna Biggs, "Top 10 Books About Working Life," *Guardian*, April 29, 2015.

Talcott Parsons's famous essay "The School Class as a Social System" appeared in *Harvard Educational Review* 29 (1959): 297–318.

On the Peter Pan syndrome, see Dan Kiley, *The Peter Pan Syndrome: Men Who Have Never Grown Up* (New York: Avon Books, 1983); Aldous Huxley, *Island* (New York: Perennial, 1962), 184–185; Melek Kalkan, Meryem Vural Batik, Leyla Kaya, and Merve Turan, "Peter Pan Syndrome 'Men Who Don't Grow': Developing a Scale," *Men and Masculinities* 24, no. 2 (June 2021): 245–257.

The quote by José Ortega y Gasset is from "Overprotecting Parents Can Lead Children to Develop 'Peter Pan Syndrome,'" Science Daily, May 3, 2007, https://www.sciencedaily.com/releases/2007/05/070501112023.htm.

A summary of Erik Erikson's stages in life can be found in Kendra Cherry, "Erik Erikson's Stages of Psychosocial Development," Verywell Mind, August 3, 2022, https://www.verywellmind.com/erik-eriksons-stages-of-psychosocial-development-2795740.

Gary Becker's demographic theories are aptly summarized by Matthias Doepke, "Gary Becker on the Quantity and Quality of Children," *Journal of Demographic Economics* 81 (2015): 59–66. His quote comes from Gary Becker, *A Treatise on the Family* (Cambridge, MA: Harvard University Press, 1991), 144.

The quotes on the trials and tribulations of the Gilbreths are from Frank B. Gilbreth Jr. and Ernestine Gilbreth Carey, *Cheaper by the Dozen* (Binghamton, NY: Vail-Ballou Press, 1948), 2, 10, 21–22, 88; Ernestine M. Gilbreth, *Living with Our Children* (New York: W. W. Norton, 1928), 3, 11.

The statistics on women's education and children are from Gladys M. Martinez, Kimberly Daniels, and Isaedmarie Febo-Vazquez, "Fertility of Men and Women Aged 15–44 in the United States: National Survey of Family Growth, 2011–2015," *National Health Statistics Report* no. 113 (July 11, 2018).

On parental pressures and children's educational plans, see Carl O'Brien, "Parents Warned of Obsession with Sending Children to University," *Irish Times,* May 23, 2018, https://www.irishtimes.com/news/education/parents-warned-of-obsession-with-sending-children-to-university-1.3402361, including the quote from Ken Robinson; Avik Mallick, "How Obsession with Grades Harms Children's Education," India Education, 2022, https://indiaeducation.net/students-corner/how-obsession-with-grades-harms-childrens-education/; Alia Wong, "The American Obsession with Parenting," *Atlantic,* December 12, 2016, https://www.theatlantic.com/family/archive/2016/12/the-american-obsession-with-parenting/510221/.

On cultural capital and grades at school, see Paul DiMaggio, "Cultural Capital and School Success," *American Sociological Review* 47 (April 1982): 189–201.

The quote by Dr. Joseph Garberly is in "Parental Pressure and Behavior May Put Teens at Risk for Substance Use and Abuse Say Experts from Caron Treatment Centers," Globe-Newswire, March 14, 2019, https://www.globenewswire.com/news-release/2019/03/14/1754943/0/en/Parental-Pressure-and-Behavior-May-Put-Teens-at-Risk-for-Substance-Use-and-Abuse-Say-Experts-from-Caron-Treatment-Centers.html.

The quotes on the midlife crisis are from Rebecca A. Clay, "Researchers Replace Midlife Myths with Facts," *Monitor on Psychology* 34, no. 4 (April 2003): 36. See also "Midlife," *Psychology Today,* https://www.psychologytoday.com/intl/conditions/midlife; Jonathan Rauch, "The Real Roots of Midlife Crisis," *Atlantic,* December 2014, https://www.theatlantic.com/magazine/archive/2014/12/the-real-roots-of-midlife-crisis/382235/; Xu Qin, "Did Snow White Deal with Midlife Crisis?," Shine, October 16, 2020, https://www.shine.cn/feature/book/2010167822/.

On living alone and loneliness, see "Percentage of Americans Living Alone, by Age," Our World in Data, https://ourworldindata.org/grapher/percentage-of-americans-living-alone-by-age?time=1900.2018; "Social Isolation, Loneliness in Older People Pose Health Risks," National Institute on Aging, https://www.nia.nih.gov/news/social-isolation-loneliness-older-people-pose-health-risks. On loneliness during retirement, see "How to Combat Loneliness in Older Age," Gransnet, https://www.gransnet.com/relationships/older-people-feeling-lonely-making-new-friends; James Sullivan, "The Financial and Human Cost of Loneliness in Retirement," *Journal of Accountancy Newsletter / CPA Insider,* January 21, 2020, https://www.journalofaccountancy.com/newsletters/2020/jan/financial-consequences-isolation-senior-clients.html; Oejin Shin, Sojung Park, Takashi Amano, Eunsun Kwon, and BoRin Kim, "Nature of Retirement and Loneliness: The Moderating Roles of Social Support," *Journal of Applied Gerontology* 39, no. 12 (2020): 1292–1302; Esteban Calvo, Kelly Haverstick, and Steven A. Sass, "Gradual Retirement, Sense of Control, and Retirees' Happiness," *Research on Aging* 31, no. 1 (2009): 112–135.

On Walter Gropius and Frank Gilbreth, see Mauro F. Guillén, *The Taylorized Beauty of the Mechanical: Scientific Management and the Rise of Modernist Architecture* (Princeton, NJ: Princeton University Press, 2006).

On intergenerational dynamics, see "Intergenerational Solidarity and Needs of Future Generations," United Nations, August 5, 2013, https://sustainabledevelopment.un.org/content/documents/2006future.pdf; Michael J. Urick, Elaine C. Hollensbe, Suzanne S. Masterson, and Sean T. Lyons, "Understanding and Managing Intergenerational Conflict: An Examination of Influences and Strategies," *Work, Aging and Retirement* 3, no. 2 (April 2017): 166–185; "Inheriting Climate Change," Climate One, https://www.climateone.org/audio/inheriting-climate-change-0; Bruce Gibney, *A Generation of Sociopaths: How the Baby Boomers Betrayed America* (New York: Hachette Books, 2017).

2. SOARING LONGEVITY AND HEALTH

The best history is James C. Riley, *Rising Life Expectancy: A Global History* (Cambridge, England: Cambridge University Press, 2001). The quote appears on page 1. The London causes of death throughout history are reported on page 17.

On centenarian Stalin, see Neil G. Bennett and Lea Keil Garson, "The Centenarian Question and Old-Age Mortality in the Soviet Union, 1959–1970," *Demography* 20, no. 4 (November 1983): 587–606; Neil G. Bennett and Lea Keil Garson, "Extraordinary Longevity in the Soviet Union: Fact or Artifact?," *Gerontologist* 6, no. 4 (August 1986): 358–361; Lea Keil Garson, "The Centenarian Question: Old-Age Mortality in the Soviet Union, 1897 to 1970," *Population Studies* 45, no. 2 (July 1991): 265–278.

Historical American life expectancy data are available from "Life Expectancy in the USA, 1900–1998," University of California, Berkeley, https://u.demog.berkeley.edu /~andrew/1918/figure2.html.

The data on the life expectancy of male elites is from J. P. Griffin, "Changing Life Expectancy Throughout History," *Journal of the Royal Society of Medicine* 101, no. 12 (December 2008): 577.

On life expectancy around the world, see Aaron O'Neill, "Life Expectancy in the United Kingdom 1765–2020," Statista, https://www.statista.com/statistics/1040159/life -expectancy-united-kingdom-all-time/; "Life Expectancy by Age," Infoplease, https: //www.infoplease.com/us/health-statistics/life-expectancy-age-1850–2011; Lauren Medina, Shannon Sabo, and Jonathan Vespa, "Living Longer: Historical and Projected Life Expectancy in the United States, 1960 to 2060," *Current Population Reports,* February 2020, https://www.census.gov/content/dam/Census/library/publications /2020/demo/p25-1145.pdf; Raphael Minder, "Spain's Formula to Live Forever," *Foreign Policy,* July 4, 2019, https://foreignpolicy.com/2019/07/04/spains-formula -to-live-forever/; Steven Johnson, "How Humanity Gave Itself an Extra Life," *New York Times Magazine,* April 27, 2021.

On the fountain of youth, see Herodotus, *The Histories,* book III, http://www.perseus .tufts.edu/hopper/text?doc=Perseus%3Atext%3A1999.01.0126%3Abook%3D3; "Myth of the Source: Historical References," Acción Cultura Española, https://www .accioncultural.es/virtuales/florida/eng/search/myth_history.html; Tad Friend, "Silicon Valley's Quest to Live Forever," *New Yorker,* March 27, 2017; Jocelyn Kaiser, "Google X Sets Out to Define Healthy Human," *Science,* July 28, 2014; Eva Hamrud, "Scientists Think We Can 'Delay' the Aging Process, but How Far Can We Actually Go?," Science Alert, April 3, 2021; Adam Gopnik, "Can We Live Longer but Stay Younger?," *New Yorker,* May 13, 2019.

The information on "deaths of despair" in the U.S. is from Anne Case and Angus Deaton, "Rising Morbidity and Mortality in Midlife among White Non-Hispanic Americans in the 21st Century," *Proceedings of the National Academy of Sciences* 112, no. 49 (November 2, 2015); Alan B. Krueger, "Where Have All the Workers Gone?," paper prepared for "The Elusive 'Great' Recovery: Causes and Implications for Future Business Cycle

Dynamics," Sixtieth Annual Economic Conference, Federal Reserve Bank of Boston, Boston, MA, October 14, 2016, https://www.bostonfed.org/-/media/Documents /economic/conf/great-recovery-2016/Alan-B-Krueger.pdf.

The section on changing rates of mortality by gender due to work is based on UN, *World Population Prospects: 2019 Revision;* Bertrand Desjardins, "Why Is Life Expectancy Longer for Women Than It Is for Men?," *Scientific American,* August 30, 2004; Rochelle Sharpe, "Women's Longevity Falling in Some Parts of the U.S., Stress May Be Factor," *Connecticut Health,* November 12, 2012, http://c-hit.org/2012/11/12/womens-longevity -falling-in-some-parts-of-u-s-stress-may-be-factor/; Irma T. Elo et al., "Trends in Non-Hispanic White Mortality in the United States by Metropolitan-Nonmetropolitan Status and Region, 1990–2016," *Population and Development Review* 45, no. 3 (2019): 549–583; Arun S. Hendi, "Trends in Education-Specific Life Expectancy, Data Quality, and Shifting Education Distributions: A Note on Recent Research," *Demography* 54, no. 3 (2017): 1203–1213; Monica Potts, "What's Killing Poor White Women?," *American Prospect,* September 3, 2013.

On COVID-19 mortality rate by race, see Tamara Rushovich, Marion Boulicault, and Heather Shattuck-Heidorn, "Sex Disparities in COVID-19 Mortality Vary Across US Racial Groups," *Journal of General Internal Medicine* 36 (2021): 1696–1701.

The statistics on single motherhood are from "Single Mother Statistics," Single Mother Guide, May 17, 2021, https://singlemotherguide.com/single-mother-statistics/.

The statistics on life expectancy adjusted by health status are from "Healthy Life Expectancy at Birth," UN, https://www.un.org/esa/sustdev/natlinfo/indicators /methodology_sheets/health/health_life_expectancy.pdf.

The Jan-Pieter Jansen quote is from Josephine Cumbo, "'Their House is on Fire': The Pension Crisis Sweeping the World," *Financial Times,* November 17, 2019.

Average retirement ages data come from Brendan Shaw, "Five Generations in the Workplace," Shawview Consulting, June 7, 2019, https://www.shawview.com/post/2019 /06/07/an-historical-moment-five-generations-in-the-workplace.

The government report is *Intergenerational Fairness and Provision Committee Report* (London: House of Lords, January 21, 2021), https://lordslibrary.parliament.uk /intergenerational-fairness-and-provision-committee-report/. See also Aart-Jan Riekhoff, "Pension Reforms, the Generational Welfare Contract and Preferences for Pro-Old Welfare Policies in Europe," *Social Policy & Administration* 55, no. 3 (December 2020): 501–518.

The London bus strikes of the 1950s are documented in "London Buses on the Streets, 1940s and 1950s," https://www.1900s.org.uk/1940s-london-buses.htm; "Bus Drivers and Their Special Skills, 1940s and 1950s," https://www.1900s.org.uk/1940s-london -bus-drivers.htm.

3. THE RISE AND FALL OF
THE NUCLEAR FAMILY

The data on U.S. and international households are from the Bureau of the Census, "American Families and Living Arrangements: 2021," tables H1 and FG3, https://www.census.gov/data/tables/2021/demo/families/cps-2021.html; Stephanie Kramer, "U.S. Has World's Highest Rate of Children Living in Single-Parent Households," Pew Research Center, December 12, 2019, https://www.pewresearch.org/fact-tank/2019/12/12/u-s-children-more-likely-than-children-in-other-countries-to-live-with-just-one-parent/.

The quotes on the nuclear family are from Margaret Mead and Ken Heyman, *Family* (New York: Macmillan, 1965), 77–78; David Brooks, "The Nuclear Family Was a Mistake," *Atlantic,* March 2020; Joe Pinsker, "If the Nuclear Family Has Failed, What Comes Next?," *Atlantic,* March 2020.

The quotes from women's magazines come from Francesca M. Cancian and Steven L. Gordon, "Changing Emotion Norms in Marriage: Love and Anger in U.S. Women's Magazines Since 1900," *Gender and Society* 2, no. 3 (September 1988): 308–342. The quote from Robert N. Bellah, Richard Madsen, William M. Sullivan, Ann Swidler, and Steven M. Tipton, *Habits of the Heart: Individualism and Commitment in American Life* (Berkeley: University of California Press, 1985) is on page 6. The quotes from Robert D. Putnam, *Bowling Alone: The Collapse and Revival of American Community* (New York: Simon & Schuster, 2000) are on pages 183, 277.

The data on family structure and single mothers come from OECD Family Database, https://www.oecd.org/els/family/database.htm#structure; Huizhong Wu, "Denied Benefits, Chinese Single Moms Press for Change," *Associated Press,* March 15, 2021, https://apnews.com/article/china-single-moms-denied-benefits-d7c841920b21331e7c18ca4f40e69b6a; Vivian Wang, "For China's Single Mothers, a Road to Recognition Paved with False Starts," *New York Times,* May 31, 2021; Kanksha Raina, "The Joys and Struggles of Being a Single Mother in India," *Kool Kanya,* July 28, 2020, https://blogs.koolkanya.com/the-joys-and-struggles-of-being-a-single-mother-in-india/; Bella DePaulo, *How We Live Now: Redefining Home and Family in the 21st Century* (New York: Simon & Schuster, 2015).

On *Little House on the Prairie,* see Diana Bruk, "11 Reasons 'Little House on the Prairie' Was Once the Best Show on Television," *Country Living,* November 12, 2014, https://www.countryliving.com/life/a6263/little-house-on-the-prairie/.

On South Korea's *I Live Alone* reality show, see Sam Kim, "South Korea Crosses a Population Rubicon in Warning to the World," *Bloomberg,* May 26, 2021.

On living alone, see Bella DePaulo, "Living Alone: Men and Women, Young to Old, Around the World," *Psychology Today,* February 28, 2020, https://www.psychologytoday.com/us/blog/living-single/202002/living-alone-men-and-women-young-old-around-the-world; Albert Esteve, David S. Reher, Rocío Treviño, Pilar Zueras, and Anna Turu, "Living Alone over the Life Course: Cross-National: Variations on an Emerging Issue," *Population and Development Review* 46, no. 1 (2019): 169–189; Eric Kilnenberg, *Going Solo: The Extraordinary Rise and Surprising Appeal of Living Alone* (New York: Duckworth Books, 2013).

On adults living with their parents, see Richard Fry, Jeffrey S. Passel, and D'Vera Cohn, "A Majority of Young Adults in the U.S. Live with Their Parents for the First Time Since the Great Depression," Pew Research Center, September 4, 2020, https://www.pewresearch.org/fact-tank/2020/09/04/a-majority-of-young-adults-in-the-u-s-live-with-their-parents-for-the-first-time-since-the-great-depression/; "When Are They Ready to Leave the Nest?," Eurostat, August 12, 2020, https://ec.europa.eu/eurostat/web/products-eurostat-news/-/edn-20200812–1; "The Ominous 'Kangaroo' Generation in Korea," Newsnpr, November 7, 2021, https://www.newsnpr.org/the-ominous-kangaroo-generation-in-korea-parents-do-not-let-their-children-be-independent-until-the-age-of-40-they-still-have-no-intention-of-leaving-the-house/; "Census Data Shows More than 42% of South Koreans in their 30s Are Unmarried," Allkpop, September 29, 2021, https://www.allkpop.com/article/2021/09/census-data-shows-more-than-42-of-south-koreans-in-their-30s-are-unmarried; Christina Newberry, "Adult Children At Home? Learn Strategies for Making It Work—Including How to Word a Contract for Adult Children Living at Home That Makes the Rules Clear!," Adult Children Living at Home, https://adultchildrenlivingathome.com/. The South Korean quotes come from the Newsnpr article above.

The quotes from Bella DePaulo's *How We Live Now: Redefining Home and Family in the 21st Century,* Kindle edition (New York: Atria Books, 2015) are on pages 5–6.

The ILGA map on sexual orientation laws is at https://ilga.org/maps-sexual-orientation-laws. The "language is a prison" quote is at https://www.reddit.com/r/Showerthoughts/comments/3qghcp/language_is_a_prison_we_cannot_break_out_of_it_is/.

On gender language and inequality, see "The Subtle Ways Language Shapes Us," BBC, https://www.bbc.com/culture/article/20201006-are-some-languages-more-sexist-than-others; Jennifer L. Prewitt-Freilino, T. Andrew Caswell, and Emmi K. Laakso, "The Gendering of Language: A Comparison of Gender Equality in Countries with Gendered, Natural Gender, and Genderless Languages," *Sex Roles* 66, nos. 3–4 (February 2011): 268–281.

On multigenerational households, see Robert Habiger, "Multigenerational Living: A Personal Experience," Dekker Perich Sabatini, https://www.dpsdesign.org/blog/multigenerational-living-a-personal-experience; Peter Muennig, Boshen Jiao, and Elizabeth Singer, "Living with Parents or Grandparents Increases Social Capital and Survival: 2014 General Social Survey—National Death Index," *SSM Population Health* 4 (April 2018): 71–75; James Tapper, "All Under One Roof: The Rise and Rise of Multigenerational Life," *Guardian,* March 10, 2019; Ian Marcus Corbin, "A Return to Multigenerational Living," Institute for Family Studies, June 22, 2020, https://ifstudies.org/blog/a-return-to-multi-generational-living; D'Vera Cohn et al., "Financial Issues

Top the List of Reasons U.S. Adults Live in Multigenerational Homes," Pew Research Center, March 24, 2022, https://www.pewresearch.org/fact-tank/2018/04/05/a-record-64-million-americans-live-in-multigenerational-households/; *Family Matters: Multigenerational Living Is on the Rise and Here to Stay* (Washington, DC: Generations United, 2021), https://www.gu.org/app/uploads/2021/04/21-MG-Family-Report-WEB.pdf; Gemma Burgess and Kathryn Muir, "The Increase in Multigenerational Households in the UK: The Motivations for and Experiences of Multigenerational Living," *Housing, Theory and Society* 37, no. 3 (2020): 322–338; Shannon Guzman, "Multigenerational Housing on the Rise, Fueled by Economic and Social Changes," AARP Public Policy Institute, June 2019, https://www.aarp.org/content/dam/aarp/ppi/2019/06/multigenerational-housing.doi.org.10.26419–2Fppi.00071.001.pdf; Daphne Lofquist, "Multigenerational Households," U.S. Census Bureau, working paper #2013–20, https://www.census.gov/content/dam/Census/library/working-papers/2013/acs/lofquist-01.pdf.

On communes and utopias, see Rosabeth Moss Kanter, *Community and Commitment* (Cambridge, MA: Harvard University Press, 1972).

4. REBELS WITHOUT A CAUSE?

On parental pressure on teenagers, see Janet Sasson Edgette, "Let's Stop Stressing Out Our Kids with Career Choice Pressure," *Philadelphia Inquirer,* March 11, 2019; Elena Blanco-Suarez, "The Myths About the Teenage Brain," *Psychology Today,* March 19, 2019, https://www.psychologytoday.com/us/blog/brain-chemistry/201903/the-myths-about-the-teenage-brain; Richard Wike, "Americans Say Kids Need More Pressure in School, Chinese Say Less," Pew Research Center, August 22, 2013, https://www.pewresearch.org/fact-tank/2013/08/22/americans-say-kids-need-more-pressure-in-school-chinese-say-less/; Amy Morin, "The Dangers of Putting Too Much Pressure on Kids," Verywell Family, September 22, 2020, https://www.verywellfamily.com/the-dangers-of-putting-too-much-pressure-on-kids-1094823.

On student performance, see PISA 2018 results, https://www.oecd.org/pisa/PISA-results_ENGLISH.png; "Dropout Rates," National Center for Education Statistics, https://nces.ed.gov/fastfacts/display.asp?id=16; H. Dryler, "Parental Role Models, Gender, and Educational Choice," *British Journal of Sociology* 49, no. 3 (September 1998): 375–398; Grace Chen, "Parental Involvement Is Key to Student Success," Public School Review, August 14, 2021, https://www.publicschoolreview.com/blog/parental-involvement-is-key-to-student-success.

On college decisions, see John Katzman and Steve Cohen, "Why Parents Pick the Wrong Colleges for Their Kids," *Time,* April 14, 2017; Kristin van Ogtrop, "A Letter of Apology to a Son Graduating from College," *Time,* April 13, 2017; Anna Raskind, "Major Problems: How to Choose a Major Under Pressure," *Columbia Daily Spectator,* April 21, 2016; Leighann Camarero, "When It Comes to Choosing a Major, College Students Feel the Pressure," WAMC Northeast Public Radio, April 4, 2013, https://www.wamc.org /post/when-it-comes-choosing-major-college-students-feel-pressure; Editorial Board, "Do Parentals Pressure Career Choices?," *Ledger,* November 14, 2018; Sonu Kumari Singh, "Academic and Psychological Consequences of Imposed Career Choices," master's thesis, National Institute of Technology, Rourkela, India, May 2015, https://core .ac.uk/download/pdf/80147549.pdf.

On perfectionism, see Rachel Simmons, "Perfectionism Among Teens Is Rampant (and We're Not Helping)," *Washington Post,* January 25, 2018; Thomas Curran and Andrew P. Hill, "Perfectionism Is Increasing Over Time: A Meta-Analysis of Birth Cohort Differences from 1989 to 2016," *Psychological Bulletin* 145, no. 4 (2019): 410–429.

The story of Alexandra Morgan Gruber is based on her U.S. Senate testimony, "No Place to Grow Up," May 19, 2015, United States Finance Committee, https://www.finance .senate.gov/imo/media/doc/Gruber%20Testimony.pdf.

The data on college assistance programs by state are from "Tuition Waivers by State," University of Washington, https://depts.washington.edu/fostered/tuition-waivers -state.

The study on recovering addicts was authored by David Eddie et al., "From Working on Recovery to Working in Recovery," *Journal of Substance Abuse and Treatment* 113 (June 2020).

On skills in the labor force, see "The Professional and Technical Workforce: By the Numbers," AFL-CIO Department for Professional Employees, September 27, 2021, https: //www.dpeaflcio.org/factsheets/the-professional-and-technical-workforce-by-the -numbers; David J. Deming, "The Growing Importance of Social Skills in the Labor Market," *Quarterly Journal of Economics* 132, no. 4 (November 2017): 1593–1640; J. D. Mayer, R. D. Roberts, and S. R. Barsade, "Human Abilities: Emotional Intelligence," *Annual Review of Psychology* 59 (2008): 507–536; *The Future of Jobs* (Geneva: World Economic Forum, January 2016), http://www3.weforum.org/docs/WEF_Future_of _Jobs.pdf.

The Calton Pu quote is from Nicole Krueger, "Preparing Students for Jobs That Don't Exist," ISTE, August 31, 2021, https://www.iste.org/explore/ISTE-blog/Preparing -students-for-jobs-that-don%27t-exist.

The quotes from work and technology experts are from "The Future of Jobs and Jobs Training," Pew Research Center, May 3, 2017, https://www.pewresearch.org/internet /2017/05/03/the-future-of-jobs-and-jobs-training/; National Academies of Science, Engineering, and Medicine, *Information Technology and the U.S. Workforce* (Washington, DC: National Academies Press, 2017), https://www.nap.edu/read/24649 /chapter/1.

The quote by Picasso is from William Fifield, "Pablo Picasso: A Composite Interview," *Paris Review* 32 (summer-fall 1964).

On financial literacy and functional illiteracy, see Annamaria Lusardi and Olivia S. Mitchell, "The Economic Importance of Financial Literacy: Theory and Evidence," *Journal of Economic Literature* 52, no. 1 (2014): 5–44; Meredith Cicerchia and Chris

Freeman, "How Common Is Functional Illiteracy?," Touch-type Read and Spell, https://www.readandspell.com/functional-illiteracy.

On learning foreign languages, see "Which Countries Are Best at English as a Second Language?," World Economic Forum, November 2019, https://www.weforum.org/agenda/2019/11/countries-that-speak-english-as-a-second-language. See also Mauro F. Guillén, "The Real Reasons to Support Language Study," *Chronicle of Higher Education,* July 27, 2009, https://www.chronicle.com/article/the-real-reasons-to-support-language-study/.

The quote by Walter Long is from Byron Pitts, "Battling the Scourge of Illiteracy," CBS News, October 4, 2009, https://www.cbsnews.com/news/battling-the-scourge-of-illiteracy/; Daniel Lattier, "32 Million U.S. Adults Are 'Functionally Illiterate' . . . What Does That Even Mean?," Intellectual Takeout, August 26, 2015, https://www.intellectualtakeout.org/blog/32-million-us-adults-are-functionally-illiterate-what-does-even-mean/; "National Assessment of Adult Literacy (NAAL)," National Center for Education Statistics, https://nces.ed.gov/naal/; "Program for the International Assessment of Adult Competencies," National Center for Education Statistics, https://nces.ed.gov/surveys/piaac/; "Survey of Adult Skills," OECD, https://www.oecd.org/skills/piaac/.

5. THREE CAREERS IN A LIFETIME

On career switching, see Stacy Rapacon, "Career Change Is the New Normal of Working," CNBC, April 27, 2016, https://www.cnbc.com/2016/04/26/career-change-is-the-new-normal-of-working.html; Helen Barrett, "Plan for Five Careers in a Lifetime," *Financial Times,* September 5, 2017.

On the future of online education, see "The Future of Jobs and Jobs Training," Pew Research Center, May 3, 2017, https://www.pewresearch.org/internet/2017/05/03/the-future-of-jobs-and-jobs-training/; Emma Jacobs and Aimee Keane, "Career Changers: Cracking It as a Coder," *Financial Times,* August 30, 2018, including the quotes by Hannah Cross and Martha Chambers; https://www.ft.com/content/1ee55290–963e-11e8-b67b-b8205561c3fe; "Creativity Peaks in Your 20s and 30s," BBC News, April 27, 2019, https://www.bbc.com/news/newsbeat-48077012.

On technology and job destruction, see Andrew J. Chapin, "Forget Robots, Blockchain Technology May Be the Real Threat to Your Job," *Observer,* November 18, 2018, https://observer.com/2018/11/blockchain-smart-contracts-middle-management-jobs/; "Resoundingly Human: Robots on the Job—What's the Real Impact for Their Human Counterparts?," Knowledge at Wharton, November 6, 2020, https://ai.wharton.upenn.edu/news-stories/resoundingly-human-robots-on-the-job-whats-the-real-impact-for-their-human-counterparts/; Joe McKendrick, "It's Managers, Not Workers, Who Are Losing Jobs to AI and Robots, Study Shows," *Forbes,* November 15, 2020, https://www.forbes.com/sites/joemckendrick/2020/11/15

/its-managers-not-workers-who-are-losing-jobs-to-ai-and-robots-study-shows/?sh
=22fd3ce520d5; *Technology and the Future of the Government Workforce* (Walldorf,
Germany: SAP, 2020), https://www.instituteforgovernment.org.uk/sites/default
/files/publications/tech-future-government-workforce.pdf; "The Future of Public
Service," Deloitte, https://www2.deloitte.com/us/en/pages/public-sector/articles
/future-of-public-service.html.

For seniors and education, see "China Focus: Silver-Haired Students Rise Against
Population Ageing," XinhuaNet, May 8, 2017, http://www.xinhuanet.com//english
/2017–05/08/c_136266199.htm; Neha Thirani Bagri, "China's Seniors Are Lining up
to Go Back to College," Quartz, May 9, 2017, https://qz.com/978805/chinas-seniors
-are-lining-up-to-go-back-to-college/; *Tech and the Modern Grandparent* (Washington, DC: AARP, 2019), https://www.aarp.org/content/dam/aarp/research/surveys
_statistics/life-leisure/2019/aarp-grandparenting-study-technology-fact-sheet.doi
.10.26419–2Fres.00289.016.pdf; Peter Rinderud, "Seniors and Technology During
Covid-19," Ericsson, January 26, 2021, https://www.ericsson.com/en/blog/2021/1
/seniors-and-technology-during-covid; Laurie Quinn, "Going Back to College After
50: The New Normal?," *Forbes,* July 1, 2018; Jacob Share, "Career Changes After 40:
True Stories of Real People Who Succeeded," JobMob, April 4, 2019, https://jobmob
.co.il/blog/career-changes-after-40-success-stories/; "Is It Too Late to Become a
Doctor? Not According to Today's Medical Students," St. George's University Medical School, May 20, 2021, https://www.sgu.edu/blog/medical/becoming-a-doctor
-later-in-life/.

On the average number of jobs over people's lifetime, see "Number of Jobs, Labor Market Experience, Marital Status, and Health," Bureau of Labor Statistics, August 31,
2021, https://www.bls.gov/news.release/pdf/nlsoy.pdf; "Average Time Spent with
One Employer in European Countries 2020," Statista, August 4, 2021, https://www
.statista.com/statistics/1209552/average-time-spent-with-one-employer-in-europe/.

For the multigenerational workplace, see "Managing the Multigenerational Workplace,"
January 1, 2014, Future of Work Hub, https://www.futureofworkhub.info/allcontent
/2014/1/1/managing-the-multigenerational-workplace; Caroline Ngonyo Njoroge
and Rashad Yazdanifard, "The Impact of Social and Emotional Intelligence on Employee Motivation in a Multigenerational Workplace," *Global Journal of Management
and Business Research* 14, no. 3 (2014); Eddy S. Ng and Emma Parry, "Multigenerational Research in Human Resource Management," in *Review in Personnel and
Human Resources Management* (Bingley, England: Emerald, 2016), 1–41; "The Hartford's Reverse Mentoring Program," *Profiles in Diversity Journal,* July 1, 2013, https:
//diversityjournal.com/11474-the-hartfords-reverse-mentoring-program/; Carol
Hymowitz, "The Tricky Task of Managing the New, Multigenerational Workplace,"
Wall Street Journal, August 12, 2018; David Mallon, Yves Van Durme, and Maren
Hauptmann, "The Postgenerational Workforce: From Millennials to Perennials,"
Deloitte, May 15, 2020, https://www2.deloitte.com/us/en/insights/focus/human
-capital-trends/2020/leading-a-multigenerational-workforce.html; "The Perennial

Mindset in the Era of Ageless with Gina Pell and Susan Hoffman," Arts Research Center, University of California, Berkeley, https://arts.berkeley.edu/the-perennial -mindset-in-the-era-of-ageless-with-gina-pell-and-susan-hoffman/; Lindsey Pollak, *The Remix: How to Lead and Succeed in the Multigenerational Workplace* (New York: Harper Business, 2019).

For millennials as a label, see "Most Millennials Resist the 'Millennial' Label," Pew Research Center, September 3, 2015, https://www.pewresearch.org/politics/2015/09 /03/most-millennials-resist-the-millennial-label/.

The Peter Cappelli quote is from Carol Hymowitz, "The Tricky Task of Managing the New, Multigenerational Workplace," *Wall Street Journal,* August 12, 2018. See also Peter Cappelli and Bill Novelli, *Managing the Older Worker: How to Prepare for the New Organizational Order* (Boston, MA: Harvard Business Review Press, 2010).

The Preziosi, Weisman, and Feinberg quotes are from "Company Culture and the Multigenerational Workforce," Built In, May 10, 2021, https://builtin.com/company -culture/multigenerational-workforce.

6. REIMAGINING RETIREMENT

On objections to retirement, see Eric Brotman, "Why Retirement Is a Bad Idea Financially and Psychologically," *Forbes,* June 30, 2020, https://www.forbes.com /sites/ericbrotman/2020/06/30/why-retirement-is-a-bad-idea-financially-and -psychologically/?sh=4cbc5ce53c76.

The interviews with Toni and Toby are from Don Ezra, "#56 Interviews about Retirement," *Life After Full-Time Work* (blog), 2017, https://donezra.com/56-interviews -about-retirement/.

For retirement's impact on health, see Iris van der Heide et al., "Is Retirement Good for Your Health? A Systematic Review of Longitudinal Studies," *Academic BMC Public Health* 13, no. 1 (2013): 1–22; Elizabeth Mokyr Horner et al., "The Impact of Retirement on Health," *MBC Health Services Research* 16 (2016): 1–9; Ranu Sewdas, "Association Between Retirement and Mortality: Working Longer, Living Longer?," *Journal of Epidemiology and Community Health* 74 (2020): 473–480; *Living in the Covid-19 Pandemic: The Health, Finances, and Retirement Prospects of Four Generations* (Cedar Rapids, IA: Transamerica Center for Retirement Studies, August 2021), https://transamericacenter.org/docs/default-source/retirement-survey-of-workers /tcrs2021_sr_four-generations-living-in-a-pandemic.pdf.

On how seniors spend their time, see "American Time Use Survey," Bureau of Labor Statistics, https://www.bls.gov/TUS/CHARTS/OLDER.HTM; Jasmin Collier, "Excessive Daily TV at Older Age Tied to Poorer Memory," *Medical News Today,* March 1, 2019, https://www.medicalnewstoday.com/articles/324598; Gretchen Livingston, "Americans 60 and Older Are Spending More Time in Front of Their Screens Than a Decade Ago," Pew Research Center, June 18, 2019, https://www.pewresearch.org

/fact-tank/2019/06/18/americans-60-and-older-are-spending-more-time-in-front
-of-their-screens-than-a-decade-ago/; AJ Dellinger, "How the Elderly Spend Their
Time with Screens," Mic, August 15, 2019, https://www.mic.com/life/screen-time
-is-higher-for-the-elderly-than-younger-people-new-data-reports-18660210; Edward
C. Baig, "Worried About Increased Screen Time? Think About Its Quality," AARP,
April 6, 2020, https://www.aarp.org/home-family/personal-technology/info-2020
/increased-screen-time.html, including Marick quote; Katharine G. Abraham and
Susan N. Houseman, "Policies to Improve Workforce Services for Older Americans,"
Economic Studies at Brookings, November 2020, https://www.brookings.edu/wp
-content/uploads/2020/11/ES-11.19.20-Abraham-Houseman.pdf.

On retirement around the world, see "At 54, China's Average Retirement Age Is Too
Low," *Economist*, June 24, 2021; Kasper Lippert-Rasmussen, "The EU and Age Discrimination: Abolishing Mandatory Retirement!," Twelve Stars, March 7, 2019, https:
//www.twelvestars.eu/post/kasper-lippert-rasmussen.

On seniors and employment growth, see William R. Emmons, "Older Workers Ac-
counted for All Net Employment Growth in Past 20 Years," Federal Reserve Bank
of St. Louis, February 1, 2021, https://www.stlouisfed.org/on-the-economy/2021
/february/older-workers-accounted-all-net-employment-growth; Jo Ann Jenkins,
"It's Time to Rethink Aging and Retirement, AARP's Jenkins Says," *Barron's*, May
17, 2021; Nicole Maestas, "Back to Work: Expectations and Realizations of Work
after Retirement," *Journal of Human Resources* 45, no. 3 (summer 2010): 718–748;
Nicole Maestas, "Why Are People Unretiring?," Retirement Wisdom, August 2, 2018,
https://www.retirementwisdom.com/podcasts/why-are-people-unretiring-nicole
-maestas/.

On work after retirement, see Sherry E. Sullivan and Adram Al Ariss, "Employment
After Retirement: A Review Framework for Future Research," *Journal of Management*
45, no. 1 (January 2019): 262–284; Zaria Gorvett, "What If We Have to Work Until
We're 100?," BBC, July 16, 2018, https://www.bbc.com/worklife/article/20180710
-whats-it-like-working-past-your-100th-birthday, including the quote by Jane Falkingham.

On seniors, technology, and remote work, see Lisa Michaels, "How Is Workplace
Technology Supporting an Ageing Workforce," DiversityQ, August 7, 2020, https:
//diversityq.com/how-is-workplace-technology-supporting-an-ageing-workforce
-1509859/; Kerry Hannon, "5 Reasons Working from Home Benefits Older
Workers—and Their Employers," AARP, June 9, 2020, https://www.aarp.org/work
/working-at-50-plus/info-2020/telework-benefits.html; Caitlin Powell, "Older People Who Work from Home More Likely to Stay in the Workforce, ONS Finds," *People
Management*, August 31, 2021, https://www.peoplemanagement.co.uk/news/articles
/older-people-work-from-home-more-likely-stay-workforce-ons#gref.

On gig jobs, see Eileen Applebaum, Arne Kalleberg, and Hye Jin Rho, "Nonstan-
dard Work Arrangements and Older Americans, 2005–2017," Economic Policy Institute, February 28, 2019, https://www.epi.org/publication/nonstandard-work

-arrangements-and-older-americans-2005–2017/; "UK's Gig Economy Workforce Has Doubled Since 2016," TUC, June 28, 2019, https://www.tuc.org.uk/news/uks -gig-economy-workforce-has-doubled-2016-tuc-and-feps-backed-research-shows; Damjan Jugovic Spajic, "The Future of Employment: 30 Telling Gig Economy Sta- tistics," SmallBizGenius, May 26, 2021, https://www.smallbizgenius.net/by-the -numbers/gig-economy-statistics/#gref; Andrew Fennell, "Gig Economy Statistics UK," StandOutCV, January 2022, https://standout-cv.com/gig-economy-statistics -uk; Elaine Pofeldt, "Why Older Workers Are Embracing the Gig Economy," *Forbes*, August 30, 2017, https://www.forbes.com/sites/elainepofeldt/2017/08/30/why -older-workers-are-embracing-the-gig-economy/?sh=193903aa42ce; Leonardo Castañeda, "Boomers, Not Millennials, May Be the Most Active Generation in the Gig Economy," *Mercury News,* June 28, 2019, including the description of the Wonolo study.

For COVID-19 and retirement inequality, see Brett Arends, "How the Covid Crisis Is Making Retirement Inequality Worse," MarketWatch, September 11, 2021, https:// www.marketwatch.com/story/how-the-covid-crisis-is-making-retirement-inequality -worse-11631201005; Owen Davis et al., "The Pandemic Retirement Surge Increased Retirement Inequality," Schwartz Center for Economic Policy Analysis, June 1, 2021, https://www.economicpolicyresearch.org/jobs-report/the-pandemic-retirement -surge-increased-retirement-inequality; Mark Miller, "America's Retirement Race Gap, and Ideas for Closing It," *New York Times,* August 14, 2020.

7. INHERITING AT ONE HUNDRED

The quote by Charles Dickens is from *Our Mutual Friend* (1864–1865), chapter 11, available from Project Gutenberg, https://www.gutenberg.org/cache/epub/883 /pg883-images.html.

For longevity and inheritance expectations, see Richard Venturi, "Inherited Wealth in Greying Societies," France Stratégie, July 6, 2017, https://www.strategie.gouv.fr /english-articles/inherited-wealth-greying-societies; Amy Feldman, "When Lon- gevity Upends Trusts," *Forbes*, November 29, 2014; Amy Fontinelle, "Why Millen- nials Should Not Rely on an Inheritance," MassMutual, July 28, 2020, https://blog .massmutual.com/post/why-millennials-should-not-rely-on-an-inheritance; "Survey of Consumer Finances (SCF)," Board of Governors of the Federal Reserve System, https://www.federalreserve.gov/econres/aboutscf.htm; Will Kenton, "Average Inheritance: How Much Are Retirees Leaving to Heirs?," NewRetirement, June 29, 2020, https://www.newretirement.com/retirement/average-inheritance-how -much-are-retirees-leaving-to-heirs/; Nicolas Gattig, "'Inheritance Mother': Tack- ling Taboo of Caring for Elderly Parents," *Japan Times,* August 12, 2017; "Ameriprise Study: Family Financial Discussions Go Smoother Than Anticipated, but Unrealis- tic Inheritance Expectations Persist," BusinessWire, March 15, 2017, https://www

.businesswire.com/news/home/20170315005007/en/Ameriprise-Study-Family
-Financial-Discussions-Go-Smoother-Than-Anticipated-But-Unrealistic-Inheritance
-Expectations-Persist, including Keckler quote; "Despite Good Intentions, Millennials and Gen Z Are Demonstrating Unrealistic Expectations About Their Financial Futures," BusinessWire, August 13, 2018, https://www.businesswire.com/news
/home/20180813005101/en/Despite-Good-Intentions-Millennials-and-Gen-Z
-Are-Demonstrating-Unrealistic-Expectations-About-Their-Financial-Futures, including Charles Schwab quote; "Over-Optimistic UK Adults Overestimating Their
Inheritance," Just, https://www.wearejust.co.uk/waj-archive/ARCHIVED-my-home
-my-future/ARCHIVED-inheritance-expectations/; "Millennials 'Misjudging Inher-
intance Windfall,'" Week, May 10, 2019; Gail Johnson, "Nearly Half of Canadians
Are Banking on an Inheritance to Meet Their Financial Goals. What Are the Dangers?," Globe and Mail, October 22, 2019; Edward Jones, "Canadians Are Banking
on an Inheritance as Many Struggle to Meet Their Financial Goals," Newswire Canada, September 30, 2019, https://www.newswire.ca/news-releases/edward-jones
-survey-canadians-are-banking-on-an-inheritance-as-many-struggle-to-meet-their
-financial-goals-834230408.html; Mary R. Tomlinson, "Gen Y Housing Aspirations
Could Depend on a Housing Inheritance," Future Justice issue paper, https://www
.futurejustice.com.au/reports/pdf/GenY-Housing-Inheritance-issue-paper.pdf; "The
Inheritance Expectation," Eldernet, October 12, 2021, https://www.eldernet.co.nz
/gazette/the-inheritance-expectation-experts-say-spend-it-while-you-can/; Jay Zagorsky, "Do People Save or Spend Their Inheritances? Understanding What Happens
to Inherited Wealth," Journal of Family and Economic Issues 34, no. 1 (March 2013):
64–76.

On the intergenerational contact around the world, see Misa Izuhara, "Care and Inheritance: Japanese and English Perspectives on the 'Generational Contract,'" Ageing &
Society 22, no. 1 (January 2002): 61–77; Yun Sheng, "Little Emperors," London Review
of Books 38, no. 10 (May 19, 2016); Christina Zhou, "One-Child Policy: A Look Inside
the Struggles and Benefits of China's 'Little Emperor' Generation," ABC News Australia, February 3, 2018, https://www.abc.net.au/news/2018–02–03/the-struggles
-and-benefits-of-chinas-little-emperor-generation/9323300; Tanza Loudenback,
"The Typical American Heir Is Now a Middle-Class 50-Something Who Puts the
Money Toward Retirement," Business Insider, November 21, 2019, https://www
.businessinsider.com/personal-finance/older-americans-get-more-inheritances-use
-for-retirement-2019–11, including the Lincoln Plews quote.

On Samsung's Lee family, see Joyce Lee and Keekyoung Yang, "Samsung's Lee Family
to Pay More Than $10.8 Bln Inheritance Tax," Reuters, April 28, 2021, https://www
.reuters.com/business/samsungs-lee-family-pay-more-than-12-trln-won-inheritance
-taxes-2021–04–28/; Choe Sang-Hun, "An Inheritance Tax Bill You 'Can't Fathom':
$10.8 Billion," New York Times, April 28, 2021; Bae Hyunjung, "Samsung Estate Sparks
Debate on Inheritance Tax," Korea Herald, May 11, 2021.

On inheritance taxes and inequality, see Inheritance Taxation in OECD Countries (Paris:

OECD, 2021), 74–75; Facundo Alvaredo, Bertrand Garbinti, and Thomas Piketty, "On the Share of Inheritance in Aggregate Wealth: Europe and the USA, 1900–2010," *Economica* 84, no. 334 (April 2017): 239–260; Mikael Elinder, Oscar Erixson, and Daneil Waldenstrom, "Inheritance and Wealth Inequality: Evidence from Population Registers," *Journal of Public Economics* 165 (September 2018): 17–30; Meredith Haggerty, "The Impact of Inheritance," Vox, March 23, 2021, https://www.vox.com/the-highlight/22320272/inheritance-money-wealth-transfer-estate-tax; "Inheritance for All," Friedrich Ebert Stiftung, March 31, 2020, https://www.ips-journal.eu/interviews/inheritance-for-all-4207/, including the quote by Piketty; Eric Levitz, "Will 'the Great Wealth Transfer' Trigger a Millennial Civil War?," *New York,* July 18, 2021, https://nymag.com/intelligencer/2021/07/will-the-great-wealth-transfer-spark-a-millennial-civil-war.html.

For the impact of remarrying on inheritance, see Gretchen Livingston, "The Demographics of Remarriage," Pew Research Center, November 14, 2014, https://www.pewresearch.org/social-trends/2014/11/14/chapter-2-the-demographics-of-remarriage/; Sarah O'Brien, "Remarried After Having Kids? Here Are Tips to Avoid Accidentally Disinheriting Them," CNBC, January 17, 2019, https://www.cnbc.com/2019/01/17/estate-planning-for-second-marriages-when-you-have-kids.html; Jamie M. Lewis and Rose M. Kreider, "Remarriage in the United States," United States Census Bureau Report Number ACS-30, March 10, 2015, https://www.census.gov/library/publications/2015/acs/acs-30.html; Tammy La Gorce, "When Your Parents Remarry, Everyone Is Happy, Right?," *New York Times,* March 22, 2018, including the quotes on this topic.

For women and inheritance throughout history, see Suzanne McGee and Heidi Moore, "Women's Rights and Their Money: A Timeline from Cleopatra to Lilly Ledbetter," *Guardian,* August 11, 2014; "Women, Business, and the Law Database," World Bank, https://wbl.worldbank.org/en/wbl; Pooneh Baghai et al., "Women as the Next Wave of Growth in US Wealth Management," McKinsey, July 29, 2020, https://www.mckinsey.com/industries/financial-services/our-insights/women-as-the-next-wave-of-growth-in-us-wealth-management; "Women's Wealth 2030: Parity, Power, and Purpose," UBS, March 8, 2021, https://www.ubs.com/global/en/wealth-management/women/2021/women-wealth-parity-power-purpose.html; "How Women's Wealth Is Driving Economic Change," Barclays, March 6, 2020, https://privatebank.barclays.com/news-and-insights/womens-rising-wealth/; "The Face of Wealth and Legacy: How Women Are Redefining Wealth, Giving, and Legacy Planning," RBC Wealth Management, https://www.rbcwealthmanagement.com/gb/en/research-insights/the-new-face-of-wealth-and-legacy-how-women-are-redefining-wealth-giving-and-legacy-planning/detail/; Warren Lewis, "Majority of Women Planning on Leaving an Inheritance Unlikely to Seek Advice," Financial Reporter, October 5, 2021, https://www.financialreporter.co.uk/finance-news/majority-of-women-planning-on-leaving-an-inheritance-unlikey-to-seek-financial-advice.html, including Mealing quote; Tanita Jamil, "The Inheritance Challenge Facing Women

in the Sandwich Generation," St. James's Place, January 7, 2021, https://www.sjp.co
.uk/news/how-to-manage-inheritance; "$8.5 Billion Inheritance Skipping a Genera-
tion Every Year," One Family, August 7, 2019, https://www.onefamily.com/our-story
/media-centre/2019/8–5-billion-inheritance-skipping-a-generation-every-year/.

8. A GAME CHANGER FOR WOMEN

For women, motherhood, and the biological clock, see Carley Fortune, "The Career
Advice I Wish I Got Before Having a Baby," Refinery29, July 23, 2020, https://www
.refinery29.com/en-gb/2020/07/9929316/career-advice-for-new-mothers; Richard
Cohen, "The Clock Is Ticking for the Career Woman," *Washington Post,* March 16,
1978; Moira Weigel, "The Foul Reign of the Biological Clock," *Guardian,* May 10,
2016; Quoctrung Bui and Claire Cain Miller, "The Age That Women Have Babies:
How a Gap Divides America," *New York Times,* August 4, 2018, including quote by
Heather Rakin; Melinda Mills et al., "Why Do People Postpone Parenthood?," *Human
Reproduction Update* 17, no. 6 (November–December 2011): 848–860.

For women's careers, see Sharon Mavin, "Women's Career in Theory and Practice:
Time for Change?," *Women in Management Review* 16, no. 4 (2011): 183–192; Patrick
Ishizuka and Kelly Musick, "Occupational Inflexibility and Women's Employment
During the Transition to Parenthood," *Demography* 58, no. 4 (221): 1249–1274.

For women's work and stress, see "Women More Likely to Be Stressed Than Men," Priory, https://www.priorygroup.com/blog/why-are-stress-levels-among-women-50
-higher-than-men, including Mohring quote; Nancy Beauregard et al., "Gendered
Pathways to Burnout: Results from the SALVEO Study," *Annals of Work Exposures
and Health* 2, no. 4 (May 2018): 426–437; "For Mothers in the Workplace, a Year
(and Counting) Like No Other," McKinsey, May 5, 2021, https://www.mckinsey.com
/featured-insights/diversity-and-inclusion/for-mothers-in-the-workplace-a-year-and
-counting-like-no-other.

For more on women's careers, see Marianne Cooper, "Mothers' Careers Are at Extraordinary Risk Right Now," *Atlantic,* October 1, 2020, https://www.theatlantic
.com/family/archive/2020/10/pandemic-amplifying-bias-against-working-mothers
/616565/; Michelle Fox, "Men Have Been Promoted 3 Times More Than Women
During the Pandemic, Study Finds," CNBC, October 13, 2020, https://www.cnbc
.com/2020/10/13/pandemic-fallout-men-got-3-times-more-promotions-than
-women.html, including Qualtrics/theBoardlist study; Caitlin Powell, "Could Working from Home Stall Women's Careers?," *People Management,* November 15, 2021,
https://www.peoplemanagement.co.uk/news/articles/could-working-from-home
-stall-womens-careers#gref, including Dr. Stephenson quote.

Allison's story is from Jen Gann, "6 Women on How They've Been Treated at Work After
Having Kids," *New York,* June 13, 2018.

On the motherhood penalty, see Shelley Zalis, "The Motherhood Penalty: Why We're

Losing Our Best Talent to Caregiving," *Forbes,* February 22, 2019; *The Pursuit of Gender Equality: An Uphill Battle* (Paris: OECD, 2017), figures 12.3, 12.4, and 12.5; Henrik Kleven, Camille Landais, and Jakob Egholt Sogaard, "Children and Gender Inequality: Evidence from Denmark," National Bureau of Economic Research, working paper 24219; Claire Cain Miller, "The Motherhood Penalty vs. the Fatherhood Bonus," *New York Times,* September 6, 2014, including Budig quote; Katja Möhring, "Is There a Motherhood Penalty in Retirement Income in Europe?," *Ageing & Society* 38, no. 2 (December 2018): 2560–2589; M. Gough and M. Noonan, "A Review of the Motherhood Wage Penalty in the United States," *Sociology Compass* 7, no. 4 (2013): 328–342; M. J. Budig and P. England, "The Wage Penalty for Motherhood," *American Sociological Review* 66 (2001): 204–225; M. J. Budig, J. Misra, and I. Boeckmann, "The Motherhood Penalty in Cross-National Perspective: The Importance of Work-Family Policies and Cultural Attitudes," *Social Politics: International Studies in Gender, State & Society* 19, no. 2 (2012): 163–193; *The Pursuit of Gender Equality: An Uphill Battle,* figure 13.14; Gann, "6 Women," including the Sally quotes; Joan R. Kahn, Javier Garcia-Manglano, and Suzanne M. Bianchi, "The Motherhood Penalty at Midlife," *Journal of Marriage & Family* 76, no. 1 (February 2014): 56–72.

On mothers' guilt of not working, see Katie Martin, "When Women Choose Children Over a Career," *Atlantic,* December 19, 2016, https://www.theatlantic.com/business /archive/2016/12/opting-out/500018/.

On the "mommy track," see Felice N. Schwartz, "Management Women and the New Facts of Life," *Harvard Business Review,* January–February 1989; Tamar Lewin, "'Mommy Career Track' Sets Off a Furor," *New York Times,* March 8, 1989; Lisa Endlich Heffernan, "Want to Keep Mothers in the Workforce? Make It Possible for Them to Stay," Vox, May 7, 2015, https://www.vox.com/2015/5/4/8523753/mommy -track, including examples of Vodafone and IBM; Cathy Barrera, "The Economics of the 'Mommy Track' Explain Why Parental Leave Isn't Enough," Quartz, February 6, 2018, https://qz.com/work/1189295/the-economics-of-the-mommy-track-explain -why-offering-parental-leave-isnt-enough/.

For public policies and women's careers, see Melinda Mills, "Why Do People Postpone Parenthood?"

On teenage mothers, see Courtney Pellegrino, "The Lived Experiences of Teenage Mothers That Foster Resiliency," doctor of education thesis, Northeastern University, Boston, MA, August 2014, including Stassi's quote, page 56, https://repository .library.northeastern.edu/files/neu:336610/fulltext.pdf; "Reproductive Health: Teen Pregnancy," Centers for Disease Control and Prevention, November 15, 2021, https: //www.cdc.gov/teenpregnancy/about/index.htm.

The story of Erica Alfaro is based on Eric Breier, "From Teen Mom to College Graduate," California State University at San Marcos, May 8, 2017, https://news.csusm.edu/from -teen-mom-to-college-graduate/.

The data on teen pregnancies and births is from "Trends in Teen Pregnancies and

Childbearing," U.S. Department of Health & Human Services, https://opa.hhs.gov/adolescent-health/reproductive-health-and-teen-pregnancy/trends-teen-pregnancy-and-childbearing; "Early Childbearing," UNICEF, May 2021, https://data.unicef.org/topic/child-health/adolescent-health/; Josephine Nabugoomu, Gloria K. Seruwagi, and Rhoa Hanning, "What Can Be Done to Reduce the Prevalence of Teen Pregnancy in Rural Eastern Uganda?," *Reproductive Health* 17, no. 134 (2020); Nana Yaa Konadu Gyesaw and Augustine Ankomah, "Experiences of Pregnancy and Motherhood Among Teenage Mothers in a Suburb of Accra, Ghana," *International Journal of Women's Health* 5 (2013): 773–780; "National Single Parent Day," U.S. Bureau of the Census, https://www.census.gov/newsroom/stories/single-parent-day.html.

For women returning to school, see Andrew J. Hostetler, Stephen Sweet, and Phyllis Moen, "Gendered Career Paths: A Life Course Perspective on Returning to School," *Sex Roles* 56 (2007): 85–103; Amy B. Valente, "Back on the Career Path: A Qualitative Study of Employment Transitions for Women Who Take a Career Break and Their Re-Entry Experiences," doctoral thesis, Northeastern University, Boston, MA, December 2019, https://repository.library.northeastern.edu/files/neu:m044ww78b/fulltext.pdf; Zoe May Simpson, "The Return of Teen Mothers to the Formal School System," doctoral thesis, University of Sheffield, August 2010, https://etheses.whiterose.ac.uk/14998/1/555516.pdf; Linnea Lynne Watson, "Educational Resiliency in Teen Mothers," doctoral dissertation, University of Northern Colorado, Greeley, CO, January 12, 2014, https://digscholarship.unco.edu/cgi/viewcontent.cgi?article=1272&context=dissertations; Zarina Chogan and Malose Langa, "Teenage Mothers Talk About Their Experience of Teenage Motherhood," *Agenda: Empowering Women for Gender Equity* 25, no. 3 (2011): 87–95, including the Sue quote, page 91; "10 Teen Pregnancy Quotes," Texas Adoption Center, December 12, 2019, including the quote from the fifteen-year-old mother, https://www.texasadoptioncenter.org/blog/teen-pregnancy-quotes/.

9. THE POSTGENERATIONAL CONSUMER MARKET

For marketing and generations, see "Marketing to People Based on Their 'Generation' Will Ultimately Fail," Dragonfly Marketing, https://dragonflymarketing.com.au/marketing-people-based-generation-will-ultimately-fail/; Laura Slattery, "Advertisers' Portrayal of Older People Isn't Just Alienating, It's Self-Defeating," *Irish Times*, October 25, 2021, including the Odgers quote; Sonya Matejko, "How to Bridge the Age Gap in Marketing," *Forbes*, October 15, 2021; Alexandra Pastore, "Blurring the Lines for Multigenerational Appeal," WWD, January 7, 2021, https://wwd.com/business-news/business-features/multigenerational-appeal-1234690602/.

For millennials, stereotypes, and popular culture, see Jeff J. Butler, "Where Did the Avocado Toast Millennial Stereotype Come From?," April 12, 2019, https://jeffjbutler.com/2019/04/12/where-did-the-avocado-toast-millennial-stereotype-come-from/;

Ash Collyer, "Generational Stereotypes Are 'Insulting, Recycled and Not True,'" Rhino Interiors Group, June 12, 2018, https://www.rhinooffice.co.uk/blog/generational-stereotypes; Tom Wolfe, "The 'Me' Decade and the Third Great Awakening," *New York*, April, 8 2008; Jean Twenge, "Millennials: the Me Me Me Generation," *Time*, May 20, 2013.

For ageism and critiques of the concept of generation, see Stéphane P. Francioli and Michael S. North, "Youngism: The Content, Causes, and Consequences of Prejudices Toward Younger Adults," *Journal of Experimental Psychology: General* 150, no. 12 (2021): 2591–2612; "The Whys and Hows of Generations Research," Pew Research Center, September 3, 2015, https://www.pewresearch.org/politics/2015/09/03/the-whys-and-hows-of-generations-research/; A. Bell and K. Jones, "The Impossibility of Separating Age, Period and Cohort Effects," *Social Science & Medicine* 93 (2013): 163–165; Stacy M. Campbell et al., "Fuzzy but Useful Constructs: Making Sense of the Differences Between Generations," *Work, Aging and Retirement* 3, no. 2 (April 2017): 130–139; P. J. Urwin and E. Parry, "The Evidence Base for Generational Differences: Where Do We Go from Here?," WestminsterResearch, 2017, https://westminsterresearch.westminster.ac.uk/download/f9124d9430b69b3df89f8a631919e4a56795e04cde20a95d33139865d2bcba21/200052/Generations%20paper%20for%20WAR%20v4%2024116.pdf; Cort W. Rudolph et al., "Generations and Generational Differences: Debunking Myths in Organizational Science and Practice and Paving New Paths Forward," *Journal of Business and Psychology* 36 (2021): 945–967.

For ageism, women, and marketing, see Tamar Miller, "It's Time for the Fashion Industry to Stop Ignoring Older Women," Swaay, June 22, 2020, https://swaay.com/ageism-fashion-industry-older-women; "Ageism in Marketing Is Not Only Harmful; It's Bad for Business," *Forbes*, January 3, 2020, including Rocks quote; Patrick Coffee, "Age Discrimination Is the Biggest Hidden Bias in Advertising—and It's Gotten Worse During the Pandemic," Business Insider, June 30, 2021, https://www.businessinsider.com/the-ad-industrys-silent-battle-against-ageism-2021–6?r=US&IR=T, including second Rocks quote; Georganna Simpson, "L'Oréal and Vogue Challenge Beauty Perceptions After 50," Campaign, https://www.campaignlive.co.uk/article/loreal-vogue-challenge-beauty-perceptions-50/1587434; Aimée McLaughlin, "Is Advertising Finally Addressing Its Age Problem?," *CreativeReview*, November 9, 2021, https://www.creativereview.co.uk/advertising-age-problem/, including McGuire quote; "Ageism Is Rife in Marketing," Longevity, August 12, 2021, https://www.longevity.technology/ageism-is-rife-in-marketing/, including Weiss quote.

For consumption and marketing at advanced ages, see Mari Shibata, "The Untapped Potential of the 'Longevity Economy,'" BBC, October 10, 2019, https://www.bbc.com/worklife/article/20190930-the-untapped-potential-of-the-longevity-economy; Jeff Beer, "Why Marketing to Seniors Is So Terrible," *Fast Company*, June 5, 2019, including the Chatterjee quote; Robert Zniva and Wolfgang Weitzl, "It's Not How Old You Are but How You Are Old: A Review on Aging and Consumer Behavior," *Management*

Review Quarterly 66 (2016): 267–297; Pastore, "Blurring the Lines," including the Drabicky and Martin quote.

On the granfluencers, see "How 'Granfluencers' Are Shaking Up Social Media Representation and Influencer Marketing," PR Daily, December 31, 2021, https://www .prdaily.com/how-granfluencers-are-shaking-up-social-media-representation-and -influencer-marketing/; "The Rise of the Granfluencer," Social Standard, https://www .sostandard.com/blogs/the-rise-of-the-granfluencer/; Kantaro Komiya, "Grandparents Gone Viral," Rest of World, https://restofworld.org/2021/social-media-isnt-just -for-young-people/; Kait Shea, "The Golden Age of Influence: Eight 'Granfluencers' Shaking Up Consumers' Social Media Feeds," Event Marketer, March 28, 2022, https: //www.eventmarketer.com/article/social-media-granfluencers-eight-types/; Carlo Pizzati, "Aging Influencers, Chinese Grandmas Are Social Media Hit," World Crunch, September 3, 2021, https://worldcrunch.com/culture-society/-aging-influencers -grandmas-in-china.

The quotes about TikTok are from Lindsay Dodgson, "TikTokers Are Dancing with Their Grandparents for Content, and It Could Help Curb the Pandemic of Loneliness Among Older People," Insider, June 11, 2020, https://www.insider.com/how-tiktok -brings-grandparents-and-grandchildren-together-2020–6; Sydney Page, "Grandparents Are Dancing with Their Grandkids on TikTok. People Can't Get Enough," *Washington Post,* May 14, 2020.

For multigenerational households and marketing, see Scott McKenzie, "Nielsen: The Rise of Multigeneration Homes and the New Gatekeepers Within," Drum, August 4, 2020, https://www.thedrum.com/opinion/2020/08/04/nielsen-the-rise-multi -generation-homes-and-the-new-gatekeepers-within; Sharon Vinderine, "Multigenerational Households Are Influencing North American Retail Trends," *Entrepreneur,* November 6, 2018, https://www.entrepreneur.com/growing-a-business /multigenerational-households-are-influencing-north-american/322144.

For statistics on Uber and Airbnb, see "Celebrating Airbnb's 60+ Host Community," Airbnb blog, https://blog.atairbnb.com/celebrating-airbnbs-60-host -community; "Airbnb Statistics, User Counts, Facts & News (2022)," DMR, https: //expandedramblings.com/index.php/airbnb-statistics/; "Uber Revenue and Usage Statistics," BuildFire, https://buildfire.com/uber-statistics/.

The perennials quotes are from Pastore, "Blurring the Lines."

On Nike, see Carol Kuruvilla, "'Iron Nun' Proves Youth Is Unlimited in Nike Ad," HuffPost, August 15, 2016, https://www.huffingtonpost.co.uk/entry/iron-nun-proves -youth-is-unlimited-in-nike-ad_n_57b209e1e4b0718404123f79; Miriam Tremelling, "The Iron Nun Inspires Us All in Nike's 'Unlimited Youth,'" Campaign, August 23, 2016, https://www.campaignlive.co.uk/article/iron-nun-inspires-us-nikes-unlimited -youth/1406682.

On Mercedes-Benz, see "Mercedes-Benz 'Grow Up' Campaign: Tapping into an Urban Subculture," Advertising + Marketing, April 18, 2018, https://www.marketing -interactive.com/mercedes-benz-grow-up-campaign-tapping-into-an-urban

-subculture; "Your Shot: Diving Deeper Into Mercedes-Benz's Compelling 'Grow Up' Series," Little Black Book, https://www.lbbonline.com/news/your-shot-diving -deeper-into-mercedes-benzs-compelling-grow-up-series.

On CoverGirl, see "CoverGirl Embraces Inclusivity in Their New Campaign by Droga5," MPC, https://archive.mpcadvertising.com/our-work/all/covergirl-i-am-what-i-make -up; Ruby Boddington, "CoverGirl Releases Biggest Reinvention in Brand's 60-Year History: I Am What I Make Up," It's Nice That, October 16, 2017, https://www .itsnicethat.com/news/covergirl-i-am-what-i-make-up-graphic-design-161017.

The Sarah Rabia quote is from Beer, "Why Marketing to Seniors Is So."

On multigenerational marketing, see Jessica Kriegel, "Why Marketing to Millennials and Other Generations Is Pointless," *Forbes*, November 25, 2015; Heidi Zak, "How to Successfully Market One Product to Multiple Generations," Medium, July 23, 2019, https://medium.com/swlh/how-to-successfully-market-one-product-to-multiple -generations-7c23428d11ee, including the example of ThirdLove; Sam Bradley, "How Do You Solve a Problem Like . . . Ageism in the Marketing Business?," Drum, June 1, 2021, https://www.thedrum.com/news/2021/06/01/how-do-you-solve -problem-ageism-the-marketing-business, including quotes on agencies and Ollie Scott; Matthew Schwartz, "Finding the Common Threads Is Key for Generational Marketing," ANA, June 23, 2020, https://www.ana.net/blogs/show/id/mm-blog -2019–12-common-threads-for-generational-marketing, including the Schwartz quote; "'Parentmorphosis'—Progressive's Latest Ad Campaign Reminds Us . . . We're All Becoming Our Parents," UTA Social, March 29, 2017, https://utasocial .wordpress.com/2017/03/29/parentmorphosis-progressives-latest-ad-campaign -reminds-us-were-all-becoming-our-parents/; Paul Talbot, "How Marketers Can Engage with Different Generations," *Forbes*, November 11, 2021, including Goddard quotes.

10. TOWARD A POSTGENERATIONAL SOCIETY OF PERENNIALS

The Miura quotes are from "80-Year-Old Japanese Man Yuichiro Mirua Becomes Oldest to Conquer Mount Everest," *Independent,* May 23, 2013; Kara Goldfarb, "He Was the Oldest Man to Climb Mount Everest—10 Years Later He Beat His Own Record," All That's Interesting, May 14, 2018, https://allthatsinteresting.com/yuichiro-miura. See also "About Miura Everest 2013 Project," Miura Everest 2013, http://miura -everest2013.com/pdf/project_english_130322.pdf.

The Mead quote is from Millard Dale Baughman, *Teacher's Treasury of Stories for Every Occasion* (Englewood Cliffs, NJ: Prentice-Hall, 1958), 69.

The Drucker quote is at Goodreads, https://www.goodreads.com/quotes/861169-we -now-accept-the-fact-that-learning-is-a-lifelong.

On the World Values Survey's study on attitudes toward ageism, see Alana Officer et al.,

"Ageism, Healthy Life Expectancy and Population Ageing: How Are They Related?," *International Journal of Environmental Research and Public Health* 17, no. 9 (2020): 3159; Michael S. North and Susan T. Fiske, "A Prescriptive, Intergenerational-Tension Ageism Scale: Succession, Identity, and Consumpion (SIC)," *Psychological Assessment* 25, no. 3 (September 2013): 706–713. The original data are at "Online Data Analysis," World Values Survey, https://www.worldvaluessurvey.org/WVSOnline.jsp.

The quote by Huth is from Joe Kita, "Workplace Age Discrimination Still Flourishes in America," AARP, December 30, 2019, https://www.aarp.org/work/working-at-50-plus/info-2019/age-discrimination-in-america.html.

The Toffler quote is from Susan Ratcliffe, *Oxford Essential Quotations* (Oxford, England: Oxford University Press, 2016).

The quote by Kopervas is from Sam Bradley, "How Do You Solve a Problem Like . . . Ageism in the Marketing Business?," Drum, June 1, 2021, https://www.thedrum.com/news/2021/06/01/how-do-you-solve-problem-ageism-the-marketing-business.

The statistics on U.S. online-only students are from the National Center for Education Statistics, https://nces.ed.gov/programs/digest/d21/tables/dt21_311.15.asp.

The quote by Olipcia is from *Global Report of Ageism* (New York: United Nations, 2021), 125, https://www.who.int/teams/social-determinants-of-health/demographic-change-and-healthy-ageing/combatting-ageism/global-report-on-ageism.

On age discrimination and population aging, see David Neumark, "Strengthen Age Discrimination Protections to Help Confront the Challenge of Population Aging," Brookings Institution, November 19, 2020, https://www.brookings.edu/research/strengthen-age-discrimination-protections-to-help-confront-the-challenge-of-population-aging/.

The AARP 2019 study is described by G. Oscar Anderson, "Mentorship and the Value of a Multigenerational Workforce," AARP, January 2019, https://www.aarp.org/research/topics/economics/info-2019/multigenerational-work-mentorship.html.

The Whitman quote is from Kerry Hannon, "Forget 'OK, Boomer'—Workplaces of the Future Will Be Multigenerational," MarketWatch, December 16, 2019, https://www.marketwatch.com/story/forget-ok-boomer-workplaces-of-the-future-will-be-multigenerational-2019–12–16.

The data on college enrollments by age come from the OECD's Education Database, https://data.oecd.org/education.htm.

The data on online learning by age come from the Statista database.

The AARP survey of executives was conducted by Rebecca Perron and published as *Global Insights on a Multigenerational Workforce* (Washington, DC: AARP Research, August 2020).

The Deloitte survey is quoted in Gildas Poirel and Michela Coppola, "Wrong Numbers," Deloitte, https://www2.deloitte.com/us/en/insights/focus/technology-and-the-future-of-work/post-pandemic-talent-strategy-generations-in-the-workplace.html.

On multigenerational marketing in the entertainment industry, see Natalie Oganesyan,

"Entertainment Executives See Return to Multi-Generational Viewing," Yahoo! News, October 2, 2020, https://www.yahoo.com/now/entertainment-executives-see-return -multi-201447044.html.

The Canadian brand 19/99 is featured in Lisa Payne, "New Multigenerational Beauty Brand Targets Ages 19 to 99," Stylus, https://www.stylus.com/new-multigenerational -beauty-brand-targets-ages-19-to-99.

INDEX